THE RIVERMAN

"Admire Your Handiwork!" She Told Him. "You are Rapidly
Bringing Me to 'Tell the Truth and Shame the Devil'"

THE RIVERMAN

BY

STEWART EDWARD WHITE

ILLUSTRATIONS BY N. C. WYETH AND
CLARENCE F. UNDERWOOD

NEW YORK
THE McCLURE COMPANY
MCMVIII

LIST OF ILLUSTRATIONS

THE RIVERMAN

I

THE time was the year 1872, and the place a bend in the river above a long pond terminating in a dam. Beyond this dam, and on a flat lower than it, stood a two-story mill structure. Save for a small, stump-dotted clearing, and the road that led from it, all else was forest. Here in the bottom-lands, following the course of the stream, the hardwoods grew dense, their uppermost branches just beginning to spray out in the first green of spring. Farther back, where the higher lands arose from the swamp, could be discerned the graceful frond of white pines and hemlock, and the sturdy tops of Norways and spruce.

A strong wind blew up the length of the pond. It ruffled the surface of the water, swooping down in fan-shaped, scurrying cat's-paws, turning the dark-blue surface as one turns the nap of velvet. At the upper end of the pond it even succeeded in raising quite respectable wavelets, which *lap lap lapped* eagerly against a barrier of floating logs that filled completely the mouth of the inlet river. And behind this barrier were other logs, and yet others, as far as the eye could see, so that the entire surface of the stream was carpeted by the brown timbers. A man could have walked down the middle of that river as down a highway.

On the bank, and in a small woods-opening, burned two fires, their smoke ducking and twisting under the buffeting of the wind. The first of these fires occupied a shallow trench dug for its accommodation, and was overarched by a rustic framework from which hung several pails, kettles,

3

and pots. An injured-looking, chubby man in a battered brown derby hat moved here and there. He divided his time between the utensils and an indifferent youth—his "cookee." The other, and larger, fire centred a rectangle composed of tall racks, built of saplings and intended for the drying of clothes. Two large tents gleamed white among the trees.

About the drying-fire were gathered thirty-odd men. Some were half-reclining before the blaze; others sat in rows on logs drawn close for the purpose; still others squatted like Indians on their heels, their hands thrown forward to keep the balance. Nearly all were smoking pipes.

Every age was represented in this group, but young men predominated. All wore woollen trousers stuffed into leather boots reaching just to the knee. These boots were armed on the soles with rows of formidable sharp spikes or caulks, a half and sometimes even three quarters of an inch in length. The tight driver's shoe and "stagged" trousers had not then come into use. From the waist down these men wore all alike, as though in a uniform, the outward symbol of their calling. From the waist up was more latitude of personal taste. One young fellow sported a bright-coloured Mackinaw blanket jacket; another wore a red knit sash, with tasselled ends; a third's fancy ran to a bright bandana about his neck. Head-gear, too, covered wide variations of broader or narrower brim, of higher or lower crown; and the faces beneath those hats differed as everywhere the human countenance differs. Only when the inspection, passing the gradations of broad or narrow, thick or thin, bony or rounded, rested finally on the eyes, would the observer have caught again the caste-mark which stamped these men as belonging to a distinct order, and separated them essentially from other men in other occupations. Blue and brown and black and gray these eyes were, but all steady and clear with the steadiness and clarity that comes to those whose daily work compels them under penalty to pay close and undeviating attention to their surroundings. This is true of sailors, hunters, plainsmen, cowboys, and tugboat captains. It was especially true of the old-fashioned river-driver, for a misstep, a miscalculation, a moment's forgetfulness of the sullen forces shifting and changing about him could mean for him maiming or destruction. So, finally, to one of an imaginative bent, these eyes, like the " cork boots," grew to seem part of the uniform, one of the marks of their caste, the outward symbol of their calling.

" Blow, you son of a gun! " cried disgustedly one young fellow with a red bandana, apostrophising the wind. " I wonder if there's *any* side of this fire that ain't smoky! "

" Keep your hair on, bub," advised a calm and grizzled old-timer. " There's never no smoke on the *other* side of the fire—whichever that happens to be. And as for wind —she just makes holiday for the river-hogs."

" Holiday, hell! " snorted the younger man. " We ought to be down to Bull's Dam before now——"

" And Bull's Dam is half-way to Redding," mocked a reptilian and red-headed giant on the log, " and Redding is the happy childhood home of——"

The young man leaped to his feet and seized from a pile of tools a peavy—a dangerous weapon, like a heavy cant-hook, but armed at the end with a sharp steel shoe.

" That's about enough! " he warned, raising his weapon, his face suffused and angry. The red-headed man, quite unafraid, rose slowly from the log and advanced, bare-handed, his small eyes narrowed and watchful.

But immediately a dozen men interfered.

" Dry up! " advised the grizzled old-timer—Tom North by name. " You, Purdy, set down ; and you, young squirt, subside! If you're going to have ructions, why, have 'em, but not on drive. If you don't look out, I'll set you both to rustling wood for the doctor."

At this threat the belligerents dropped muttering to their places. The wind continued to blow, the fire continued to flare up and down, the men continued to smoke, exchanging from time to time desultory and aimless remarks. Only Tom North carried on a consecutive, low-voiced conversation with another of about his own age.

" Just the same, Jim," he was saying, " it is a little tough on the boys—this new sluice-gate business. They've been sort of expectin' a chance for a day or two at Redding, and now, if this son of a gun of a wind hangs out, I don't know when we'll make her. The shallows at Bull's was always bad enough, but this is worse."

" Yes, I expected to pick you up 'way below," admitted Jim, whose " turkey," or clothes-bag, at his side proclaimed him a newcomer. " Had quite a tramp to find you."

" This stretch of slack water was always a terror," went on North, " and we had fairly to pike-pole every stick through when the wind blew; but now that dam's backed the water up until there reely ain't no current at all. And this breeze has just stopped the drive dead as a smelt."

" Don't opening the sluice-gates give her a draw? " inquired the newcomer.

" Not against this wind—and not much of a draw, anyway, I should guess."

" How long you been hung? "

" Just to-day. I expect Jack will be down from the rear shortly. Ought to see something's wrong when he runs against the tail of this jam of ours."

At this moment the lugubrious, round-faced man in the derby hat stepped aside from the row of steaming utensils he had been arranging.

" Grub pile," he remarked in a conversational tone of voice.

The group arose as one man and moved upon the heap of cutlery and of tin plates and cups. From the open fifty-pound lard pails and kettles they helped themselves liber-ally; then retired to squat in little groups here and there near the sources of supply. Mere conversation yielded to an industrious silence. Sadly the cook surveyed the scene, his arms folded across the dirty white apron, an immense mental reservation accenting the melancholy of his coun-tenance. After some moments of contemplation he mixed a fizzling concoction of vinegar and soda, which he drank. His rotundity to the contrary notwithstanding, he was ravaged by a gnawing dyspepsia, and the sight of six eggs eaten as a side dish to substantials carried consternation to his interior.

So busily engaged was each after his own fashion that nobody observed the approach of a solitary figure down the highway of the river. The man appeared tiny around the upper bend, momently growing larger as he approached. His progress was jerky and on an uneven zigzag, accord-ing as the logs lay, by leaps, short runs, brief pauses, as a riverman goes. Finally he stepped ashore just below the camp, stamped his feet vigorously free of water, and ap-proached the group around the cooking-fire.

No one saw him save the cook, who vouchsafed him a stately and lugubrious inclination of the head.

The newcomer was a man somewhere about thirty years of age, squarely built, big of bone, compact in bulk. His face was burly, jolly, and reddened rather than tanned by long exposure. A pair of twinkling blue eyes and a humor-ously quirked mouth redeemed his countenance from com-monplaceness.

He spread his feet apart and surveyed the scene.

"Well, boys," he remarked at last in a rollicking big voice, "I'm glad to see the situation hasn't spoiled your appetites."

At this they looked up with a spontaneous answering grin. Tom North laid aside his plate and started to arise.

"Sit still, Tom," interposed the newcomer. "Eat hearty. I'm going to feed yet myself. Then we'll see what's to be done. I think first thing you'd better see to having this wind turned off."

After the meal was finished, North and his principal sauntered to the water's edge, where they stood for a minute looking at the logs and the ruffled expanse of water below.

"Might as well have sails on them and be done with it," remarked Jack Orde reflectively. "Couldn't hold 'em any tighter. It's a pity that old mossback had to put in a mill. The water was slack enough before, but now there seems to be no current at all."

"Case of wait for the wind," agreed Tom North. "Old Daly will be red-headed. He must be about out of logs at the mill. The flood-water's going down every minute, and it'll make the riffles above Redding a holy fright. And I expect Johnson's drive will be down on our rear most any time."

"It's there already. Let's go take a look," suggested Orde.

They picked their way around the edge of the pond to the site of the new mill.

"Sluice open all right," commented Orde. "Thought she might be closed."

"I saw to that," rejoined North in an injured tone.

"'Course," agreed Orde, "but he might have dropped her shut on you between times, when you weren't looking."

He walked out on the structure and looked down on the smooth water rushing through.

"Ought to make a draw," he reflected. Then he laughed. "Tom, look here," he called. "Climb down and take a squint at this."

North clambered to a position below.

"The son of a gun!" he exclaimed.

The sluice, instead of bedding at the natural channel of the river, had been built a good six feet above that level; so that, even with the gates wide open, a "head" of six feet was retained in the slack water of the pond.

"No wonder we couldn't get a draw," said Orde. "Let's hunt up old What's-his-name and have a pow-wow."

"His name is plain Reed," explained North. "There he comes now."

"Sainted cats!" cried Orde, with one of his big, rollicking chuckles. "Where did you catch it?"

The owner of the dam flapped into view as a lank and lengthy individual dressed in loose, long clothes and wearing a-top a battered old "plug" hat, the nap of which seemed all to have been rubbed off the wrong way.

As he bore down on the intruders with tremendous, nervous strides, they perceived him to be an old man, white of hair, cadaverous of countenance, with thin, straight lips, and burning, fanatic eyes beneath stiff and bushy brows.

"Good-morning, Mr. Reed," shouted Orde above the noise of the water.

"Good-morning, gentlemen," replied the apparition.

"Nice dam you got here," went on Orde.

Reed nodded, his fiery eyes fixed unblinking on the riverman.

"But you haven't been quite square to us," said Orde. "You aren't giving us much show to get our logs out."

"How so?" snapped the owner, his thin lips tightening.

"Oh, I guess you know, all right," laughed Orde, clambering leisurely back to the top of the dam. "That sluice is a good six foot too high."

"Is that so!" cried the old man, plunging suddenly into a craze of excitement. "Well, let me tell you this, Mr. Man, I'm giving you all the law gives you, and that's the

natural flow of the river, and not a thing more will you
get! You that comes to waste and destroy, to arrogate
unto yourselves the kingdoms of the yearth and all the
fruits thereof, let me tell you you can't override Simeon
Reed! I'm engaged here in a peaceful and fittin' operation,
which is to feed the hungry by means of this grist-mill,
not to rampage and bring destruction to the noble forests
God has planted! I've give you what the law gives you,
and nothin' more!"

Somewhat astonished at this outbreak, the two rivermen
stood for a moment staring at the old man. Then a steely
glint crept into Orde's frank blue eye and the corners of
his mouth tightened.

"We want no trouble with you, Mr. Reed," said he,
"and I'm no lawyer to know what the law requires you
to do and what it requires you not to do. But I do know
that this is the only dam on the river with sluices built up
that way, and I do know that we'll never get those logs
out if we don't get more draw on the water. Good-day."

Followed by the reluctant North he walked away, leaving
the gaunt figure of the dam owner gazing after them, his
black garments flapping about him, his hands clasped behind his back, his ruffled plug hat thrust fr n his forehead.

"Well!" burst out North, when they were out of hearing.

"Well!" mimicked Orde with a laugh.

"Are you going to let that old high-banker walk all
over you?"

"What are you going to do about it, Tom? It's his
dam."

"I don't know. But you ain't going to let him hang
us up here all summer——"

"Sure not. But the wind's shifting. Let's see what the
weather's like to-morrow. To-day's pretty late."

II

THE next morning dawned clear and breathless. Before daylight the pessimistic cook was out, his fire winking bravely against the darkness. His only satisfaction of the long day came when he aroused the men from the heavy sleep into which daily toil plunged them. With the first light the entire crew were at the banks of the river.

As soon as the wind died the logs had begun to drift slowly out into the open water. The surface of the pond was covered with the scattered timbers floating idly. After a few moments the clank of the bars and ratchet was heard as two of the men raised the heavy sluice-gate on the dam. A roar of water, momently increasing, marked the slow rise of the barrier. A very imaginative man might then have made out a tendency forward on the part of those timbers floating nearest the centre of the pond. It was a very sluggish tendency, however, and the men watching critically shook their heads.

Four more had by this time joined the two men who had raised the gate, and all together, armed with long pike poles, walked out on the funnel-shaped booms that should concentrate the logs into the chute. Here they prodded forward the few timbers within reach, and waited for more.

These were a long time coming. Members of the driving crew leaped shouting from one log to another. Sometimes, when the space across was too wide to jump, they propelled a log over either by rolling it, paddling it, or projecting it by the shock of a leap on one end. In accomplishing these feats of tight-rope balance, they stood upright and graceful, quite unconscious of themselves, their bodies accustomed by long habit to nice and instant obedience to the almost unconscious impulses of the brain. Only their eyes, intent, preoccupied, blazed out by sheer will-power the unstable path their owners should follow. Once at the forefront of the drive, the men began vigorously to urge the logs forward. This they accomplished almost entirely by main strength, for the sluggish current gave them little aid. Under the pressure of their feet as they pushed against their implements, the logs dipped, rolled, and plunged. Nevertheless, they worked as surely from the decks of these unstable craft as from the solid earth itself.

In this manner the logs in the centre of the pond were urged forward until, above the chute, they caught the slightly accelerated current which should bring them down to the pike-pole men at the dam. Immediately, when this stronger influence was felt, the drivers zigzagged back up stream to start a fresh batch. In the meantime a great many logs drifted away to right and left into stagnant water, where they lay absolutely motionless. The moving of them was deferred for the " sacking crew," which would bring up the rear.

Jack Orde wandered back and forth over the work, his hands clasped behind his back, a short pipe clenched between his teeth. To the edge of the drive he rode the logs, then took to the bank and strolled down to the dam. There he stood for a moment gazing aimlessly at the water making over the apron, after which he returned to the work. No cloud obscured the serene good-nature of his face. Meeting Tom North's troubled glance, he grinned broadly.

" Told you we'd have Johnson on our necks," he remarked, jerking his thumb up river toward a rapidly approaching figure.

This soon defined itself as a tall, sun-reddened, very blond individual with a choleric blue eye.

"What in hell's the matter here?" he yelled, as soon as he came within hearing distance.

Orde made no reply, but stood contemplating the newcomer with a flicker of amusement.

"What in hell's the matter?" repeated the latter violently.

"Better go there and inquire," rejoined Orde drolly. "What ails you, Johnson?"

"We're right at your rear," cried the other, "and you ain't even made a start gettin' through this dam! We'll lose the water next! Why in hell ain't you through and gone?"

"Keep your shirt on," advised Orde. "We're getting through as fast as we can. If you want these logs pushed any faster, come down and do it yourself."

Johnson vouchsafed no reply, but splashed away over the logs, examining in detail the progress of the work. After a little he returned within hailing distance.

"If you can't get out logs, why do you take the job?" he roared, with a string of oaths. "If you hang my drive, damn you, you'll catch it for damages! It's gettin' to a purty pass when any old highbanker from anywheres can get out and play jackstraws holdin' up every drive in the river! I tell you our mills need logs, and what's more they're agoin' to *git* them!"

He departed in a rumble of vituperation.

Orde laughed humorously at his foreman.

"Johnson gets so mad sometimes, his skin cracks," he remarked. "However," he went on more seriously, "there's a heap in what he means, if there ain't so much in what he says. I'll go labour with our old friend below."

He regained the bank, stopped to light his pipe, and sauntered, with every appearance of leisure, down the bank, past the dam, to the mill structure below.

Here he found the owner occupying a chair tilted back against the wall of the building. His ruffled plug hat was thrust, as usual, well away from his high and narrow forehead; the long broadcloth coat fell back to reveal an unbuttoned waistcoat; the flapping black trousers were hitched up far enough to display woollen socks wrinkled about bony shanks. He was whittling a pine stick, which he held pointing down between his spread knees, and conversing animatedly with a young fellow occupying another chair at his side.

" And there comes one of 'em now," declaimed the old man dramatically.

Orde nodded briefly to the stranger, and came at once to business.

" I want to talk this matter over with you," he began. " We aren't making much progress. We can't afford to hang up the drive, and the water is going down every day. We've got to have more water. I'll tell you what we'll do: If you'll let us cut down the new sill, we'll replace it in good shape when we get all our logs through."

" No, sir ! " promptly vetoed the old man.

" Well, we'll give you something for the privilege. What do you think is fair ? "

" I tell ye I'll give you your legal rights, and not a cent more," replied the old man, still quietly, but with quivering nostrils.

" What is your name ? " asked Orde.

" My name is Reed, sir."

" Well, Mr. Reed, stop and think what this means. It's a more serious matter than you think. In a little while the water will be so low in the river that it will be impossible to take out the logs this year. That means a large loss, of course, as you know."

" I don't know nothin' about the pesky business, and I don't want to," snorted Reed.

" Well, there's borers, for one thing, to spoil a good many of the logs. And think what it will mean to the mills. No logs means no lumber. That is bankruptcy for a good many who have contracts to fulfil. And no logs means the mills must close. Thousands of men will be thrown out of their jobs, and a good many of them will go hungry. And with the stream full of the old cutting, that means less to do next winter in the woods—more men throw ᵢ out. Getting out a season's cut with the flood-water is a ᵖretty serious matter to a great many people, and if you insist on holding us up here in this slack water the situation will soon become alarming."

" Ye finished? " demanded Reed grimly.

" Yes," replied Orde.

The old man cast from him his half-whittled piece of pine. He closed his jack-knife with a snap and thrust it in his pocket. He brought to earth the front legs of his chair with a thump, and jammed his ruffled plug hat to its proper place.

" And if the whole kit and kaboodle of ye starved outright," said he, " it would but be the fulfillin' of the word of the prophet who says, ' So will I send upon you famine and evil beasts, and they shall bereave thee, and pestilence and blood shall pass through thee; and I will bring the sword upon thee. I the Lord have spoken it ! ' "

" That's your last word? " inquired Orde.

" That's my last word, and my first. Ye that make of God's smilin' land waste places and a wilderness, by your own folly shall ye perish."

" Good-day," said Orde, whirling on his heel without further argument.

The young man, who had during this colloquy sat an interested and silent spectator, arose and joined him. Orde looked at his new companion a little curiously. He was a very slender young man, taut-muscled, taut-nerved, but impassive in demeanour. He possessed a shrewd, thin face, steel-gray, inscrutable eyes behind glasses. His costume was quite simply an old gray suit of business clothes and a gray felt hat. At the moment he held in his mouth an unlighted and badly chewed cigar.

"Nice, amiable old party," volunteered Orde with a chuckle.

"Seems to be," agreed the young man drily.

"Well, I reckon we'll just have to worry along without him," remarked Orde, striking his steel caulks into the first log and preparing to cross out into the river where the work was going on.

"Wait a minute," said the young fellow. "Have you any objections to my hanging around a little to watch the work? My name is Newmark—Joseph Newmark. I'm out in this country a good deal for my health. This thing interests me."

"Sure," replied Orde, puzzled. "Look all you want to. The scenery's free."

"Yes. But can you put me up? Can I get a chance to stay with you a little while?"

"Oh, as far as I'm concerned," agreed Orde heartily. "But," he supplemented with one of his contagious chuckles, "I'm only river-boss. You'll have to fix it up with the doctor—the cook, I mean," he explained, as Newmark look puzzled. "You'll find him at camp up behind that brush. He's a slim, handsome fellow, with a jolly expression of countenance."

He leaped lightly out over the bobbing timbers, leaving Newmark to find his way.

In the centre of the stream the work had been gradually

slowing down to a standstill with the subsidence of the first rush of water after the sluice-gate was opened. Tom North, leaning gracefully against the shaft of a peavy, looked up eagerly as his principal approached.

"Well, Jack," he inquired, "is it to be peace or war?"

"War," replied Orde briefly.

III

AT this moment the cook stepped into view, and, making a trumpet of his two hands, sent across the water a long, weird, and not unmusical cry. The men at once began slowly to drift in the direction of the camp. There, when the tin plates had all been filled, and each had found a place to his liking, Orde addressed them. His manner was casual and conversational.

"Boys," said he, "the old mossback who owns that dam has come up here loaded to scatter. He's built up the sill of that gate until we can't get a draw on the water, and he refuses to give, lend, or sell us the right to cut her out. I've made him every reasonable proposition, but all I get back is quotations from the prophets. Now, we've got to get those logs out—that's what we're here for. A fine bunch of whitewater birlers we'd look if we got hung up by an old mossback in a plug hat. Johnny Sims, what's the answer?"

"Cut her out," grinned Johnny Sims briefly.

"Correct!" replied Orde with a chuckle. "Cut her out. But, my son, it's against the law to interfere with another man's property."

This was so obviously humourous in intent that its only reception consisted of more grins from everybody.

"But," went on Orde more seriously, "it's quite a job. We can't work more than six or eight men at it at a time. We got to work as fast as we can before the old man can interfere."

"The nearest sheriff's at Spruce Rapids," commented some one philosophically.

" We have sixty men, all told," said Orde. " We ought to be able to carry it through."

He filled his plate and walked across to a vacant place. Here he found himself next to Newmark.

" Hello ! " he greeted that young man, " fixed it with the doctor all right? "

" Yes," replied Newmark, in his brief, dry manner, " thanks ! I think I ought to tell you that the sheriff is not at Spruce Rapids, but at the village—expecting trouble."

Orde whistled, then broke into a roar of delight.

" Boys," he called, " old Plug Hat's got the sheriff right handy. I guess he sort of expected we'd be thinking of cutting through that dam. How'd you like to go to jail? "

" I'd like to see any sheriff take us to jail, unless he had an army with him," growled one of the river-jacks.

" Has he a posse? " inquired Orde of Newmark.

" I didn't see any; but I understood in the village that the governor had been advised to hold State troops in readiness for trouble."

Orde fell into a brown study, eating mechanically. The men began an eager and somewhat truculent discussion full of lawless and bloodthirsty suggestion. Some suggested the kidnapping and sequestration of Reed until the affair should be finished.

" How'd he get hold of his old sheriff, then? " they inquired with some pertinence.

Orde, however, paid no attention to all this talk, but continued to frown into space. At last his face cleared, and he slapped down his tin plate so violently that the knife and fork jumped off into the dirt.

" I have it ! " he cried aloud.

But he would not tell what he had. After the noon hour he instructed a half-dozen men to provide themselves with saws, axes, picks, and shovels, and all marched in the direction of the mill.

When within a hundred yards or so of that structure the advancing riverman saw the lank, black figure of the mill owner flap into sight, astride a bony old horse, and clatter away, coat-tails flying, up the road and into the waiting forest.

"Now, boys!" cried Orde crisply. "He'll be back in an hour with the sheriff. Lively!" He rapidly designated ten men of his crew. "You boys get to work and make things hum. Get as much done as you can before the sheriff comes."

"He'll have to bring all of Spruce County to get me," commented one of those chosen, spitting on his hands.

"Me, too!" said others.

"Now, listen," said Orde, holding them with an impressive gesture. "When that sheriff comes, with or without a posse, I want you to go peaceably. Understand?"

"Cave in? Not much!" cried Purdy.

"See here," and Orde drew them aside to an earnest, low-voiced conversation that lasted several minutes. When he had finished he clapped each of them on the back, and all moved off, laughing, to the dam.

"Now, boys," he commanded the others, "no row without orders. Understand? If there's going to be a fight, I'll give you the word when."

The chopping crew descended to the bottom of the sluice, the gate of which had been shut, and began immediately to chop away at the apron. As the water in the pond above had been drawn low by the morning's work, none overflowed the gate, so the men were enabled to work dry. Below the apron, of course, had been filled in with earth and stones. As soon as the axe-men had effected an entry to this deposit, other men with shovels and picks began to remove the filling.

The work had continued nearly an hour when Orde commanded the fifty or more idlers back to camp.

" Get out, boys," he ordered. " The sheriff will be here
pretty quick now, and I don't want any row. Get out of
sight."

" And leave them to fight her out alone? Guess not! "
grumbled a tall, burly individual with a red face.

Orde immediately walked directly to this man.

" Am I bossing this drive, or am I not? " he demanded.
The riverman growled something.

Smack! Smack! sounded Orde's fists. The man, taken
by surprise, went down in a heap, but immediately re-
bounded to his feet as though made of rubber. But Orde
had seized a peavy, and stood over against his antagonist,
the murderous weapon upraised.

" Lie down, you hound, or I'll brain you! " he roared at
the top strength of his great voice. " Want fight, do you?
Well, you won't have to wait till the sheriff gets here!
You make a move! "

For a full half minute the man crouched breathless,
and Orde, his ruddy face congested, held his threatening attitude. Then he dropped his peavy and stepped
aside.

" March! " he commanded. " Get your turkey and hit
the hay trail. You'll get your time at Redding."

The man sullenly arose and slouched away, grumbling
under his breath. Orde watched him from sight, then turned
to the silent group, a new crispness in his manner.

" Well? " he demanded.

Hesitating, they turned to the river trail, leaving the ten
still working at the sluice. When well within the fringe
of the brush, Orde called a halt. His customary good-
humour seemed quite restored.

" Now, boys," he commanded, " squat down and lay low.
You give me an ache! Don't you suppose I got this thing
all figured out? If fight would do any good, you know
mighty well I'd fight. And the boys won't be in jail any

longer than it takes to get a wire to Daly to bail them out. Smoke up, and don't bother."

They filled their pipes and settled down to an enjoyment of the situation. Ordinarily from very early in the morning until very late at night the riverman is busy every instant at his dangerous and absorbing work. Those affairs which do not immediately concern his task—as the swiftness of rapids, the state of flood, the curves of streams, the height of water, the obstructions of channels, the quantities of logs—pass by the outer fringe of his consciousness, if indeed they reach him at all. Thus, often he works all day up to his waist in a current bearing the rotten ice of the first break-up, or endures the drenching of an early spring rain, or battles the rigours of a belated snow with apparent indifference. You or I would be exceedingly uncomfortable; would require an effort of fortitude to make the plunge. Yet these men, absorbed in the mighty problems of their task, have little attention to spare to such things. The cold, the wet, the discomfort, the hunger, the weariness, all pass as shadows on the background. In like manner the softer moods of the spring rarely penetrate through the concentration of faculties on the work. The warm sun shines; the birds by thousands flutter and twitter and sing their way north; the delicate green of spring, showered from the hand of the passing Sower, sprinkles the tops of the trees, and gradually sifts down through the branches; the great, beautiful silver clouds sail down the horizon like ships of a statelier age, as totally without actual existence to these men. The logs, the river—those are enough to strain all the faculties a man possesses, and more.

So when, as now, a chance combination of circumstances brings them leisure to look about them, the forest and the world of out-of-doors comes to them with a freshness impossible for the city dweller to realise. The surroundings are accustomed, but they bring new messages. To most of them, these impressions never reach the point of coherency. They brood, and muse, and expand in the actual and figurative warmth, and proffer the general opinion that it is a damn fine day!

Another full half hour elapsed before the situation developed further. Then Tom North's friend Jim, who had gathered his long figure on the top of a stump, unclasped his knees and remarked that old Plug Hat was back.

The men arose to their feet and peered cautiously through the brush. They saw Reed, accompanied by a thick-set man whom some recognised as the sheriff of the county, approach the edge of the dam. A moment later the working crew mounted to the top, stacked their tools neatly, resumed their coats and jackets, and departed up the road in convoy of the sheriff.

A gasp of astonishment broke from the concealed rivermen.

" Well, I'll be damned! " ejaculated one. " What arc we comin' to? That's the first time I ever see one lonesome sheriff gather in ten river-hogs without the aid of a gatlin' or an ambulance! What's the matter with that chickenlivered bunch, anyway? "

Orde watched them, his eyes expressionless, until they had disappeared in the fringe of the forest. Then he turned to the astonished group.

" Jim," said he, " and you, Ellis, and you, and you, and you, and you, get to work on that dam. And remember this, if you are arrested, go peaceably. Any resistance will spoil the whole game."

The men broke into mingled cheers and laughter as the full significance of Orde's plan reached them. They streamed back to the dam, where they perched proffering advice and encouragement to those about to descend.

Immediately, however, Reed was out, his eyes blazing either side his hawk nose.

" Here! " he cried, " quit that! I'll have ye arrested! "

" Arrest ahead," replied Orde coldly.

Reed stormed back and forth for a moment, then departed at full speed up the road.

" Now, boys, get as much done as possible," urged Orde. " We better get back in the brush, or he may try to take in the whole b'iling of us on some sort of a blanket warrant."

" How about the other boys? " inquired North.

" I gave one of them a telegram to send to Daly," replied Orde. " Daly will be up to bail them out."

Once more they hid in the woods; and again, after a longer interval, the mill owner and the sheriff reappeared. Reed appeared to be expostulating violently, and a number of times pointed up river; but the sheriff went ahead stolidly to the dam, summoned those working below, and departed up the road as before. Reed stood uncertain until he saw the rivermen beginning to re-emerge from the brush, then followed the officer at top speed.

Without the necessity of command, a half-dozen men leaped down on the apron. The previous crews had made considerable progress in weakening the heavy supports. As soon as these should be cut out and the backing removed, the mere sawing through of the massive sill should carry away the whole obstruction.

" Next time will decide it," remarked Orde. " If the sheriff brings a posse and sits down to lay for us, of course we won't be able to get near to finish the job."

" I didn't think that of George Morris," commented Sims in an aggrieved way. " He was a riverman himself once before he was sheriff."

" He's got to obey orders, and serve a warrant when it's issued, of course," replied Orde to this. " What did you expect? "

At the end of another hour, which brought the time to

four o'clock, the sheriff made his third appearance—this time in a side-bar buggy.

"I wish I dared join that confab," said Orde, "and hear what's going on, but I'm afraid he'd jug me sure."

"He wouldn't jug me," spoke up Newmark. "I'll go down."

"Bully for you!" agreed Orde.

The young man departed in his precise, methodical manner, picking his way rather mincingly among the inequalities of the trail. In spite of the worn and wrinkled condition of his garments, they retained something of a city hang and smartness that sharply differentiated their wearer from even the well-dressed citizens of a smaller town. They seemed to match the refined, shrewd, but cold intelligence of his lean and nervous face.

About sunset he returned from a scene which the distant spectators had watched with breathless interest. It was in essence only a repetition of the two that had preceded it, but Reed had evidently gone almost to the point of violence in his insistence, and the sheriff had shaken him off rudely. Finally, Morris and his six prisoners had trailed away. The sheriff and North's friend occupied the seat of the buggy, while the other five trudged peaceably alongside. Once again Reed clattered away on his bony steed, but this time ahead of the official party.

With a whoop the river crew, now reduced to a scant dozen, rushed down to meet the too deliberate Newmark.

"Well?" they demanded, crowding about him.

"Reed wanted the sheriff to stay and protect the dam," reported Newmark in his brief, dry manner. "Sheriff refused. Said his duty was simply to arrest on warrant, and as often as Reed got out warrants, he'd serve them. Reed said, then, he should get a posse and hunt up Orde and the rest of them. Sheriff replied that as far as he could see, the terms of his warrant were covered by the men he found working on the dam. Reed demanded protection. Sheriff said for him to get an injunction, and it would be enforced."

"Well, that's all right," interjected Orde with satisfaction. "We'll have her cut through before he gets that injunction, and I guess I've got men enough here and down river to get through before we're *all* arrested."

"Yes," said Newmark, "that's all very well. But now he's gone to telegraph the governor to send the troops."

Orde whistled a jig tune.

"Kind of expected that, boys," said he. "Let's see. The next train out from Redding— They'll be here by five in the morning at soonest. Hope it'll be later."

"What will you do?" asked Newmark.

"Take chances," replied Orde. "All you boys get to work. Zeke," he commanded one of the cookees, "go up road, and report if Morris comes back. I reckon this time we'll have to scatter if he comes after us. I hope we won't have to, though. Like to keep everything square on account of this State troop business."

The sun had dropped below the fringe of trees, which immediately etched their delicate outlines against a pale, translucent green sky. Two straight, thin columns of smoke rose from the neglected camp-fires. Orde, glancing around him, noticed these.

"Doctor," he commanded sharply, "get at your grub! Make some coffee right off, and bring it down. Get the lanterns from the wanigan, and bring them to the dam. Come on, boys!"

Over a score of men attacked the sluice-way, for by now part of the rear crew had come down river. The pond above had recovered its volume. Water was beginning to trickle over the top of the gate. In a short time progress became difficult, almost impossible. The men worked up to their knees in swift water. They could not see, and the strokes of axe or pick lost much of their force against the liquid. Dusk fell. The fringe of the forest became mysterious in its velvet dark. Silver streaks, of a supernal calm, suggested the reaches of the pond. Above, the sky's day surface unfolded and receded and dissolved and melted away until, through the pale afterglow, one saw beyond into the infinities. Down by the sluice a dozen lanterns flickered and blinked yellow against the blue-blackness of the night.

After some time Orde called his crew off and opened the sluice-gates. The water had become too deep for effective work, and a half hour's flow would reduce the pressure. The time was occupied in eating and in drying off about the huge fire the second cookee had built close at hand.

" Water cold, boys? " asked Orde.

" Some," was his reply.

" Want to quit? " he inquired, with mock solicitude.

" Nary quit."

Orde's shout of laughter broke the night silence of the whispering breeze and the rushing water.

" We'll stick to 'em like death to a dead nigger," was his comment.

Newmark, having extracted a kind of cardigan jacket from the bag he had brought with him as far as the mill, looked at the smooth, iron-black water and shivered.

When the meal was finished, the men lit their pipes and went back to work philosophically. With entire absorption in the task, they dug, chopped, and picked. The dull sound of blows, the gurgle and trickle of the water, the occasional grunt or brief comment of a riverman alone broke the calm of evening. Now that the sluice-gate was down and the water had ceased temporarily to flow over it, the work went faster. Orde, watching with the eye of an expert, vouchsafed to the taciturn Newmark that he thought they'd make it.

Near midnight, however, a swaying lantern was seen approaching. Orde, leaping to his feet with a curse at the boy on watch, heard the sound of wheels. A moment later, Daly's bulky form stepped into the illumination of the fire.

Orde wandered over to where his principal stood peering about him.

" Hullo! " said he.

" Oh, there you are! " cried Daly angrily. " What in hell you up to here? "

" Running logs," replied Orde coolly.

" Running logs! " shouted Daly, tugging at his overcoat pocket, and finally producing a much-folded newspaper. " How about this? "

Orde unfolded the paper and lowered it to the campfire. It was an extra, screaming with wood type. He read it deliberately over.

WAR!

the headline ran.

RIOTING AND BLOODSHED IN THE WOODS
RIVERMEN AND DAM OWNERS CLASH!

There followed a vague and highly coloured statement to the effect that an initial skirmish had left the field in possession of the rivermen, in spite of the sheriff and a large posse, but that troops were being rushed to the spot, and that this " high-handed defiance of authority " would undoubtedly soon be suppressed. It concluded truthfully with the statement that the loss of life was as yet unknown.

Orde folded up the paper and handed it back.

" Don't you know any better than to get into that kind of a row down here? " Daly had been saying. " Do you want to bring us up for good here? Don't you realise that this isn't the northern peninsula? What are you trying to do, any way?"

"Sure I do," replied Orde placidly. "Come along here till I show you the situation."

Ten minutes later, Daly, relieved in his mind, was standing by the fire drinking hot coffee and laughing at Orde's description of Reed's plug hat.

To Orde's satisfaction, the sheriff did not reappear. Reed evidently now pinned his faith to the State troops.

All night the work went on, the men spelling each other at intervals of every few hours. By three o'clock the main abutments had been removed. The gate was then blocked to prevent its fall when its nether support should be withdrawn, and two men, leaning over cautiously, began at arm's-length to deliver their axe-strokes against the middle of the sill-timbers of the sluice itself, notching each heavy beam deeply that the force of the current might finally break it in two. The night was very dark, and very still. Even the night creatures had fallen into the quietude that precedes the first morning hours. The muffled, spaced blows of the axes, the low-voiced comments or directions of the workers, the crackle of the fire ashore were thrown by contrast into an undue importance. Men in blankets, awaiting their turn, slept close to the blaze.

Suddenly the vast silence of before dawn was broken by a loud and exultant yell from one of the axemen. At once the two scrambled to the top of the dam. The blanketed figures about the fire sprang to life. A brief instant later the snapping of wood fibres began like the rapid explosions of infantry fire; a crash and bang of timbers smote the air; and then the river, exultant, roaring with joy, rushed from its pent quietude into the new passage opened for it. At the same moment, as though at the signal, a single bird, premonitor of the yet distant day, lifted up his voice, clearly audible above the tumult.

Orde stormed into the camp up stream, his eyes bright, his big voice booming exultantly.

"Roll out, you river-hogs!" he shouted to those who had worked out their shifts earlier in the night. "Roll out, you web-footed sons of guns, and hear the little birds sing praise!"

Newmark, who had sat up the night through, and now shivered sleepily by the fire, began to hunt around for the bed-roll he had, earlier in the evening, dumped down somewhere in camp.

"I suppose that's all," said he. "Just a case of run logs now. I'll turn in for a little."

But Orde, a thick slice of bread half-way to his lips, had frozen in an attitude of attentive listening.

"Hark!" said he.

Faint, still in the depths of the forest, the wandering morning breeze bore to their ears a sound whose difference from the louder noises nearer at hand alone rendered it audible.

"The troops!" exclaimed Orde.

He seized a lantern and returned down the trail, followed eagerly by Newmark and every man in camp.

"Troops coming!" said Orde to Daly.

The men drew a little to one side, watching the dim line of the forest, dark against the paling sky. Shadows seemed to stir in its blackness. They heard quite distinctly the clink of metal against metal. A man rode out of the shadow and reined up by the fire. "Halt!" commanded a harsh voice. The rivermen could make out the troops—three or four score of them—standing rigid at attention. Reed, afoot now in favour of the commanding officer, pushed forward.

"Who is in charge here?" inquired the officer crisply.

"I am," replied Orde, stepping forward.

"I wish to inquire, sir, if you have gone mad to counsel your men to resist civil authority?"

" I have not resisted civil authority," replied Orde respectfully.

" It has been otherwise reported."

" The reports have been false. The sheriff of this county has arrested about twenty of my men single-handed and without the slightest trouble."

" Mr. Morris," cried the officer sharply.

" Yes," replied the sheriff.

" Is what this man says true? "

" It sure is. Never had so little fuss arrestin' rivermen before in my life."

The officer's face turned a slow brick-red. For a moment he said nothing, then exploded with the utmost violence.

" Then why the devil am I dragged up here with my men in the night? " he cried. " Who's responsible for this insanity, anyway? Don't you know," he roared at Reed, who that moment swung within his range of vision, " that I have no standing in the presence of civil law? What do you mean getting me up here to your miserable little backwoods squabbles? "

Reed started to say something, but was immediately cut short by the irate captain.

" I've nothing to do with that; settle it in court. And what's more, you'll have something yourself to settle with the State! About, face! Forward, march! "

The men faded into the gray light as though dissolved by it.

A deep and respectful silence fell upon the men, which was broken by Orde's solemn and dramatic declamation.

> " The King of France and twice ten thousand men
> Marched up the hill, and then marched down again,"

he recited; then burst into his deep roar of laughter.

" Now you see, boys," he said, digging his fists into his

eyes, "if you'd put up a row, what we'd have got into. No blue-coats in mine, thank you. Well, push the grub pile, and then get at those logs. It's a case of flood-water now."

But Reed, having recovered from his astonishment, had still his say.

"I tell ye, I'm not done with ye yet," he threatened, shaking his bony forefinger in Orde's face. "I'll sue ye for damages, and I'll *git* 'em, too."

"See here, you old mossback," said Orde, thrusting his bulky form to the fore, "you sue just as soon as you want to. You can't get at it any too quick to suit us. But just now you get out of this camp, and you stay out. You're an old man, and we don't want to be rough with you, but you're biting off more than you can chew. Skedaddle!"

Reed hesitated, waving his long arms about, flail-like, as though to begin a new oration.

"Now, do hop along," urged Orde. "We'll pay you any legitimate damages, of course, but you can't expect to hang up a riverful of logs just on a notion. And we're sick of you. Oh, hell, then! See here, you two; just see that this man leaves camp."

Orde turned square on his heel. Reed, after a glance at the two huge rivermen approaching, beat a retreat to his mill, muttering and wrathful still.

"Well, good-bye, boys," said Daly, pulling on his overcoat; "I'll just get along and bail the boys out of that village calaboose. I reckon they've had a good night's rest. Be good!"

The fringe of trees to eastward showed clearly against the whitening sky. Hundreds of birds of all kinds sang in an ecstasy. Another day had begun. Already men with pike-poles were guiding the sullen timbers toward the sluice-way.

IV

WHEN Newmark awoke once more to interest in affairs, the morning was well spent. On the river the work was going forward with the precision of clockwork. The six-foot lowering of the sluice-way had produced a fine current, which sucked the logs down from above. Men were busily engaged in "sacking" them from the sides of the pond toward its centre, lest the lowering water should leave them stranded. Below the dam the jam crew was finding plenty to do in keeping them moving in the white-water and the shallows. A fine sun, tempered with a prophetic warmth of later spring, animated the scene. Reed had withdrawn to the interior of his mill, and appeared to have given up the contest.

Some of the logs shot away down the current, running freely. To these the crews were not required to pay any attention. With luck, a few of the individual timbers would float ten, even twenty, miles before some chance eddy or fortuitous obstruction would bring them to rest. Such eddies and obstructions, however, drew a constant toll from the ranks of the free-moving logs, so that always the volume of timbers floating with the current diminished, and always the number of logs caught and stranded along the sides of the river increased. To restore these to the faster water was the especial province of the last and most expert crew—the rear.

Orde discovered about noon that the jam crew was having its troubles. Immediately below Reed's dam ran a long chute strewn with boulders, which was alternately a shal-

33

low or a stretch of white-water according as the stream
rose or fell. Ordinarily the logs were flushed over this
declivity by opening the gate, behind which a head of water
had been accumulated. Now, however, the efficiency of the
gate had been destroyed. Orde early discovered that he
was likely to have trouble in preventing the logs rushing
through the chute from grounding into a bad jam on the
rapids below.

For a time the jam crew succeeded in keeping the
" wings " clear. In the centre of the stream, however, a
small jam formed, like a pier. Along the banks logs
grounded, and were rolled over by their own momentum
into places so shallow as to discourage any hope of re-
floating them unless by main strength. As the sluicing of
the nine or ten million feet that constituted this particular
drive went forward, the situation rapidly became worse.

" Tom, we've got to get flood-water unless we want to
run into an awful job there," said Orde to the foreman.
" I wonder if we can't drop that gate 'way down to get
something for a head."

The two men examined the chute and the sluice-gate
attentively for some time.

" If we could clear out the splinters and rubbish, we
might spike a couple of saplings on each side for the gate
to slide down into," speculated North. " Might try her on."

The logs were held up in the pond, and a crew of men
set to work to cut away, as well as they might in the
rush of water, the splintered ends of the old sill and apron.
It was hard work. Newmark, watching, thought it im-
practicable. The current rendered footing impossible, so
all the work had to be done from above. Wet wood gripped
the long saws vice-like, so that a man's utmost strength
could scarcely budge them. The water deadened the force
of axe-blows. Nevertheless, with the sure persistence of the
riverman, they held to it. Orde, watching them a few

moments, satisfied himself that they would succeed, and so departed up river to take charge of the rear.

This crew he found working busily among some overflowed woods. They were herding the laggards of the flock. The subsidence of the water consequent upon the opening of the sluice-gate had left stranded and in shallows many hundreds of the logs. These the men sometimes, waist deep in the icy water, owing to the extreme inequality of the bottom, were rolling over and over with their peavies until once more they floated. Some few the rivermen were forced to carry bodily, ten men to a side, the peavies clamped in as handles. When once they were afloat, the task became easier. From the advantage of deadwood, stumps, or other logs the " sackers " pushed the unwieldy timbers forward, leaping, splashing, heaving, shoving, until at last the steady current of the main river seized the logs and bore them away. With marvellous skill they topped the dripping, bobby, rolling timbers, treading them over and over, back and forth, in unconscious preservation of equilibrium.

There was a good deal of noise and fun at the rear. The crew had been divided, and a half worked on either side the river. A rivalry developed as to which side should advance fastest in the sacking. It became a race. Momentary success in getting ahead of the other fellow was occasion for exultant crowing, while a mishap called forth ironic cheers and catcalls from the rival camp. Just as Orde came tramping up the trail, one of the rivermen's caulks failed to " bite " on an unusually smooth, barked surface. His foot slipped; the log rolled; he tried in vain to regain his balance, and finally fell in with a heavy splash.

The entire river suspended work to send up a howl of delight. As the unfortunate crawled out, dripping from head to foot, he was greeted by a flood of sarcasm and profane inquiry that left no room for even his acknowledged talents of repartee. Cursing and ashamed, he made

his way ashore over the logs, spirting water at every step.
There he wrung out his woollen clothes as dry as he could,
and resumed work.

Hardly had Orde the opportunity to look about at the
progress making, however, before he heard his name
shouted from the bank. Looking up, to his surprise he saw
the solemn cook waving a frantic dish-towel at him. Nothing could induce the cook to attempt the logs.

"What is it, Charlie?" asked Orde, leaping ashore and
stamping the loose water from his boots.

"It's all off," confided the cook pessimistically. "It's no
good. He's stopped us now."

"What's off? Who's stopped what?"

"Reed. He's druv the men from the dam with a shotgun. We might as well quit."

"Shotgun, hey!" exclaimed Orde. "Well, the old son
of a gun!" He thought a moment, his lips puckered as
though to whistle; then, as usual, he laughed amusedly.
"Let's go take a look at the army," said he.

He swung away at a round pace, followed rather breath-
lessly by the cook. The trail led through the brush across
a little flat point, up over a high bluff where the river
swung in, down to another point, and across a pole trail
above a marsh to camp.

A pole trail consists of saplings laid end to end, and
supported three or four feet above wet places by means
of sawbuck-like structures at their extremities. To a riverman or a tight-rope dancer they are easy walks. All others
must proceed cautiously in contrite memory of their sins.

Orde marched across the first two lengths confidently
enough. Then he heard a splash and lamentations. Turning, he perceived Charlie, covered with mud, in the act
of clambering up one of the small trestles.

"Ain't got no caulks!" ran the lamentations. "The ——
of a —— of a pole-trail, anyways!"

He walked ahead gingerly, threw his hands aloft, bent forward, then suddenly protruded his stomach, held out one foot in front of him, spasmodically half turned, and then, realising the case hopeless, wilted like a wet rag, to clasp the pole trail both by arm and leg. This saved him from falling off altogether, but swung him underneath, where he hung like the sloths in the picture-books. A series of violent wriggles brought him, red-faced and panting, astride the pole, whence, his feelings beyond mere speech, he sadly eyed his precious derby, which lay, crown up, in the mud below.

Orde contemplated the spectacle seriously.

" Sorry I haven't got time to enjoy you just now, Charlie," he remarked. " I'd take it slower, if I were you."

He departed, catching fragments of vows anent never going on any more errands for nobody, and getting his time if ever again he went away from his wanigan.

Orde stopped short outside the fringe of brush to utter another irrepressible chuckle of amusement.

The centre of the dam was occupied by Reed. The old man was still in full regalia, his plug hat fuzzier than ever, and thrust even farther back on his head, his coat-tails and loose trousers flapping at his every movement as he paced back and forth with military precision. Over his shoulder he carried a long percussion-lock shotgun. Not thirty feet away, perched along the bank, for all the world like a row of cormorants, sat the rivermen, watching him solemnly and in silence.

" What's the matter? " inquired Orde, approaching.

The old man surveyed him with a snort of disgust.

" If the law of the land don't protect me, I'll protect myself, sir," he proclaimed. " I give ye fair warning! I ain't a-going to have my property interfered with no more."

" But surely," said Orde, " we have a right to run our logs through. It's an open river."

" And hev ye been running your logs through? " cried the old man excitedly. " Hev ye? First off ye begin to tear down my dam; and then, when the river begins a-roarin' and a-ragin' through, then you tamper with my improvements furthermore, a-lowerin' the gate and otherwise a-modifyin' my structure."

Orde stepped forward to say something further. Immediately Reed wheeled, his thumb on the hammer.

" All right, old Spirit of '76," replied Orde. " Don't shoot; I'll come down."

He walked back to the waiting row, smiling quizzically.

" Well, you calamity howlers, what do you think of it? "

Nobody answered, but everybody looked expectant.

" Think he'd shoot? " inquired Orde of Tom North.

" I know he would," replied North earnestly. " That crazy-headed kind are just the fellers to rip loose."

" I think myself he probably would," agreed Orde.

" Surely," spoke up Newmark, " whatever the status of the damage suits, you have the legal right to run your logs."

Orde rolled a quizzical eye in his direction.

" Per-fect-ly correct, son," he drawled, " but we're engaged in the happy occupation of getting out logs. By the time the law was all adjusted and a head of steam up, the water'd be down. In this game, you get out logs first, and think about law afterward."

" How about legal damages? " insisted Newmark.

" Legal damages! " scoffed Orde. " Legal damages! Why, we count legal damages as part of our regular expenses—like potatoes. It's lucky it's so," he added. " If anybody paid any attention to legal technicalities, there'd never be a log delivered. A man always has enemies."

" Well, what are you going to do? " persisted Newmark.

Orde thrust back his felt hat and ran his fingers through his short, crisp hair.

"There you've got me," he confessed, "but, if necessary, we'll pile the old warrior."

He walked to the edge of the dam and stood looking down current. For perhaps a full minute he remained there motionless, his hat clinging to one side, his hand in his hair. Then he returned to the grimly silent rivermen.

"Boys," he commanded briefly, "get your peavies and come along."

He led the way past the mill to the shallows below.

"There's a trifle of wading to do," he announced. "Bring down two logs—fairly big—and hold them by that old snag," he ordered. "Whoa-up! Easy! Hold them end on—no, pointing up stream—fix 'em about ten foot apart—that's it! George, drive a couple of stakes each side of them to hold 'em. Correct! Now, run down a couple dozen more and pile them across those two—side on to the stream, of course. Roll 'em up—that's the ticket!"

Orde had been splashing about in the shallow water, showing where each timber was to be placed. He drew back, eyeing the result with satisfaction. It looked rather like a small and bristly pier.

Next he cast his eye about and discovered a partially submerged boulder on a line with the newly completed structure. Against this he braced the ends of two more logs, on which he once more caused to be loaded at right angles many timbers. An old stub near shore furnished him the basis of a third pier. He staked a thirty-inch butt for a fourth; and so on, until the piers, in conjunction with the small centre jam already mentioned, extended quite across the river.

All this was accomplished in a very short time, and immediately below the mill, but beyond sight from the sluice-gate of the dam.

"Now, boys," commanded Orde, "shove off some shore logs, and let them come down."

"We'll have a jam sure," objected Purdy stupidly.

"No, my son, would we?" mocked Orde. "I surely hope not!"

The stray logs floating down with the current the rivermen caught and arranged to the best possible advantage about the improvised piers. A good riverman understands the correlation of forces represented by saw-logs and water-pressure. He knows how to look for the key-log in breaking jams; and by the inverse reasoning, when need arises he can form a jam as expertly as Koosy-oonek himself—that bad little god who brings about the disagreeable and undesired—"who hides our pipes, steals our last match, and brings rain on the just when they want to go fishing."

So in ten seconds after the shore logs began drifting down from above, the jam was taking shape. Slowly it formed, low and broad. Then, as the water gathered pressure, the logs began to slip over one another. The weight of the topmost sunk those beneath to the bed of the stream. This to a certain extent dammed back the water. Immediately the pressure increased. More logs were piled on top. The piers locked the structure. Below the improvised dam the water fell almost to nothing, and above it, swirling in eddies, grumbling fiercely, bubbling, gurgling, searching busily for an opening, the river, turned back on itself, gathered its swollen and angry forces.

"That will do, boys," said Orde with satisfaction.

He led the way to the bank and sat down. The men followed his example. Every moment the water rose, and each instant, as more logs came down the current, the jam became more formidable.

"Nothing can stand that pressure," breathed Newmark, fascinated.

" The bigger the pressure the tighter she locks," replied Orde, lighting his pipe.

The high bank where the men sat lay well above the reach of the water. Not so the flat on which stood Reed's mill. In order to take full advantage of the water-power developed by the dam, the old man had caused his structure to be built nearly at a level with the stream. Now the river, backing up, rapidly overflowed this flat. As the jam tightened by its own weight and the accumulation of logs, the water fairly jumped from the lowest floor of the mill to the one above.

Orde had not long to wait for Reed's appearance. In less than five minutes the old man descended on the group, somewhat of his martial air abated, and something of a vague anxiety manifest in his eye.

" What's the matter here? " he demanded.

" Matter? " inquired Orde easily. " Oh, nothing much, just a little jam."

" But it's flooding my mill! "

" So I perceive," replied Orde, striking a match.

" Well, why don't you break it? "

" Not interested."

The old warrior ran up the bank to where he could get a good view of his property. The water was pouring into the first-floor windows.

" Here! " he cried, running back. " I've a lot of grain up-stairs. It'll be ruined! "

" Not interested," repeated Orde.

Reed was rapidly losing control of himself.

" But I've got a lot of money invested here! " he shouted. " You miserable blackguard, you're ruining me! "

Orde replaced his pipe.

Reed ran back and forth frantically, disappeared, returned bearing an antiquated pike-pole, and single-handed and alone attacked the jam!

Astonishment and delight held the rivermen breathless for a moment. Then a roar of laughter drowned even the noise of the waters. Men pounded each other on the back, rolled over and over, clutching handfuls of earth, struggled weak and red-faced for breath as they saw against the sky-line of the bristling jam the lank, flapping figure with the old plug hat pushing frantically against the immovable statics of a mighty power. The exasperation of delay, the anxiety lest success be lost through the mulish and narrow-minded obstinacy of one man, the resentment against another obstacle not to be foreseen and not to be expected in a task redundantly supplied with obstacles of its own—these found relief at last.

"By Jove!" breathed Newmark softly to himself. "Don Quixote and the windmills!" Then he added vindictively, "The old fool!" although, of course, the drive was not his personal concern.

Only Orde seemed to see the other side. And on Orde the responsibility, uncertainty, and vexation had borne most heavily, for the success of the undertaking was in his hands. With a few quick leaps he had gained the old man's side.

"Look here, Reed," he said kindly, "you can't break this jam. Come ashore now, and let up. You'll kill yourself."

Reed turned to him, a wild light in his eye.

"Break it!" he pleaded. "You're ruining me. I've got all my money in that mill."

"Well," said Orde, "we've got a lot of money in our logs too. You haven't treated us quite right."

Reed glanced frantically toward the flood up stream.

"Come," said Orde, taking him gently by the arm. "There's no reason you and I shouldn't get along together all right. Maybe we're both a little hard-headed. Let's talk it over."

He led the old man ashore, and out of earshot of the rivermen.

At the end of ten minutes he returned.

" War's over, boys! " he shouted cheerfully. " Get in and break that jam."

At once the crew swarmed across the log barrier to a point above the centre pier. This they attacked with their peavies, rolling the top logs off into the current below. In less than no time they had torn out quite a hole in the top layer. The river rushed through the opening. Immediately the logs in the wings were tumbled in from either side. At first the men had to do all of the work, but soon the river itself turned to their assistance. Timbers creaked and settled, or rose slightly buoyant as the water loosened the tangle. Men trod on the edge of expectation. Constantly the logs shifted, and as constantly the men shifted also, avoiding the upheavals and grindings together, wary eyes estimating the correlation of the forces into whose crushing reach a single misstep would bring them. The movement accelerated each instant, as the music of the play hastens to the climax. Wood fibres smashed. The whole mass seemed to sink down and forward into a boiling of waters. Then, with a creak and a groan, the jam moved, hesitated, moved again; finally, urged by the frantic river, went out in a majestic crashing and battering of logs.

At the first movement Newmark expected the rivermen to make their escape. Instead, they stood at attention, their peavies poised, watching cat-eyed the symptoms of the break. Twice or thrice several of the men, observing something not evident to Newmark's unpractised eye, ran forward, used their peavies vigorously for a moment or so, and stood back to watch the result. Only at the very last, when it would seem that some of them must surely be caught, did the river-jacks, using their peavy-shafts as balancing poles, zigzag calmly to shore across the plunging logs. Newmark seemed impressed.

"That was a close shave," said he to the last man ashore.

"What?" inquired the riverman. "Didn't see it. Somebody fall down?"

"Why, no," explained Newmark; "getting in off those logs without getting caught."

"Oh!" said the man indifferently, turning away.

The going out of the jam drained the water from the lower floors of the mill; the upper stories and the grain were still safe.

By evening the sluice-gate had been roughly provided with pole guides down which to slide to the bed of the river. The following morning saw the work going on as methodically as ever. During the night a very good head of water had gathered behind the lowered gate. The rear crew brought down the afterguard of logs to the pond. The sluicers with their long pike-poles thrust the logs into the chute. The jam crew, scattered for many miles along the lower stretches, kept the drive going; running out over the surface of the river like water-bugs to thrust apart logs threatening to lock; leaning for hours on the shafts of their peavies watching contemplatively the orderly ranks as they drifted by, sleepy, on the bosom of the river; occasionally gathering, as the filling of the river gave warning, to break a jam. By the end of the second day the pond was clear, and as Charlie's wanigan was drifting toward the chute, the first of Johnson's drive floated into the head of the pond.

V

CHARLIE'S wanigan, in case you do not happen to know what such a thing may be, was a scow about twenty feet long by ten wide. It was very solidly constructed of hewn timbers, square at both ends, was inconceivably clumsy, and weighed an unbelievable number of pounds. When loaded, it carried all the bed-rolls, tents, provisions, cooking utensils, tools, and a chest of tobacco, clothes, and other minor supplies. It was managed by Charlie and his two cookees by means of pike-poles and a long sweep at either end. The pike-poles assured progress when the current slacked; the sweeps kept her head-on when drifting with the stream.

Charlie's temperament was pessimistic at best. When the wanigan was to be moved, he rose fairly to the heights of what might be called destructive prophecy.

The packing began before the men had finished breakfast. Shortly after daylight the wanigan, pushed strongly from shore by the pike-poles, was drifting toward the chute. When the heavy scow threatened to turn side-on, the sweeps at either end churned the water frantically in an endeavour to straighten her out. Sometimes, by a misunderstanding, they worked against each other. Then Charlie, raging from one to the other of his satellites, frothed and roared commands and vituperations. His voice rose to a shriek. The cookees, bewildered by so much violence, lost their heads completely. Then Charlie abruptly fell to an exaggerated calm. He sat down amidships on a pile of bags, and gazed with ostentatious indifference out over the pond. Finally, in a voice fallen almost to a whisper, and with an elaborate politeness, Charlie proffered a request that his assistants acquire the sense God gave a rooster. Newmark, who had elected to accompany the wanigan on its voyage, evidently found it vastly amusing, for his eyes twinkled behind his glasses. As the wanigan neared the sluice through which it must shoot the flood-water, the excitement mounted to fever pitch. The water boiled under the strokes of the long steering oars. The air swirled with the multitude and vigour of Charlie's commands. As many of the driving crew as were within distance gathered to watch. It was a supreme moment. As Newmark looked at the smooth rim of the water sucking into the chute, he began to wonder why he had come.

However, the noble ship was pointed right at last, and caught the faster water head-on. Even Charlie managed to look cheerful for an instant, and to grin at his passenger as he wiped his forehead with a very old, red handkerchief.

" All right now," he shouted.

Zeke and his mate took in the oars. The wanigan shot forward below the gate—

Whack! Bump! Bang! and the scow stopped so suddenly that its four men plunged forward in a miscellaneous heap, while Zeke narrowly escaped going overboard. Almost immediately the water, backed up behind the stern, began to overflow into the boat. Newmark, clearing his vision as well as he could for lack of his glasses, saw that the scow had evidently run her bow on an obstruction, and had been brought to a standstill square beneath the sluice-gate. Men seemed to be running toward them. The water was beginning to flow the entire length of the boat. Various lighter articles shot past him and disappeared over the side. Charlie had gone crazy and was grabbing at these, quite uselessly, for as fast as he had caught one thing he let it go in favour of another. The cookees, retaining some small degr e of coolness, were pushing uselessly with pike-poles.

Newmark had an inspiration. The more important matters, such as the m n's clothes-bags, the rolls of bedding, and the heavier supplies of provisions, had not yet cut loose from their moorings, although the rapid backing of the water threatened soon to convert the wanigan into a chute for nearly the full volume of the current. He seized one of the long oars, thrust the blade under the edge of a thwart astern laid the shaft of the oar across the cargo, and by resting his weight on the handle attempted to bring it down to bind the contents of the wanigan to their places. The cookees saw what he was about, and came to his assistance. Together they succeeded in bending the long hickory sweep far enough to catch its handle-end under another, forward, thwart. The second oar was quickly locked alongside the first, and not a moment too soon. A rush of water forced them all to cling for their lives. The poor old wanigan was almost buried by the river.

But now help was at hand. Two or three rivermen appeared at the edge of the chute. A moment later old man Reed ran up, carrying a rope. This, after some difficulty, was made fast to the bow of the wanigan. A dozen men ran with the end of it to a position of vantage from which they might be able to pull the bow away from the sunken obstruction, but Orde, appearing above, called a halt. After consultation with Reed, another rope was brought and the end of it tossed down to the shipwrecked crew. Orde pointed to the stern of the boat, revolving his hands in pantomime to show that the wanigan would be apt to upset if allowed to get side-on when freed. A short rope led to the top of the dam allowed the bow to be lifted free of the obstruction; a cable astern prevented the current from throwing her broadside to the rush of waters; another cable from the bow led her in the way she should go. Ten minutes later she was pulled ashore out of the eddy below, very much water-logged, and manned by a drenched and disgruntled crew.

But Orde allowed them little chance for lamentation.

"Hard luck!" he said briefly. "Hope you haven't lost much. Now get a move on you and bail out. You've got to get over the shallows while this head is on."

"That's all the thanks you get," grumbled Charlie to himself and the other three as Orde moved away. "Work, slave, get up in the night, drownd yourself——"

He happily discovered that the pails under the forward thwart had not been carried away, and all started in to bail. It was a back-breaking job, and consumed the greater part of two hours. Even at the end of that time the wanigan, though dry of loose water, floated but sluggishly.

"'Bout two ton of water in them bed-rolls and turkeys," grumbled Charlie. "Well, get at it!"

Newmark soon discovered that the progress of the wanigan was looked upon in the light of a side-show by the rivermen. Its appearance was signal for shouts of delighted and ironic encouragement; its tribulations—which at first, in the white-water, were many—the occasion for unsympathetic and unholy joy. Charlie looked on all spectators as enemies. Part of the time he merely glowered. Part of the time he tried to reply in kind. To his intense disgust, he was taken seriously in neither case.

In a couple of hours' run the wanigan had overtaken and left far behind the rear of the drive. All about floated the logs, caroming gently one against the other, shifting and changing the pattern of their brown against the blue of the water. The current flowed strongly and smoothly, but without obstruction. Everything went well. The banks slipped by silently and mysteriously, like the unrolling of a panorama—little strips of marshland, stretches of wood-

land where the great trees leaned out over the river, thickets
of overflowed swampland with the water rising and draining among roots in a strange regularity of its own. The
sun shone warm. There was no wind. Newmark wrung out
his outer garments, and basked below the gunwale. Zeke
and his companion pulled spasmodically on the sweeps.
Charlie, having regained his equanimity together with his
old brown derby, which he came upon floating sodden in
an eddy, marched up and down the broad gunwale with
his pike-pole, thrusting away such logs as threatened interference.

"Well," said he at last, "we better make camp. We'll
be down in the jam pretty soon."

The cookees abandoned the sweeps in favour of more
pike-poles. By pushing and pulling on the logs floating
about them, they managed to work the wanigan in close
to the bank. Charlie, a coil of rope in his hand, surveyed
the prospects.

"We'll stop right down there by that little knoll," he
announced.

He leaped ashore, made a turn around a tree, and braced
himself to snub the boat, but unfortunately he had not
taken into consideration the "two ton" of water soaked
up by the cargo. The weight of the craft relentlessly
dragged him forward. In vain he braced and struggled.
The end of the rope came to the tree; he clung for a
moment, then let go, and ran around the tree to catch it
before it should slip into the water.

By this time the wanigan had caught the stronger current at the bend and was gathering momentum. Charlie
tried to snub at a sapling, and broke the sapling; on a
stub, and uprooted the stub. Down the banks and through
the brush he tore at the end of his rope, clinging desperately, trying at every solid tree to stop the career of his
runaway, but in every instance being forced by the danger

of jamming his hands to let go. Again he lost his derby. The landscape was a blur. Dimly he made out the howls of laughter as the outfit passed a group of rivermen. Then abruptly a ravine yawned before him, and he let go just in time to save himself a fall. The wanigan, trailing her rope, drifted away.

Nor did she stop until she had overtaken the jam. There, her momentum reduced by the closer crowding of the logs, she slowed down enough so that Newmark and the cookees managed to work her to the bank and make her fast.

That evening, after the wanigan's crew had accomplished a hard afternoon's work pitching camp and drying blankets, the first of the rear drifted in very late after a vain search for camp farther up stream.

"For God's sake, Charlie," growled one, "it's a wonder you wouldn't run through to Redding and be done with it."

Whereupon Charlie, who had been preternaturally calm all the afternoon, uttered a shriek of rage, and with a carving-knife chased that man out into the brush. Nor would he be appeased to the point of getting supper until Orde himself had intervened.

"Well," said Orde to Newmark later, around the camp-fire, "how does river-driving strike you?"

"It is extremely interesting," replied Newmark.

"Like to join the wanigan crew permanently?"

"No, thanks," returned Newmark drily.

"Well, stay with us as long as you're having a good time," invited Orde heartily, but turning away from his rather uncommunicative visitor.

"Thank you," Newmark acknowledged this, "I believe I will."

"Well, Tommy," called Orde across the fire to North, "I reckon we've got to rustle some more supplies. That shipwreck of ours to-day mighty near cleaned us out of some things. Lucky Charlie held his head and locked in the bedding with those sweeps, or we'd have been strapped."

"I didn't do it," grumbled Charlie. "It was him."

"Oh!" Orde congratulated Newmark. "Good work! I'm tickled to death you belonged to that crew."

"That old mossback Reed was right on deck with his rope," remarked Johnny Simms. "That was pretty decent of him."

"Old skunk!" growled North. "He lost us two days with his damn nonsense. You let him off too easy, Jack."

"Oh, he's a poor old devil," replied Orde easily. "He means well enough. That's the way the Lord made him. He can't help how he's made."

VI

DURING the thirty-three days of the drive, Newmark, to the surprise of everybody, stayed with the
work. Some of these days were very disagreeable.
April rains are cold and persistent—the proverbs as to
showers were made for another latitude. Drenched garments are bad enough when a man is moving about and
has daylight; but when night falls, and the work is over,
he likes a dry place and a change with which to comfort
himself. Dry places there were none. Even the interior of
the tents became sodden by continual exits and entrances
of dripping men, while dry garments speedily dampened
in the shiftings of camp which, in the broader reaches of
the lower river, took place nearly every day. Men worked
in soaked garments, slept in damp blankets. Charlie cooked
only by virtue of persistence. The rivermen ate standing
up, as close to the sputtering, roaring fires as they could
get. Always the work went forward.

But there were other times when a golden sun rose each
morning a little earlier on a green and joyous world. The
river ran blue. Migratory birds fled busily northward—
robins, flute-voiced blue-birds, warblers of many species,
sparrows of different kinds, shore birds and ducks, the
sweet-songed thrushes. Little tepid breezes wandered up and
down, warm in contrast to the faint snow-chill that even
yet lingered in the shadows. Sounds carried clearly, so that
the shouts and banter of the rivermen were plainly audible
up the reaches of the river. Ashore moist and aggressive
green things were pushing up through the watery earth

52

Several Bad Jams Relieved the Monotony

from which, in shade, the last frost had not yet departed. At camp the fires roared invitingly. Charlie's grub was hot and grateful. The fir beds gave dreamless sleep.

Newmark followed the work of the log-drive with great interest. All day long he tramped back and forth—on jam one day, on the rear the next. He never said much, but watched keenly, and listened to the men's banter both on the work and about the evening's fire as though he enjoyed it. Gradually the men got used to him, and ceased to treat him as an outsider. His thin, eager face, his steel-blue, inquiring eyes behind the glasses, his gray felt hat, his lank, tense figure in its gray, became a familiar feature. They threw remarks to him, to which he replied briefly and drily. When anything interesting was going on, somebody told him about it. Then he hurried to the spot, no matter how distant it might be. He used always the river trail; he never attempted to ride the logs.

He seemed to depend most on observation, for he rarely asked any questions. What few queries he had to proffer, he made to Orde himself, waiting sometimes until evening to interview that busy and good-natured individual. Then his questions were direct and to the point. They related generally to the advisability of something he had seen done; only rarely did they ask for explanation of the work itself. That Newmark seemed capable of puzzling out for himself.

The drive, as has been said, went down as far as Redding in thirty-three days. It had its share of tribulation. The men worked fourteen and sixteen hours at times. Several bad jams relieved the monotony. Three dams had to be sluiced through. Problems of mechanics arose to be solved on the spot; problems that an older civilisation would have attacked deliberately and with due respect for the seriousness of the situation and the dignity of engineering. Orde solved them by a rough-and-ready but very effective rule of thumb. He built and abandoned structures

which would have furnished opportunity for a winter's discussion to some committees; just as, earlier in the work,
the loggers had built through a rough country some hundreds of miles of road better than railroad grade, solid in
foundation, and smooth as a turnpike, the quarter of which
would have occupied the average county board of super-
visors for five years. And while he was at it, Orde kept
his men busy and satisfied. Your white-water birler is not
an easy citizen to handle. Yet never once did the boss
appear hurried or flustered. Always he wandered about,
his hands in his pockets, chewing a twig, his round, wind-
reddened face puckered humorously, his blue eyes twinkling, his square, burly form lazily relaxed. He seemed to
meet his men almost solely on the plane of good-natured
chaffing. Yet the work was done, and done efficiently, and
Orde was the man responsible.

The drive of which Orde had charge was to be delivered
at the booms of Morrison and Daly, a mile or so above the
city of Redding. Redding was a thriving place of about
thirty thousand inhabitants, situated on a long rapids some
forty miles from Lake Michigan. The water-power developed from the rapids explained Redding's existence. Most
of the logs floated down the river were carried through to
the village at the lake coast, where, strung up the river
for eight or ten miles, stood a dozen or so big saw-mills,
with concomitant booms, yards, and wharves. Morrison and
Daly, however, had built a saw and planing mill at Redding, where they supplied most of the local trade and that
of the surrounding country-side.

The drive, then, was due to break up as soon as the
logs should be safely impounded.

The last camp was made some six or eight miles above
the mill. From that point a good proportion of the rivermen, eager for a taste of the town, tramped away down
the road, to return early in the morning, more or less

runk, but faithful to their job. One or two did not eturn.

Among the revellers was the cook, Charlie, commonly :alled The Doctor. The rivermen early worked off the effects of their rather wild spree, and turned up at noon chipper as larks. Not so the cook. He moped about disconsolately all day; and in the evening, after his work had been finished, he looked so much like a chicken with the pip that Orde's attention was attracted.

" Got that dark-brown taste, Charlie? " he inquired with mock solicitude.

The cook mournfully shook his head.

" Large head? Let's feel your pulse. Stick out your tongue, sonny."

" I ain't been drinking, I tell you! " growled Charlie.

" Drinking! " expostulated Orde, horrified. " Of course not! I hope none of *my* boys ever take a drink! But that lemon-pop didn't agree with your stomach—now did it, Charlie? "

" I tell you I only had two glasses of beer! " cried Charlie, goaded, " and I can prove it by Johnny Challan."

Orde turned to survey the pink-cheeked, embarrassed young boy thus designated.

" How many glasses did Johnny Challan have? " he inquired.

" He didn't drink none to speak of," spoke up the boy.

" Then why this joyless demeanour? " begged Orde.

Charlie grumbled, fiercely inarticulate; but Johnny Challan interposed with a chuckle of enjoyment.

" He got ' bunked.' "

" Tell us! " cried Orde delightedly.

" It was down at McNeill's place," explained Johnny Challan, encouraged by the interest of his audience. " They was a couple of sports there who throwed out three cards on the table and bet you couldn't pick the jack. They

showed you where the jack was before they throwed, and
it surely looked like a picnic, but it wasn't."

"Three-card monte," said Newmark.

"How much?" asked Simms.

"About fifty dollars," replied the boy.

Orde turned on the disgruntled cook.

"And you had fifty in your turkey, camping with this
outfit of hard citizens!" he cried. "You ought to lose it."

Johnny Challan was explaining to his companions exactly how the game was played.

"It's a case of keep your eye on the card, I should think,"
said big Tim Nolan. "If you got a quick enough eye to
see him flip the card around, you ought to be able to
pick her."

"That's what this sport said," agreed Challan. "'Your
eye agin my hand,' says he."

"Well, I'd like to take a try at her," mused Tim.

But at this point Newmark broke into the discussion.

"Have you a pack of cards?" he asked in his dry, in-
cisive manner.

Somebody rummaged in a turkey and produced the remains of an old deck.

"I don't believe this is a full deck," said he, "and I
think they's part of two decks in it."

"I only want three," assured Newmark, reaching his
hand for the pack.

The men crowded around close, those in front squatting,
those behind looking over their shoulders.

Newmark cleared a cracker-box of drying socks and drew
it to him.

"These three are the cards," he said, speaking rapidly.
"There is the jack of hearts. I pass my hands—so. Pick
the jack, one of you," he challenged, leaning back from
the cracker-box on which lay the three cards, back up.
"Any of you," he urged. "You, North."

The Doctor

Thus directly singled out, the foreman leaned forward and rather hesitatingly laid a blunt forefinger on one of the bits of pasteboard.

Without a word, Newmark turned it over. It was the ten of spades.

"Let me try," interposed Tim Nolan, pressing his big shoulders forward. "I bet I know which it was that time; and I bet I can pick her next time."

"Oh, yes, you *bet*!" shrugged Newmark. "And that's where the card-sharps get you fellows every time. Well, pick it," said he, again deftly flipping the cards.

Nolan, who had watched keenly, indicated one without hesitation. Again it proved to be the ten of spades.

"Anybody else ambitious?" inquired Newmark.

Everybody was ambitious; and the young man, with inexhaustible patience, threw out the cards, the corners of his mouth twitching sardonically at each wrong guess.

At length he called a halt.

"By this time I'd have had all your money," he pointed out. "Now, I'll pick the jack."

For the last time he made his swift passes and distributed the cards. Then quite calmly, without disturbing the three on the cracker-box, he held before their eyes the jack of hearts.

An exclamation broke from the interested group. Tim Nolan, who was the nearest, leaned forward and turned over the three on the board. They were the eight of diamonds and two tens of spades.

"That's how the thing is worked nine times out of ten," announced Newmark. "Once in a while you'll run against a straight game, but not often."

"But you showed us the jack every time before you throwed them!" puzzled Johnny Simms.

"Sleight of hand," explained Newmark. "The simplest kind of palming."

VII

AFTER the men had been paid off, perhaps a dozen
of them hung around the yards awaiting evening
and the rendezvous named by Orde. The rest
drifted away full of good intentions, but did not show
up again. Orde himself was busy up to the last moment,
but finally stamped out of the office just as the boarding-
house bell rang for supper. He surveyed what remained
of his old crew and grinned.

"Well, boys, ready for trouble?" he greeted them.
"Come on."

They set out up the long reach of Water Street, their
steel caulks biting deep into the pitted board-walks.

For nearly a mile the street was flanked solely by lumberyards, small mills, and factories. Then came a strip of
unimproved land, followed immediately by the wooden,
ramshackle structures of Hell's Half-Mile.

In the old days every town of any size had its Hell's
Half-Mile, or the equivalent. Saginaw boasted of its Cata-
combs; Muskegon, Alpena, Port Huron, Ludington, had
their "Pens," "White Rows," "River Streets," "Kilyub-
bin," and so forth. They supported row upon row of saloons, alike stuffy and squalid; gambling hells of all sorts;
refreshment "parlours," where drinks were served by
dozens of "pretty waiter-girls," and huge dance-halls.

The proprietors of these places were a bold and un-
scrupulous lot. In their everyday business they had to deal
with the most dangerous rough-and-tumble fighters this
country has ever known; with men bubbling over with the

joy of life, ready for quarrel if quarrel also spelled fun, drinking deep, and heavy-handed and fearless in their cups. But each of these rivermen had two or three hundred dollars to "blow" as soon as possible. The pickings were good. Men got rich very quickly at this business. And there existed this great advantage in favour of the dive-keeper: nobody cared what happened to a riverman. You could pound him over the head with a lead pipe, or drug his drink, or choke him to insensibility, or rob him and throw him out into the street, or even drop him tidily through a trap-door into the river flowing conveniently beneath. Nobody bothered—unless, of course, the affair was so bungled as to become public. The police knew enough to stay away when the drive hit town. They would have been annihilated if they had not. The only fly in the divekeeper's ointment was that the riverman would fight back.

And fight back he did, until from one end of his street to the other he had left the battered evidences of his skill as a warrior. His constant heavy lifting made him as hard as nails and as strong as a horse; the continual demand on his agility in riding the logs kept him active and prevented him from becoming muscle-bound; in his wild heart was not the least trace of fear of anything that walked, crawled, or flew. And he was as tireless as machinery, and apparently as indifferent to punishment as a man cast in iron.

Add to this a happy and complete disregard of consequences—to himself or others—of anything he did, and, in his own words, he was a "hard man to nick."

As yet the season was too early for much joy along Hell's Half-Mile. Orde's little crew, and the forty or fifty men of the drive that had preceded him, constituted the rank and file at that moment in town. A little later, when all the drives on the river should be in, and those of its tribu-

taries, and the men still lingering at the woods camps, at
least five hundred woods-weary men would be turned loose.
Then Hell's Half-Mile would awaken in earnest from its
hibernation. The lights would blaze from day to day. From
its opened windows would blare the music, the cries of
men and women, the shuffle of feet, the noise of fighting,
the shrieks of wild laughter, curses deep and frank and
unashamed, songs broken and interrupted. Crews of men,
arms locked, would surge up and down the narrow sidewalks, their little felt hats cocked one side, their heads
back, their fearless eyes challenging the devil and all his
works—and getting the challenge accepted. Girls would flit
across the lit windows like shadows before flames, or stand
in the doorways hailing the men jovially by name. And
every few moments, above the roar of this wild inferno,
would sound the sudden crash and the dull blows of combat. Only, never was heard the bark of the pistol. The
fighting was fierce, and it included kicking with the sharp
steel boot-caulks, biting and gouging; but it barred knives
and firearms. And when Hell's Half-Mile was thus in full
eruption, the citizens of Redding stayed away from Water
Street after dark. " Drive's in," said they, and had business
elsewhere. And the next group of rivermen, hurrying
toward the fun, broke into an eager dog-trot. " Taking the
old town apart to-night," they told each other. " Let's get
in the game."

To-night, however, the street was comparatively quiet.
The saloons were of modified illumination. In many of
them men stood drinking, but in a sociable rather than a
hilarious mood. Old friends of the two drives were getting
together for a friendly glass. The barkeepers were list-
lessly wiping the bars. The " pretty waiter-girls " gossiped
with each other and yawned behind their hands. From several doorways Orde's little compact group was accosted
by the burly saloonkeepers.

" Hullo, boys! " said they invariably, " glad to see you back. Come in and have a drink on me."

Well these men knew that one free drink would mean a dozen paid for. But the rivermen merely shook their heads.

" Huh! " sneered one of the girls. " Them's no river-jacks! Them's just off the hay trail, I bet! "

But even this time-honoured and generally effective taunt was ignored.

In the middle of the third block Orde wheeled sharp to the left down a dark and dangerous-looking alley. Another turn to the right brought him into a very narrow street. Facing this street stood a three-story wooden structure, into which led a high-arched entrance up a broad half-flight of wooden steps. This was McNeill's.

As Orde and his men turned into the narrow street, a figure detached itself from the shadow and approached. Orde uttered an exclamation.

" You here, Newmark? " he cried.

" Yes," replied that young man. " I want to see this through."

" With those clothes? " marvelled Orde. " It's a wonder some of these thugs haven't held you up long ago! I'll get Johnny here to go back with you to the main street."

" No," argued Newmark, " I want to go in with you."

" It's dangerous," explained Orde. " You're likely to get slugged."

" I can stand it if you can," returned Newmark.

" I doubt it," said Orde grimly. " However, it's your funeral. Come on, if you want to."

McNeill's lower story was given over entirely to drinking. A bar ran down all one side of the room. Dozens of little tables occupied the floor. " Pretty waiter-girls " were prepared to serve drinks at these latter—and to share in them, at a commission. The second floor was a theatre, and the third a dance-hall. Beneath the building were still viler depths. From this basement the riverman and the shanty boy generally graduated penniless, and perhaps unconscious, to the street. Now, your lumber-jack did not customarily arrive at this stage without more or less lively doings en route; therefore McNeill's maintained a force of fighters. They were burly, sodden men, in striking contrast to the clean-cut, clear-eyed rivermen, but strong in their experience and their discipline. To be sure, they might not last quite as long as their antagonists could—a whisky training is not conducive to long wind—but they always lasted plenty long enough. Sand-bags and brass knuckles helped some, ruthless singleness of purpose counted, and team work finished the job. At times the storm rose high, but up to now McNeill had always ridden it.

Orde and his men entered the lower hall, as though sauntering in without definite aim. Perhaps a score of men were in the room. Two tables of cards were under way— with a great deal of noisy card-slapping that proclaimed the game merely friendly. Eight or ten other men wandered about idly, chaffing loudly with the girls, pausing to overlook the card games, glancing with purposeless curiosity at the professional gamblers sitting quietly behind their various lay-outs. It was a dull evening.

Orde wandered about with the rest, a wide, good-natured smile on his face.

"Start your little ball to rolling for that," he instructed the roulette man, tossing down a bill. "Dropped again!" he lamented humorously. "Can't seem to have any luck."

He drifted on to the crap game.

"Throw us the little bones, pardner," he said. "I'll go you a five on it."

He lost here, and so found himself at the table presided over by the three-card monte men. The rest of his party, who had according to instructions scattered about the place, now began quietly to gravitate in his direction.

"What kind of a lay-out is this?" inquired Orde.

The dealer held up the three cards face out.

"What kind of an eye have you got, bub?" he asked.

"Oh, I don't know. A pretty fair eye. Why?"

"Do you think you could pick out the jack when I throw them out like this?" asked the dealer.

"Sure! She's that one."

"Well," exclaimed the gambler with a pretence of disgust, "damn if you didn't! I bet you five dollars you can't do it again."

"Take you!" replied Orde. "Put up your five."

Again Orde was permitted to pick the jack.

"You've got the best eye that's been in this place since I got here," claimed the dealer admiringly. "Here, Dennis," said he to his partner, "try if you can fool this fellow."

Dennis obligingly took the cards, threw them, and lost. By this time the men, augmented by the idlers not busy with the card games, had drawn close.

"Sail into 'em, bub," encouraged one.

Whether it was that the gamblers, expert in the reading of a man's mood and intentions, sensed the fact that Orde might be led to plunge, or whether, more simply, they were using him as a capper to draw the crowd into their game, it would be difficult to say, but twice more they bungled the throw and permitted him to win.

Newmark plucked him at the sleeve.

"You're twenty dollars ahead," he muttered. "Quit it! I never saw anybody beat this game that much before."

Orde merely shrugged him off with an appearance of growing excitement, while an *habitué* of the place, probably one of the hired fighters, growled into Newmark's ear.

"Shut up, you damn dude!" warned this man. "Keep out of what ain't none of your business."

"What limit do you put on this game, anyway?" Orde leaned forward, his eyes alight.

The two gamblers spoke swiftly apart.

"How much do you want to bet?" asked one.

"Would you stand for five hundred dollars?" asked Orde.

A dead silence fell on the group. Plainly could be heard the men's quickened breathing. The shouts and noise from the card parties blundered through the stillness. Some one tiptoed across and whispered in the ear of the nearest player. A moment later the chairs at the two tables scraped back. One of them fell violently to the floor. Their occupants joined the tense group about the monte game. All the girls drew near. Only behind the bar the white-aproned bartenders wiped their glasses with apparent imperturbability, their eyes, however, on their brass knuckles hanging just beneath the counter, their ears pricked up for the riot call.

The gambler pretended to deliberate, his cool, shifty eyes running over the group before him. A small door immediately behind him swung slowly ajar an inch or so.

"Got the money?" he asked.

"Have you?" countered Orde.

Apparently satisfied, the man nodded.

"I'll go you, bub, if I lose," said he. "Lay out your money."

Orde counted out nine fifty-dollar bills and five tens. Probably no one in the group of men standing about had realised quite how much money five hundred dollars meant until they saw it thus tallied out before them.

"All right," said the gambler, taking up the cards.

"Hold on!" cried Orde. "Where's yours?"

"Oh, that's all right," the gambler reassured him. "I'm

with the house. I guess McNeill's credit is good," he laughed.

"That may all be," insisted Orde, "but I'm putting up my good money, and I expect to see good money put up in return."

They wrangled over this point for some time, but Orde was obstinate. Finally the gamblers yielded. A canvass of the drawer, helped out by the bar and the other games, made up the sum. It bulked large on the table beside Orde's higher denominations.

The interested audience now consisted of the dozen men comprised by Orde's friends; nearly twice as many strangers, evidently rivermen; eight hangers-on of the joint, probably fighters and "bouncers"; half a dozen professional gamblers, and several waitresses. The four barkeepers still held their positions. Of these, the rivermen were scattered loosely back of Orde, although Orde's own friends had by now gathered compactly enough at his shoulder. The mercenaries and gamblers had divided, and flanked the table at either side. Newmark, a growing wonder and disgust creeping into his usually unexpressive face, recognised the strategic advantage of this arrangement. In case of difficulty, a determined push would separate the rivermen from the gamblers long enough for the latter to disappear quietly through the small door at the back.

"Satisfied?" inquired the gambler briefly.

"Let her flicker," replied Orde with equal brevity.

A gasp of anticipation went up. Quite coolly the gambler made his passes. With equal coolness and not the slightest hesitation, Orde planted his great red fist on one of the cards.

"That is the jack," he announced, looking the gambler in the eye.

"Oh, is it?" sneered the dealer. "Well, turn it over and let's see."

" No! " roared Orde. " *You turn over the other two!* "

A low oath broke from the gambler, and his face contorted in a spasm. The barkeepers slid out from behind the bar. For a moment the situation was tense and threatening. The dealer with a sweeping glance again searched the faces of those before him. In that moment, probably, he made up his mind that an open scandal must be avoided. Force and broken bones, even murder, might be all right enough under colour of right. If Orde had turned up for a jack the card on which he now held his fist, and then had attempted to prove cheating, a cry of robbery and a lively fight would have given opportunity for making way with the stakes. But McNeill's could not afford to be shown up before thirty interested rivermen as running an open-and-shut brace-game. However, the gambler made a desperate try at what he must have known was a very forlorn hope.

" That isn't the way this game is played," said he. " Show up your jack."

" It's the way I play it," replied Orde sternly. " These gentlemen heard the bet." He reached over and dexterously flipped over the other two cards. " You see, neither of these is the jack; this must be."

" You win," assented the gambler, after a pause.

Orde, his fist still on the third card, began pocketing the stakes with the other hand. The gambler reached, palm up, across the table.

" Give me the other card," said he.

Orde picked it up, laughing. For a moment he seemed to hesitate, holding the bit of pasteboard tantalisingly outstretched, as though he were going to turn also this one face up. Then, quite deliberately he looked to right and to left where the fighters awaited their signal, laughed again, and handed the card to the gambler.

At once pandemonium broke loose. The rivermen of Orde's party fairly shouted with joy over the unexpected

"I Say, Orde, I Want to Apologise to You"

trick; the employees of the resort whispered apart; the gambler explained, low-voiced and angry, his reasons for not putting up a fight for so rich a stake.

" All to the bar ! " yelled Orde.

They made a rush, and lined up and ordered their drinks. Orde poured his on the floor and took the glass belonging to the man next him.

" Get them to give you another, Tim," said he. " No knock-out drops, if I can help it."

The men drank, and some one ordered another round.

" Tim," said Orde, low-voiced, " get the crowd together and we'll pull out. I've a thousand dollars on me, and they'll sand-bag me sure if I go alone. And let's get out right off."

Ten minutes later they all stood safely on the lighted thoroughfare of Water Street.

" Good-night, boys," said Orde. " Go easy, and show up at the booms Monday."

He turned up the street toward the main part of the town. Newmark joined him.

" I'll walk a little ways with you," he explained. " And I say, Orde, I want to apologise to you. 'Most of the evening I've been thinking you the worst fool I ever saw, but you can take care of yourself at every stage of the game. The trick was good, but your taking the other fellow's drink beat it."

VIII

ORDE heard no more of Newmark—and hardly thought of him—until over two weeks later.

In the meantime the riverman, assuming the more conventional garments of civilisation, lived with his parents in the old Orde homestead at the edge of town. This was a rather pretentious two-story brick structure, in the old solid, square architecture, surrounded by a small orchard, some hickories, and a garden. Orde's father had built it when he arrived in the pioneer country from New England forty years before. At that time it was considered well out in the country. Since then the town had crept to it, so that the row of grand old maples in front shaded a stone-guttered street. A little patch of corn opposite, and many still vacant lots above, placed it, however, as about the present limit of growth.

Jack Orde was the youngest and most energetic of a large family that had long since scattered to diverse cities and industries. He and Grandpa and Grandma Orde dwelt now in the big, echoing, old-fashioned house alone, save for the one girl who called herself the " help " rather than the servant. Grandpa Orde, now above sixty, was tall, straight, slender. His hair was quite white, and worn a little long. His features were finely chiselled and aquiline. From them looked a pair of piercing, young, black eyes. In his time, Grandpa Orde had been a mighty breaker of the wilderness; but his time had passed, and with the advent of a more intensive civilisation he had fallen upon somewhat straitened ways. Grandma Orde, on the other hand, was a very small, spry old lady, with a small face,

70

a small figure, small hands and feet. She dressed in the then usual cap and black silk of old ladies. Half her time she spent at her housekeeping, which she loved, jingling about from cellar to attic store-room, seeing that Amanda, 'the " help," had everything in order. The other half she sat in a wooden " Dutch " rocking-chair by a window overlooking the garden. Her silk-shod feet rested neatly side by side on a carpet-covered hassock, her back against a gay tapestried cushion. Near her purred big Jim, a maltese rumoured to weigh fifteen pounds. Above her twittered a canary.

And the interior of the house itself was in keeping. The low ceilings, the slight irregularities of structure peculiar to the rather rule-of-thumb methods of the earlier builders, the deep window embrasures due to the thickness of the walls, the unexpected passages leading to unsuspected rooms, and the fact that many of these apartments were approached by a step or so up or a step or so down— these lent to it a quaint, old-fashioned atmosphere enhanced further by the steel engravings, the antique furnishings, the many-paned windows, and all the belongings of old people who have passed from a previous generation untouched by modern ideas.

To this house and these people Orde came direct from the greatness of the wilderness and the ferocity of Hell's Half-Mile. Such contrasts were possible even ten or fifteen years ago. The untamed country lay at the doors of the most modern civilisation.

Newmark, reappearing one Sunday afternoon at the end of the two weeks, was apparently bothered. He examined the Orde place for some moments; walked on beyond it; finding nothing there, he returned, and after some hesitation turned in up the tar sidewalk and pulled at the old-fashioned wire bell-pull. Grandma Orde herself answered the door.

At sight of her fine features, her dainty lace cap and mitts, and the stiffness of her rustling black silks, Newmark took off his gray felt hat.

"Good-afternoon," said he. "Will you kindly tell me where Mr. Orde lives?"

"This is Mr. Orde's," replied the little old lady.

"Pardon me," persisted Newmark, "I am looking for Mr. Jack Orde, and I was directed here. I am sorry to have troubled you."

"Mr. Jack Orde lives here," returned Grandma Orde. "He is my son. Would you like to see him?"

"If you please," assented Newmark gravely, his thin, shrewd face masking itself with its usual expression of quizzical cynicism.

"Step this way, please, and I'll call him," requested his interlocutor, standing aside from the doorway.

Newmark entered the cool, dusky interior, and was shown to the left into a dim, long room. He perched on a mahogany chair, and had time to notice the bookcases with the white owl atop, the old piano with the yellowing keys, the haircloth sofa and chairs, the steel engravings, and the two oil portraits, when Orde's large figure darkened the door.

For an instant the young man, who must just have come in from the outside sunshine, blinked into the dimness. Newmark, too, blinked back, although he could by this time see perfectly well.

Newmark had known Orde only as a riverman. Like most Easterners, then and now, he was unable to imagine a man in rough clothes as being anything but essentially a rough man. The figure he saw before him was decently and correctly dressed in what was then the proper Sunday costume. His big figure set off the cloth to advantage, and even his wind-reddened face seemed toned down and refined by the change in costume and surroundings.

"Oh, it's you, Mr. Newmark!" cried Orde in his hearty way, and holding out his hand. "I'm glad to see you. Where you been? Come on out of there. This is the 'company place.'" Without awaiting a reply, he led the way into the narrow hall, whence the two entered another, brighter room, in which Grandma Orde sat, the canary singing above her head.

"Mother," said Orde, "this is Mr. Newmark, who was with us on the drive this spring."

Grandma Orde laid her gold-bowed glasses and her black leather Bible on the stand beside her.

"Mr. Newmark and I spoke at the door," said she, extending her frail hand with dignity. "If you were on the drive, Mr. Newmark, you must have been one of the High Privates in this dreadful war we all read about."

Newmark laughed and made some appropriate reply. A few moments later, at Orde's suggestion, the two passed out a side door and back into the remains of the old orchard.

"It's pretty nice here under the trees," said Orde. "Sit down and light up. Where you been for the last couple of weeks?"

"I caught Johnson's drive and went on down river with him to the lake," replied Newmark, thrusting the offered cigar in one corner of his mouth and shaking his head at Orde's proffer of a light.

"You must like camp life."

"I do not like it at all," negatived Newmark emphatically, "but the drive interested me. It interested me so much that I've come back to talk to you about it."

"Fire ahead," acquiesced Orde.

"I'm going to ask you a few questions about yourself, and you can answer them or not, just as you please."

"Oh, I'm not bashful about my career," laughed Orde.

"How old are you?" inquired Newmark abruptly.

" Thirty."

" How long have you been doing that sort of thing— driving, I mean? "

" Off and on, about six years."

" Why did you go into that particular sort of thing? "

Orde selected a twig and carefully threw it at a lump in the turf.

" Because there's nothing ahead of shovelling but dirt," he replied with a quaint grin.

" I see," said Newmark, after a pause. " Then you think there's more future to that sort of thing than the sort of thing the rest of your friends go in for—law, and wholesale groceries, and banking and the rest of it? "

" There is for me," replied Orde simply.

" Yet you're merely river-driving on a salary at thirty."

Orde flushed slowly, and shifted his position.

" Exactly so—Mr. District Attorney," he said drily.

Newmark started from his absorption in his questioning and shifted his unlighted cigar.

" Does sound like it," he admitted; " but I'm not asking all this out of idle curiosity. I've got a scheme in my head that I think may work out big for us both."

" Well," assented Orde reservedly, " in that case—I'm foreman on this drive because my outfit went kerplunk two years ago, and I'm making a fresh go at it."

" Failed? " inquired Newmark.

" Partner skedaddled," replied Orde. " Now, if you're satisfied with my family history, suppose you tell me what the devil you're driving at."

He was plainly restive under the cross-examination to which he had been subjected.

" Look here," said Newmark, abruptly changing the subject, " you know that rapids up river flanked by shallows, where the logs are always going aground? "

" I do," replied Orde, still grim.

" Well, why wouldn't it help to put a string of piers down both sides, with booms between them to hold the logs in the deeper water? "

" It would," said Orde.

" Why isn't it done, then? "

" Who would do it? " countered Orde, leaning back more easily in the interest of this new discussion. " If Daly did it, for instance, then all the rest of the drivers would get the advantage of it for nothing."

" Get them to pay their share."

Orde grinned. " I'd like to see you get any three men to agree to anything on this river."

" And a sort of dam would help at that Spruce Rapids? "

" Sure! If you improved the river for driving, she'd be easier to drive. That goes without saying."

" How many firms drive logs on this stream? "

" Ten," replied Orde, without hesitation.

" How many men do they employ? "

" Driving? " asked Orde.

" Driving."

" About five hundred; a few more or less."

" Now suppose," Newmark leaned forward impressively, " suppose a firm should be organised to drive *all* the logs on the river. Suppose it improved the river with necessary piers, dams, and all the rest of it, so that the driving would be easier. Couldn't it drive with less than five hundred men, and couldn't it save money on the cost of driving? "

" It might," agreed Orde.

" You know the conditions here. If such a firm should be organised and should offer to drive the logs for these ten firms at so much a thousand, do you suppose it would get the business? "

" It would depend on the driving firm," said Orde. " You see, mill men have got to have their logs. They can't afford to take chances. It wouldn't pay."

" Then that's all right," agreed Newmark, with a gleam of satisfaction across his thin face. " Would you form a partnership with me having such an object in view? "

Orde threw back his head and laughed with genuine amusement.

" I guess you don't realise the situation," said he. " We'd have to have a few little things like distributing booms, and tugs, and a lot of tools and supplies and works of various kinds."

" Well, we'd get them."

It was now Orde's turn to ask questions.

" How much are you worth? " he inquired bluntly.

" About twenty thousand dollars," replied Newmark.

" Well, if I raise very much more than twenty thousand cents, I'm lucky just now."

" How much capital would we have to have? " asked Newmark.

Orde thought for several minutes, twisting the petal of an old apple-blossom between his strong, blunt fingers.

" Somewhere near seventy-five thousand dollars," he estimated at last.

" That's easy," cried Newmark. " We'll make a stock company—say a hundred thousand shares. We'll keep just enough between us to control the company—say fifty-one thousand. I'll put in my pile, and you can pay for yours out of the earnings of the company."

" That doesn't sound fair," objected Orde.

" You pay interest," explained Newmark. " Then we'll sell the rest of the stock to raise the rest of the money."

" If we can," interjected Orde.

" I think we can," asserted Newmark.

Orde fell into a brown study, occasionally throwing a twig or a particle of earth at the offending lump in the turf. Overhead the migratory warblers balanced right-side up or up-side down, searching busily among the new leaves,

"I'd Like to See You Get Any Three Men to Agree to
Anything on This River"

uttering their simple calls. The air was warm and soft and still, the sky bright. Fat hens clucked among the grasses. A feel of Sunday was in the air.

" I must have something to live on," said he thoughtfully at last.

" So must I," said Newmark. " We'll have to pay ourselves salaries, of course, but the smaller the better at first. You'll have to take charge of the men and the work and all the rest of it—I don't know anything about that. I'll attend to the incorporating and the routine, and I'll try to place the stock. You'll have to see, first of all, whether you can get contracts from the logging firms to drive the logs."

" How can I tell what to charge them? "

" We'll have to figure that very closely. You know where these different drives would start from, and how long each of them would take? "

" Oh, yes; I know the river pretty well."

" Well, then we'll figure how many days' driving there is for each, and how many men there are, and what it costs for wages, grub, tools—we'll just have to figure as near as we can to the actual cost, and then add a margin for profit and for interest on our investment."

" It might work out all right," admitted Orde.

" I'm confident it would," asserted Newmark. " And there'd be no harm figuring it all out, would there? "

" No," agreed Orde, " that would be fun all right."

At this moment Amanda appeared at the back door and waved an apron.

" Mr. Jack! " she called. " Come in to dinner."

Newmark looked puzzled, and, as he arose, glanced surreptitiously at his watch. Orde seemed to take the summons as one to be expected, however. In fact, the strange hour was the usual Sunday custom in the Redding of that day, and had to do with the late-church freedom of Amanda and her like.

"Come in and eat with us," invited Orde. "We'd be glad to have you."

But Newmark declined.

"Come up to-morrow night, then, at half-past six, for supper," Orde urged him. "We can figure on these things a little. I'm in Daly's all day, and hardly have time except evenings."

To this Newmark assented. Orde walked with him down the deep-shaded driveway with the clipped privet hedge on one side, to the iron gate that swung open when one drove over a projecting lever. There he said good-bye.

A moment later he entered the long dining-room, where Grandpa and Grandma Orde were already seated. An old-fashioned service of smooth silver and ivory-handled steel knives gave distinction to the plain white linen. A tea-pot smothered in a "cosey" stood at Grandma Orde's right. A sirloin roast on a noble platter awaited Grandpa Orde's knife.

Orde dropped into his place with satisfaction.

"Shut up, Cheep!" he remarked to a frantic canary hanging in the sunshine.

"Your friend seems a nice-appearing young man," said Grandma Orde. "Wouldn't he stay to dinner?"

"I asked him," replied Orde, "but he couldn't. He and I have a scheme for making our everlasting fortunes."

"Who is he?" asked grandma.

Orde dropped his napkin into his lap with a comical chuckle of dismay.

"Blest if I have the slightest idea, mother," he said. "Newmark joined us on the drive. Said he was a lawyer, and was out in the woods for his health. He's been with us, studying and watching the work, ever since."

IX

"I THINK I'll go see Jane Hubbard this evening," Orde remarked to his mother, as he arose from the table. This was his method of announcing that he would not be home for supper.

Jane Hubbard lived in a low one-story house of blue granite, situated amid a grove of oaks at the top of the hill. She was .a kindly girl, whose parents gave her free swing, and whose house, in consequence, was popular with the younger people. Every Sunday she offered to all who came a "Sunday-night lunch," which consisted of cold meats, cold salad, bread, butter, cottage cheese, jam, preserves, and the like, warmed by a cup of excellent tea. These refreshments were served by the guests themselves. It did not much matter how few or how many came.

On the Sunday evening in question Orde found about the usual crowd gathered. Jane herself, tall, deliberate in movement and in speech, kindly and thoughtful, talked in a corner with Ernest Colburn, who was just out of college, and who worked in a bank. Mignonne Smith, a plump, rather pretty little body with a tremendous aureole of hair like spun golden fire, was trying to balance a croquet-ball on the end of a ruler. The ball regularly fell off. Three young men, standing in attentive attitudes, thereupon dove forward in an attempt to catch it before it should hit the floor—which it generally did with a loud thump. A collapsed chair of slender lines stacked against the wall attested previous acrobatics. This much Orde, standing in the doorway, looked upon quite as the usual thing. Only he

missed the Incubus. Searching the room with his eyes, he
at length discovered that incoherent, desiccated, but persistent youth *vis-à-vis* with a stranger. Orde made out the
white of her gown in the shadows, the willowy outline
of her small and slender figure, and the gracious forward
bend of her head.

The company present caught sight of Orde standing in
the doorway, and suspended occupations to shout at him
joyfully. He was evidently a favourite. The strange girl
in the corner turned to him a white, long face, of which
he could see only the outline and the redness of the lips
where the lamplight reached them. She leaned slightly forward and the lips parted. Orde's muscular figure, standing
square and uncompromising in the doorway, the out-of-door
freshness of his complexion, the steadiness of his eyes
laughing back a greeting, had evidently attracted her. Or
perhaps anything was a relief from the Incubus.

" So you're back at last, are you, Jack? " drawled Jane
in her lazy, good-natured way. " Come and meet Miss
Bishop. Carroll, I want to present Mr. Orde."

Orde bowed ceremoniously into the penumbra cast by the
lamp's broad shade. The girl inclined gracefully her small
head with the glossy hair. The Incubus, his thin hands
clasped on his knee, his sallow face twisted in one of its
customary wry smiles, held to the edge of his chair with
characteristic pertinacity.

" Well, Walter," Orde addressed him genially, " are you
having a good time? "

" Yes-indeed! " replied the Incubus as though it were
one word.

His chair was planted squarely to exclude all others.
Orde surveyed the situation with good-humour.

" Going to keep the other fellow from getting a chance,
I see."

" Yes-indeed! " replied the Incubus.

Orde bent over, and with great ease lifted Incubus, chair, and all, and set him facing Mignonne Smith and the croquet-ball.

"Here, Mignonne," said he, "I've brought you another assistant."

He returned to the lamp, to find the girl, her dark eyes alight with amusement, watching him intently. She held the tip of a closed fan against her lips, which brought her head slightly forward in an attitude as though she listened. Somehow there was about her an air of poise, of absolute balanced repose quite different from Jane's rather awkward statics, and in direct contrast to Mignonne's dynamics.

"Walter is a very bright man in his own line," said Orde, swinging forward a chair, "but he mustn't be allowed any monopolies."

"How do you know I want him so summarily removed?" the girl asked him, without changing either her graceful attitude of suspended motion or the intentness of her gaze.

"Well," argued Orde, "I got him to say all he ever says to any girl—'Yes-indeed!'—so you couldn't have any more conversation from him. If you want to look at him, why, there he is in plain sight. Besides, I want to talk to you myself."

"Do you always get what you want?" inquired the girl.

Orde laughed.

"Any one can get anything he wants, if only he wants it bad enough," he asserted.

The girl pondered this for a moment, and finally lowered and opened her fan, and threw back her head in a more relaxed attitude.

"Some people," she amended. "However, I forgive you. I will even flatter you by saying I am glad you came. You look to have reached the age of discretion. I venture to say that these boys' idea of a lively evening is to throw bread about the table."

Orde flushed a little. The last time he had supped at Jane Hubbard's, that was exactly what they did do.

"They are young, of course," he said, "and you and I are very old and wise. But having a noisy, good time isn't such a great crime—or is it where you came from?"

The girl leaned forward, a sparkle of interest in her eyes.

"Are you and I going to fight?" she demanded.

"That depends on you," returned Orde squarely, but with perfect good-humour.

They eyed each other a moment. Then the girl closed her fan, and leaned forward to touch him on the arm with it.

"You are quite right not to allow me to say mean things about your friends, and I am a nasty little snip."

Orde bowed with sudden gravity.

"And they do throw bread," said he.

They both laughed. She leaned back with a movement of satisfaction, seeming to sink into the shadows.

"Now, tell me; what do you do?"

"What do I do?" asked Orde, puzzled.

"Yes. Everybody does something out West here. It's a disgrace not to do something, isn't it?"

"Oh, my business! I'm a river-driver just now."

"A river-driver?" she repeated, once more leaning forward. "Why, I've just been hearing a great deal about you."

"That so?" he inquired.

"Yes, from Mrs. Baggs."

"Oh!" said Orde. "Then you know what a drunken, swearing, worthless lot of bums and toughs we are, don't you?"

For the first time, in some subtle way she broke the poise of her attitude.

"There is Hell's Half-Mile," she reminded him.

"Oh, yes," said Orde bitterly, "there's Hell's Half-Mile! Whose fault is that? My rivermen's? My boys? Look here! I suppose you couldn't understand it, if you tried a month; but suppose you were working out in the woods nine months of the year, up early in the morning and in late at night. Suppose you slept in rough blankets, on the ground or in bunks, ate rough food, never saw a woman or a book, undertook work to scare your city men up a tree and into a hole too easy, risked your life a dozen times a week in a tangle of logs, with the big river roaring behind just waiting to swallow you; saw nothing but woods and river, were cold and hungry and wet, and so tired you couldn't wiggle, until you got to feeling like the thing was never going to end, and until you got sick of it way through in spite of the excitement and danger. And then suppose you hit town, where there were all the things you hadn't had—and the first thing you struck was Hell's Half-Mile. Say! you've seen water behind a jam, haven't you? Water-power's a good thing in a mill course, where it has wheels to turn; but behind a jam it just *rips* things—oh, what's the use talking! A girl doesn't know what it means. She couldn't understand."

He broke off with an impatient gesture. She was looking at him intently, her lips again half-parted.

"I think I begin to understand a little," said she softly. She smiled to herself. "But they are a hard and heartless class in spite of all their energy and courage, aren't they?" she drew him out.

"Hard and heartless!" exploded Orde. "There's no kinder lot of men on earth, let me tell you. Why, there isn't a man on that river who doesn't chip in five or ten dollars when a man is hurt or killed; and that means three or four days' hard work for him. And he may not know or like the injured man at all! Why——"

"What's all the excitement?" drawled Jane Hubbard

behind them. " Can't you make it a to-be-continued-in-our-next? We're 'most starved."

" Yes-indeed ! " chimed in the Incubus.

The company trooped out to the dining-room where the table, spread with all the good things, awaited them.

" Ernest, you light the candles," drawled Jane, drifting slowly along the table with her eye on the arrangements, " and some of you boys go get the butter and the milk-pitcher from the ice-box."

To Orde's relief, no one threw any bread, although the whole-hearted fun grew boisterous enough before the close of the meal. Miss Bishop sat directly across from him. He had small chance of conversation with her in the hubbub that raged, but he gained full leisure to examine her more closely in the fuller illumination. Throughout, her note was of fineness. Her hands, as he had already noticed, were long, the fingers tapering; her wrists were finely moulded, but slender, and running without abrupt swelling of muscles into the long lines of her forearm; her figure was rounded, but built on the curves of slenderness; her piled, glossy hair was so fine that though it was full of wonderful soft shadows denied coarser tresses, its mass hardly did justice to its abundance. Her face, again, was long and oval, with a peculiar transparence to the skin and a peculiar faint, healthy circulation of the blood well below the surface, which relieved her complexion of pallor, but did not give her a colour. The lips, on the contrary, were satin red, and Orde was mildly surprised, after his recent talk, to find them sensitively moulded, and with a quaint, child-like quirk at the corners. Her eyes were rather contemplative, and so black as to resemble spots.

In spite of her half-scornful references to " bread-throwing," she joined with evident pleasure in the badinage and more practical fun which struck the note of the supper. Only Orde thought to discern even in her more boisterous movements a graceful, courteous restraint, to catch in the bend of her head a dainty concession to the joy of the moment, to hear in the tones of her laughter a reservation of herself, which nevertheless was not at all a reservation, against the others.

After the meal was finished, each had his candle to blow out, and then all returned to the parlour, leaving the débris for the later attention of the " hired help."

Orde with determination made his way to Miss Bishop's side. She smiled at him.

" You see, I am a hypocrite as well as a mean little snip," said she. " I threw a little bread myself."

" Threw bread? " repeated Orde. " I didn't see you."

" The moon is made of green cheese," she mocked him, " and there are countries where men's heads do grow beneath their shoulders." She moved gracefully away toward Jane Hubbard. " Do you Western ' business men ' never deal in figures of speech as well as figures of the other sort? " she wafted back to him over her shoulder.

" I was very stupid," acknowledged Orde, following her.

She stopped and faced him in the middle of the room, smiling quizzically.

" Well? " she challenged.

" Well, what? " asked Orde, puzzled.

" I thought perhaps you wanted to ask me something."

" Why? "

" Your following me," she explained, the corners of her mouth smiling. " I had turned away——"

" I just wanted to talk to you," said Orde.

" And you always get what you want," she repeated. " Well? " she conceded, with a shrug of mock resignation. But the four other men here cut in with a demand.

" Music! " they clamoured. " We want music! "

With a nod, Miss Bishop turned to the piano, sweeping

aside her white draperies as she sat. She struck a few soft chords, and then, her long hands wandering idly and softly up and down the keys, she smiled at them over her shoulder.

" What shall it be? " she inquired.

Some one thrust an open song-book on the rack in front of her. The others gathered close about, leaning forward to see.

Song followed song, at first quickly, then at longer intervals. At last the members of the chorus dropped away one by one to occupations of their own. The girl still sat at the piano, her head thrown back idly, her hands wandering softly in and out of melodies and modulations. Watching her, Orde finally saw only the shimmer of her white figure, and the white outline of her head and throat. All the rest of the room was gray from the concentration of his gaze. At last her hands fell in her lap. She sat looking straight ahead of her.

Orde at once arose and came to her.

" That was a wonderfully quaint and beautiful thing," said he. " What was it? "

She turned to him, and he saw that the mocking had gone from her eyes and mouth, leaving them quite simple, like a child's.

" Did you like it? " she asked.

" Yes," said Orde. He hesitated and stammered awkwardly. " It was so still and soothing, it made me think of the river sometimes about dusk. What was it? "

" It wasn't anything. I was improvising."

" You made it up yourself? "

" It was myself, I suppose. I love to build myself a garden, and wander on until I lose myself in it. I'm glad there was a river in the garden—a nice, still, twilight river."

She flashed up at him, her head sidewise.

"There isn't always." She struck a crashing discord on the piano.

Every one looked up at the sudden noise of it.

"Oh, don't stop!" they cried in chorus, as though each had been listening intently.

The girl laughed up at Orde in amusement. Somehow this flash of an especial understanding between them to the exclusion of the others sent a warm glow to his heart.

"I do wish you had your harp here," said Jane Hubbard, coming indolently forward. "You just ought to hear her play the harp," she told the rest. "It's just the best thing you ever *did* hear!"

At this moment the outside door opened to admit Mr. and Mrs. Hubbard, who had, according to their usual Sunday custom, been spending the evening with a neighbour. This was the signal for departure. The company began to break up.

Orde pushed his broad shoulders in to screen Carroll Bishop from the others.

"Are you staying here?" he asked.

She opened her eyes wide at his brusqueness.

"I'm visiting Jane," she replied at length, with an affectation of demureness.

"Are you going to be here long?" was Orde's next question.

"About a month."

"I am coming to see you," announced Orde. "Good-night."

He took her hand, dropped it, and followed the others into the hall, leaving her standing by the lamp. She watched him until the outer door had closed behind him. Not once did he look back. Jane Hubbard, returning after a moment from the hall, found her at the piano again, her head slightly one side, playing with painful and accurate exactness a simple one-finger melody.

Orde walked home down the hill in company with the Incubus. Neither had anything to say; Orde because he was absorbed in thought, the Incubus because nothing occurred to draw from him his one remark. Their feet clipped sharply against the tar walks, or rang more hollow on the boards. Overhead the stars twinkled through the still-bare branches of the trees. With few exceptions the houses were dark. People " retired " early in Redding. An occasional hall light burned dimly, awaiting some one's return. At the gate of the Orde place, Orde roused himself to say good-night. He let himself into the dim-lighted hall, hung up his hat, and turned out the gas. For some time he stood in the dark, quite motionless; then, with the accuracy of long habitude, he walked confidently to the narrow stairs and ascended them. Subconsciously he avoided the creaking step, but outside his mother's door he stopped, arrested by a greeting from within.

" That you, Jack? " queried Grandma Orde.

For answer Orde pushed open the door, which stood an inch or so ajar, and entered. A dim light from a distant street-lamp, filtered through the branches of a tree, flickered against the ceiling. By its aid he made out the great square bed, and divined the tiny figure of his mother. He seated himself sidewise on the edge of the bed.

" Go to Jane's? " queried grandma in a low voice, to avoid awakening grandpa, who slept in the adjoining room.

" Yes," replied Orde, in the same tone.

" Who was there? "

" Oh, about the usual crowd."

He fell into an abstracted silence, which endured for several minutes.

" Mother," said he abruptly, at last, " I've met the girl I want for my wife."

Grandma Orde sat up in bed.

" Who is she? " she demanded.

"Her name is Carroll Bishop," said Orde, "and she's visiting Jane Hubbard."

"Yes, but *who* is she?" insisted Grandma Orde. "Where is she from?"

Orde stared at her in the dim light.

"Why, mother," he repeated for the second time that day, "blest if I know that!"

X

ORDE was up and out at six o'clock the following morning. By eight he had reported for work at Daly's mill, where, with the assistance of a portion of the river crew, he was occupied in sorting the logs in the booms. Not until six o'clock in the evening did the whistle blow for the shut-down. Then he hastened home, to find that Newmark had preceded him by some few moments and was engaged in conversation with Grandma Orde. The young man was talking easily, though rather precisely and with brevity. He nodded to Orde and finished his remark.

After supper Orde led the way up two flights of narrow stairs to his own room. This was among the gables, a chamber of strangely diversified ceiling, which slanted here and there according to the demands of the roof outside.

" Well," said he, " I've made up my mind to-day to go in with you. It may not work out, but it's a good chance, and I want to get in something that looks like money. I don't know who you are, nor how much of a business man you are or what your experience is, but I'll risk it."

" I'm putting in twenty thousand dollars," pointed out Newmark.

" And I'm putting in my everlasting reputation," said Orde. " If we tell these fellows that we'll get out their logs for them, and then don't do it, I'll be *dead* around here."

" So that's about a stand-off," said Newmark. " I'm betting twenty thousand on what I've seen and heard of you, and you're risking your reputation that I don't want to drop my money."

Orde laughed.

"And I reckon we're both right," he responded.

"Still," Newmark pursued the subject, "I've no objection to telling you about myself. New York born and bred; experience with Cooper and Dunne, brokers, eight years. Money from a legacy. Parents dead. No relatives to speak to."

Orde nodded gravely twice in acknowledgment.

"Now," said Newmark, "have you had time to do any figuring?"

"Well," replied Orde, "I got at it a little yesterday afternoon, and a little this noon. I have a rough idea." He produced a bundle of scribbled papers from his coat-pocket. "Here you are. I take Daly as a sample, because I've been with his outfit. It costs him to run and deliver his logs one hundred miles about two dollars a thousand feet. He's the only big manufacturer up here; the rest are all at Monrovia, where they can get shipping by water. I suppose it costs the other nine firms doing business on the river from two to two and a half a thousand."

Newmark produced a note-book and began to jot down figures.

"Do these men all conduct separate drives?" he inquired.

"All but Proctor and old Heinzman. They pool in together."

"Now," went on Newmark, "if we were to drive the whole river, how could we improve on that?"

"Well, I haven't got it down very fine, of course," Orde told him, "but in the first place we wouldn't need so many men. I could run the river on three hundred easy enough. That saves wages and grub on two hundred right there. And, of course, a few improvements on the river

would save time, which in our case would mean money.
We would not need so many separate cook outfits and all
that. Of course, that part of it we'd have to get right
down and figure on, and it will take time. Then, too, if
we agreed to sort and deliver, we'd have to build sorting
booms down at Monrovia."

"Suppose we had all that. What, for example, do you
reckon you could bring Daly's logs down for?"

Orde fell into deep thought, from which he emerged
occasionally to scribble on the back of his memoranda.

"I suppose somewhere about a dollar," he announced at
last. He looked up a trifle startled. "Why," he cried, "that
looks like big money! A hundred per cent!"

Newmark watched him for a moment, a quizzical smile
wrinkling the corners of his eyes.

"Hold your horses," said he at last. "I don't know anything about this business, but I can see a few things. In
the first place, close figuring will probably add a few cents
to that dollar. And then, of course, all our improvements
will be absolutely valueless to anybody after we've got
through using them. You said yesterday they'd probably stand us in seventy-five thousand dollars. Even at
a dollar profit, we'd have to drive seventy-five million
before we got a cent back. And, of course, we've got
to agree to drive for a little less than they could themselves."

"That's so," agreed Orde, his crest falling.

"However," said Newmark briskly, as he arose, "there's
good money in it, as you say. Now, how soon can you
leave Daly?"

"By the middle of the week we ought to be through
with this job."

"That's good. Then we'll go into this matter of expense
thoroughly, and establish our schedule of rates to submit
to the different firms."

Newmark said a punctilious farewell to Mr. and Mrs. Orde.

"By the way," said Orde to him at the gate, "where are you staying?"

"At the Grand."

"I know most of the people here—all the young folks. I'd be glad to take you around and get you acquainted."

"Thank you," replied Newmark, "you are very kind. But I don't go in much for that sort of thing, and I expect to be very busy now on this new matter; so I won't trouble you."

XI

THE new partners, as soon as Orde had released himself from Daly, gave all their time to working out a schedule of tolls. Orde drew on his intimate knowledge of the river and its tributaries, and the locations of the different rollways, to estimate as closely as possible the time it would take to drive them. He also hunted up Tom North and others of the older men domiciled in the cheap boarding-houses of Hell's Half-Mile, talked with them, and verified his own impressions. Together, he and Newmark visited the supply houses, got prices, obtained lists. All the evenings they figured busily, until at last Newmark expressed himself as satisfied.

"Now, Orde," said he, "here is where you come in. It's now your job to go out and interview these men and get their contracts for driving their next winter's cut."

But Orde drew back.

"Look here, Joe," he objected, "that's more in your line. You can talk business to them better than I can."

"Not a bit," negatived Newmark. "They don't know me from Adam, and they do know you, and all about you. We've got to carry this thing through at first on our face, and they'd be more apt to entrust the matter to you personally."

"All right," agreed Orde. "I'll start in on Daly."

He did so the following morning. Daly swung his bulk around in his revolving office-chair and listened attentively.

"Well, Jack," said he, "I think you're a good riverman, and I believe you can do it. I'd be only too glad to get

rid of the nuisance of it, let alone get it done cheaper.
If you'll draw up your contract and bring it in here, I'll
sign it. I suppose you'll break out the rollways?"

"No," said Orde; "we hadn't thought of doing more
than the driving and distributing. You'll have to deliver
the logs in the river. Maybe another year, after we get
better organised, we'll be able to break rollways—at a price
per thousand—but until we get a going we'll have to rush
her through."

Orde repeated this to his associate.

"That was smooth enough sailing," he exulted.

"Yes," pondered Newmark, removing his glasses and
tapping his thumb with their edge. "Yes," he repeated,
"that was smooth sailing. What was that about rollways?"

"Oh, I told him we'd expect him to break out his own,"
said Orde.

"Yes, but what does that mean exactly?"

"Why," explained Orde, with a slight stare of surprise,
"when the logs are cut and hauled during the winter, they
are banked on the river-banks, and even in the river-channel itself. Then, when the thaws come in the spring, these
piles are broken down and set afloat in the river."

"I see," said Newmark. "Well, but why shouldn't we
undertake that part of it? I should think that would be
more the job of the river-drivers."

"It would hold back our drive too much to have to stop
and break rollways," explained Orde.

The next morning they took the early train for Monrovia, where were situated the big mills and the offices
of the nine other lumber companies. Within an hour they
had descended at the small frame terminal station, and were
walking together up the village street.

Monrovia was at that time a very spread-out little place
of perhaps two thousand population. It was situated a half
mile from Lake Michigan, behind the sparsely wooded sand

hills of its shore. From the river, which had here grown to a great depth and width, its main street ran directly at right angles. Four brick blocks of three stories lent impressiveness to the vista. The stores in general, however, were low frame structures. All faced broad plank sidewalks raised above the street to the level of a waggon body. From this main street ran off, to right and left, other streets, rendered lovely by maple trees that fairly met across the way. In summer, over sidewalk and roadway alike rested a dense, refreshing dark shadow that seemed to throw from itself an odour of coolness. This was rendered further attractive by the warm spicy odour of damp pine that arose from the resilient surface of sawdust and shingles broken beneath the wheels of traffic. Back from these trees, in wide, well-cultivated lawns, stood the better residences. They were almost invariably built of many corners, with steep roofs meeting each other at all angles, with wide and ornamented red chimneys, numerous windows, and much scroll work adorning each apex and cornice. The ridge poles bristled in fancy foot-high palisades of wood. Chimneys were provided with lightning-rods. Occasionally an older structure, on square lines, recorded the era of a more dignified architecture. Everywhere ran broad sidewalks and picket fences. Beyond the better residence districts were the board shanties of the mill workers.

Orde and Newmark tramped up the plank walk to the farthest brick building. When they came to a cross street, they had to descend to it by a short flight of steps on one side, and ascend from it by a corresponding flight on the other. At the hotel, Newmark seated himself in a rocking-chair next the big window.

"Good luck!" said he.

Orde mounted a wide, dark flight of stairs that led from the street to a darker hall. The smell of stale cigars and cocoa matting was in the air. Down the dim length of this hall he made his way to a door, which without ceremony he pushed open.

He found himself in a railed-off space, separated from the main part of the room by a high walnut grill.

" Mr. Heinzman in? " he asked of a clerk.

" I think so," replied the clerk, to whom evidently Orde was known.

Orde spent the rest of the morning with Heinzman, a very rotund, cautious person of German extraction and accent. Heinzman occupied the time in asking questions of all sorts about the new enterprise. At twelve he had not in any way committed himself nor expressed an opinion. He, however, instructed Orde to return the afternoon of the following day.

" I vill see Proctor," said he.

Orde, rather exhausted, returned to find Newmark still sitting in the rocking-chair with his unlighted cigar. The two had lunch together, after which Orde, somewhat refreshed, started out. He succeeded in getting two more promises of contracts and two more deferred interviews.

" That's going a little faster," he told Newmark cheerfully.

The following morning, also, he was much encouraged by the reception his plan gained from the other lumbermen. At lunch he recapitulated to Newmark.

" That's four contracts already," said he, " and three more practically a sure thing. Proctor and Heinzman are slower than molasses about everything, and mean as pusley, and Johnson's up in the air, the way he always is, for fear some one's going to do him."

" It isn't a bad outlook," admitted Newmark.

But Heinzman offered a new problem for Orde's consideration.

" I haf talked with Proctor," said he, " and ve like your scheme. If you can deliffer our logs here for two dollars and a quarter, why, that is better as ve can do it; but how do ve know you vill do it?"

"I'll guarantee to get them here all right," laughed Orde.

"But what is your guarantee good for?" persisted Heinzman blandly, locking his fingers over his rotund little stomach. "Suppose the logs are not deliffered—what then? How responsible are you financially?"

"Well, we're investing seventy-five thousand dollars or so."

Heinzman rubbed his thumb and forefinger together and wafted the imaginary pulverisation away.

"Worth that for a judgment," said he.

He allowed a pause to ensue.

"If you vill give a bond for the performance of your contract," pursued Heinzman, "that vould be satisfactory."

Orde's mind was struck chaotic by the reasonableness of this request, and the utter impossibility of acceding to it.

"How much of a bond?" he asked.

"Twenty-fife thousand vould satisfy us," said Heinzman. "Bring us a suitable bond for that amount and ve vill sign your contract."

Orde ran down the stairs to find Newmark.

"Heinzman won't sign unless we give him a bond for performance," he said in a low tone, as he dropped into the chair next to Newmark.

Newmark removed his unlighted cigar, looked at the chewed end, and returned it to the corner of his mouth.

"Heinzman has sense," said he drily. "I was wondering if ordinary business caution was unknown out here."

"Can we get such a bond? Nobody would go on my bond for that amount."

"Mine either," said Newmark. "We'll just have to let them go and drive ahead without them. I only hope they won't spread the idea. Better get those other contracts signed up as soon as we can."

With this object in view, Orde started out early the next morning, carrying with him the duplicate contracts on which Newmark had been busy.

"Rope 'em in," advised Newmark. "It's Saturday, and we don't want to let things simmer over Sunday, if we can help it."

About eleven o'clock a clerk of the Welton Lumber Co. entered Mr. Welton's private office to deliver to Orde a note.

"This just came by special messenger," he explained.

Orde, with an apology, tore it open. It was from Heinzman, and requested an immediate interview. Orde delayed only long enough to get Mr. Welton's signature, then hastened as fast as his horse could take him across the draw-bridge to the village.

Heinzman he found awaiting him. The little German, with his round, rosy cheeks, his dot of a nose, his big spectacles, and his rotund body, looked even more than usual like a spider or a Santa Claus—Orde could not decide which.

"I haf been thinking of that bond," he began, waving a pudgy hand toward a seat, "and I haf been talking with Proctor."

"Yes," said Orde hopefully.

"I suppose you would not be prepared to gif a bond?"

"I hardly think so."

"Vell, suppose ve fix him this way," went on Heinzman, clasping his hands over his stomach and beaming through his spectacles. "Proctor and I haf talked it ofer, and ve are agreet that the probosition is a good one. Also ve think it is vell to help the young fellers along." He laughed silently in such a manner as to shake himself all over. "Ve do not vish to be too severe, and yet ve must be assured that ve get our logs on time. Now, I unterstood you to say that this new concern is a stock company."

Orde did not remember having said so, but he nodded.

"Vell, if you gif us a bond secured with stock in the new company, that would be satisfactory to us."

Orde's face cleared.

"Do you mean that, Mr. Heinzman?"

"Sure. Ve must haf some security, but ve do not vish to be too hard on you boys."

"Now, I call that a mighty good way out!" cried Orde.

"Make your contract out according to these terms, then," said Heinzman, handing him a paper, "and bring it in Monday."

Orde glanced over the slip. It recited two and a quarter as the agreed price; specified the date of delivery at Heinzman and Proctor's booms; named twenty-five thousand dollars as the amount of the bond, to be secured by fifty thousand dollars' worth of stock in the new company. This looked satisfactory. Orde arose.

"I'm much obliged to you, Mr. Heinzman," said he. "I'll bring it around Monday."

He had reached the gate to the grill before Heinzman called him back.

"By the vay," the little German beamed up at him, swinging his fat legs as the office-chair tipped back on its springs, "if it is to be a stock company, you vill be selling some of the stock to raise money, is it not so?"

"Yes," agreed Orde, "I expect so."

"How much vill you capitalise for?"

"We expect a hundred thousand ought to do the trick," replied Orde.

"Vell," said Heinzman, "ven you put it on the market, come and see me." He nodded paternally at Orde, beaming through his thick spectacles.

That evening, well after six, Orde returned to the hotel.

After freshening up in the marbled and boarded washroom, he hunted up Newmark.

"Well, Joe," said he, "I'm as hungry as a bear. Come on, eat, and I'll tell you all about it."

They deposited their hats on the racks and pushed open the swinging screen doors that led into the dining-room. There they were taken in charge by a marvellously haughty and redundant head-waitress, who signalled them to follow down through ranks of small tables watched by more stately damsels. Newmark, reserved and precise, irreproachably correct in his neat gray, seemed enveloped in an aloofness as impenetrable as that of the head-waitress herself. Orde, however, was as breezy as ever. He hastened his stride to overtake the head-waitress.

"Annie, be good!" he said in his jolly way. "We've got business to talk. Put us somewhere alone."

Newmark nodded approval, and thrust his hand in his pocket. But Annie looked up into Orde's frank, laughing face, and her lips curved ever so faintly in the condescension of a smile.

"Sure, sorr," said she, in a most unexpected brogue.

"Well, I've got 'em all," said Orde, as soon as the waitress had gone with the order. "But the best stroke of business you'd never guess. I roped in Heinzman."

"Good!" approved Newmark briefly.

"It was really pretty decent of the little Dutchman. He agreed to let us put up our stock as security. Of course, that security is good only if we win out; and if we win out, why, then he'll get his logs, so he won't have any use for security. So it's just one way of beating the devil around the bush. He evidently wanted to give us the business, but he hated like the devil to pass up his rules—you know how those old shellbacks are."

"H'm, yes," said Newmark.

The waitress sailed in through a violently kicked swinging door, bearing aloft a tin tray heaped perilously. She slanted around a corner in graceful opposition to the centrifugal, brought the tray to port on a sort of landing stage by a pillar, and began energetically to distribute small " iron-ware " dishes, each containing a dab of something. When the clash of arrival had died, Orde went on:

" I got into your department a little, too."

" How's that? " asked Newmark, spearing a baked potato.

" Heinzman said he'd buy some of our stock. He seems to think we have a pretty good show."

Newmark paused, his potato half-way to his plate.

" Kind of him," said he after a moment. " Did he sign a contract? "

" It wasn't made out," Orde reminded him. " I've the memoranda here. We'll make it out to-night. I am to bring it in Monday."

" I see we're hung up here over Sunday," observed Newmark. " No Sunday trains to Redding."

Orde became grave.

" I know it. I tried to hurry matters to catch the six o'clock, but couldn't make it." His round, jolly face fell sombre, as though a light within had been extinguished. After a moment the light returned. " Can't be helped," said he philosophically.

They ate hungrily, then drifted out into the office again, where Orde lit a cigar.

" Now, let's see your memoranda," said Newmark.

He frowned over the three simple items for some time.

" It's got me," he confessed at last.

" What? " inquired Orde.

" What Heinzman is up to."

" What do you mean? " asked Orde, turning in his chair with an air of slow surprise.

" It all looks queer to me. He's got something up his sleeve. Why should he take a bond with that security from us? If we can't deliver the logs, our company fails; that makes the stock worthless; that makes the bond worthless —just when it is needed. Of course, it's as plain as the nose on your face that he thinks the proposition a good one and is trying to get control."

" Oh, no!" cried Orde, astounded.

" Orde, you're all right on the river," said Newmark, with a dry little laugh, " but you're a babe in the woods at this game."

" But Heinzman is honest," cried Orde. " Why, he is a church member, and has a class in Sunday-school."

Newmark selected a cigar from his case, examined it from end to end, finally put it between his lips. The corners of his mouth were twitching quietly with amusement.

" Besides, he is going to buy some stock," added Orde, after a moment.

" Heinzman has not the slightest intention of buying a dollar's worth of stock," asserted Newmark.

" But why——"

" —Did he make that bluff?" finished Newmark. " Because he wanted to find out how much stock would be issued. You told him it would be a hundred thousand dollars, didn't you?"

" Why—yes, I believe I did," said Orde, pondering.

Newmark threw back his head and laughed noiselessly.

" So now he knows that if we forfeit the bond he'll have controlling interest," he pointed out.

Orde smoked rapidly, his brow troubled.

" But what I can't make out," reflected Newmark, " is why he's so sure we'll have to forfeit."

" I think he's just taking a long shot at it," suggested Orde, who seemed finally to have decided against Newmark's opinion. " I believe you're shying at mare's nests."

" Not he. He has some good reason for thinking we

won't deliver the logs. Why does he insist on putting in a date for delivery? None of the others does."

"I don't know," replied Orde. "Just to put some sort of a time limit on the thing, I suppose."

"You say you surely can get the drive through by then?"

Orde laughed.

"Sure? Why, it gives me two weeks' leeway over the worst possible luck I could have. You're too almighty suspicious, Joe."

Newmark shook his head.

"You let me figure this out," said he.

But bedtime found him without a solution. He retired to his room under fire of Orde's good-natured raillery. Orde himself shut his door, the smile still on his lips. As he began removing his coat, however, the smile died. The week had been a busy one. Hardly had he exchanged a dozen words with his parents, for he had even been forced to eat his dinner and supper away from home. This Sunday he had promised himself to make his deferred but much-desired call on Jane Hubbard—and her guest. He turned out the gas with a shrug of resignation. For the first time his brain cleared of its turmoil of calculations, of guesses, of estimates, and of men. He saw clearly the limited illumination cast downward by the lamp beneath its wide shade, the graceful, white figure against the shadow of the easy chair, the oval face cut in half by the lamp-light to show plainly the red lips with the quaint upward quirks at the corners, and dimly the inscrutable eyes and the hair with the soft shadows. With a sigh he felt asleep.

Some time in the night he was awakened by a persistent tapping on the door. In the woodsman's manner, he was instantly broad awake. He lit the gas and opened the door to admit Newmark, partially dressed over his night gown.

"Orde," said he briefly and without preliminary, "didn't

you tell me the other day that rollways were piled both on the banks and *in* the river?"

"Yes, sometimes," said Orde. "Why?"

"Then they might obstruct the river?"

"Certainly."

"I thought so!" cried Newmark, with as near an approach to exultation as he ever permitted himself. "Now, just one other thing: aren't Heinzman's rollways below most of the others?"

"Yes, I believe they are," said Orde.

"And, of course, it was agreed, as usual, that Heinzman was to break out his own rollways?"

"I see," said Orde slowly. "You think he intends to delay things enough so we can't deliver on the date agreed on."

"I know it," stated Newmark positively.

"But if he refuses to deliver the logs, no court of law will——"

"Law!" cried Newmark. "Refuse to deliver! You don't know that kind. He won't refuse to deliver. There'll just be a lot of inevitable delays, and his foreman will misunderstand, and all that. You ought to know more about that than I do."

Orde nodded, his eye abstracted.

"It's a child-like scheme," commented Newmark. "If I'd had more knowledge of the business, I'd have seen it sooner."

"I'd never have seen it at all," said Orde humbly. "You seem to be the valuable member of this firm, Joe."

"In my way," said Newmark, "you in yours. We ought to make a good team."

XII

SUNDAY afternoon, Orde, leaving Newmark to devices of his own, walked slowly up the main street, turned to the right down one of the shaded side residence streets that ended finally in a beautiful glistening sand-hill. Up this he toiled slowly, starting at every step avalanches and streams down the slope. Shortly he found himself on the summit, and paused for a breath of air from the lake.

He was just above the tops of the maples, which seen from this angle stretched away like a forest through which occasionally thrust roofs and spires. Some distance beyond a number of taller buildings and the red of bricks were visible. Beyond them still were other sand-hills, planted raggedly with wind-twisted and stunted trees. But between the brick buildings and these sand-hills flowed the river—wide, deep, and still—bordered by the steamboat landings on the town side and by fishermen's huts and net-racks and small boats on the other. Orde seated himself on the smooth, clean sand and removed his hat. He saw these things, and in imagination the far upper stretches of the river, with the mills and yards and booms extending for miles; and still above them the marshes and the flats where the river widened below the Big Bend. That would be the location for the booms of the new company—a cheap property on which the partners had already secured a valuation. And below he dropped in imagination with the slackening current until between two greater sand-hills than the rest the river ran out through the channel made by two long piers to the lake—blue, restless, immeasurable. To right and left stretched the long Michigan coast, with its low yellow hills topped with the green of twisted pines, firs, and beeches, with always its beach of sand, deep and dry to the very edge of its tideless sea, strewn with sawlogs, bark, and the ancient remains of ships.

After he had cooled he arose and made his way back to a pleasant hardwood forest of maple and beech. Here the leaves were just bursting from their buds. Underfoot the early spring flowers—the hepaticas, the anemones, the trilium, the dog-tooth violets, the quaint, early, bright green undergrowths—were just reaching their perfection. Migration was in full tide. Birds, little and big, flashed into view and out again, busy in the mystery of their northward pilgrimage, giving the appearance of secret and silent furtiveness, yet each uttering his characteristic call from time to time, as though for a signal to others of the host. The woods were swarming as city streets, yet to Orde these little creatures were as though invisible. He stood in the middle of a great multitude, he felt himself under the observation of many bright eyes, he heard the murmuring and twittering that proclaimed a throng, he sensed an onward movement that flowed slowly but steadily toward the pole; nevertheless, a flash of wings, a fluttering little body, the dip of a hasty short flight, represented the visible tokens. Across the pale silver sun of April their shadows flickered, and with them flickered the tracery of new leaves and the delicacy of the lace-like upper branches.

Orde walked slowly farther and farther into the forest, lost in an enjoyment which he could not have defined accurately, but which was so integral a portion of his nature that it had drawn him from the banks and wholesale groceries to the woods. After a while he sat down on a log and lit his pipe. Ahead the ground sloped upward. Dimly through the half-fronds of the early season he could make

out the yellow of sands and the deep complementary blue
of the sky above them. He knew the Lake to lie just beyond. With the thought he arose. A few moments later
he stood on top the hill, gazing out over the blue waters.

Very blue they were, with a contrasting snowy white
fringe of waves breaking gently as far up the coast as the
eye could reach. The beach, on these tideless waters, was
hard and smooth only in the narrow strip over which ran
the wash of the low surf. All the rest of the expanse of
sand back to the cliff-like hills lay dry and tumbled into
hummocks and drifts, from which projected here a sawlog
cast inland from a raft by some long-past storm, there a
slab, again a ship's rib sticking gaunt and defiant from the
shifting, restless medium that would smother it. And just
beyond the edge of the hard sand, following the long curves
of the wash, lay a dark, narrow line of bark fragments.

The air was very clear and crystalline. The light-houses
on the ends of the twin piers, though some miles distant,
seemed close at hand. White herring gulls, cruising against
the blue, flashed white as the sails of a distant ship. A
fresh breeze darkened the blue velvet surface of the water,
tumbled the white foam hissing up the beach, blew forward
over the dunes a fine hurrying mist of sand, and bore to
Orde at last the refreshment of the wide spaces. A woman,
walking slowly, bent her head against the force of this wind.

Orde watched her idly. She held to the better footing
of the smooth sand, which made it necessary that she retreat often before the inrushing wash, sometimes rather
hastily. Orde caught himself admiring the grace of her
deft and sudden movements, and the sway of her willowy
figure. Every few moments she turned and faced the lake,
her head thrown back, the wind whipping her garments
about her.

As she drew nearer, Orde tried in vain to catch sight
of her face. She looked down, watching the waters advance

and recede ; she wore a brimmed hat bent around her head
by means of some sort of veil tied over the top and beneath
her chin. When she had arrived nearly opposite Orde she
turned abruptly inland, and a moment later began laboriously
to climb the steep sand.

The process seemed to amuse her. She turned her head
sidewise to watch with interest the hurrying, tumbling little
cascades that slid from her every step. From time to time
she would raise her skirts daintily with the tips of her
fingers, and lean far over in order to observe with interest
how her feet sank to the ankles, and how the sand rushed
from either side to fill in the depressions. The wind carried
up to Orde low, joyous chuckles of delight, like those of
a happy child.

As though directed by some unseen guide, her course
veered more and more until it led directly to the spot where
Orde stood. When she was within ten feet of him she at
last raised her head so the young man could see something
besides the top of her hat. Orde looked plump into her
eyes.

" Hullo ! " she said cheerfully and unsurprised, and sank
down cross-legged at his feet.

Orde stood quite motionless, overcome by astonishment.
Her face, its long oval framed in the bands of the gray
veil and the down-turned brim of the hat, looked up smiling
into his. The fresh air had deepened the colour beneath
her skin and had blown loose stray locks of the fine shadow-
filled hair. Her red lips, with the quaintly up-turned corners, smiled at him with a new frankness, and the black
eyes—the eyes so black as to resemble spots—had lost their
half-indolent reserve and brimmed over quite frankly with
the joy of life. She scooped up a handful of the dry, clean
sand from either side of her, raised it aloft, and let it
trickle slowly between her fingers. The wind snatched at
the sand and sprayed it away in a beautiful plume.

"Isn't this *real* fun?" she asked him.

"Why, Miss Bishop!" cried Orde, finding his voice. "What are you doing here?"

A faint shade of annoyance crossed her brow.

"Oh, I could ask the same of you; and then we'd talk about how surprised we are, world without end," said she. "The important thing is that here is sand to play in, and there is the Lake, and here are we, and the day is charmed, and it's good to be alive. Sit down and dig a hole! We've all the common days to explain things in."

Orde laughed and seated himself to face her. Without further talk, and quite gravely, they commenced to scoop out an excavation between them, piling the sand over themselves and on either side as was most convenient. As the hole grew deeper they had to lean over more and more. Their heads sometimes brushed ever so lightly, their hands perforce touched. Always the dry sand flowed from the edges partially to fill in the result their efforts. Faster and faster they scooped it out again. The excavation thus took on the shape of a funnel. Her cheeks glowed pink, her eyes shone like stars. Entirely was she absorbed in the task. At last a tiny commotion manifested itself in the bottom of the funnel. Impulsively she laid her hand on Orde's, to stop them. Fascinated, they watched. After incredible though lilliputian upheavals, at length appeared a tiny black insect, struggling against the rolling, overwhelming sands. With great care the girl scooped this newcomer out and set him on the level ground. She looked up happily at Orde, thrusting the loose hair from in front of her eyes.

"I was convinced we ought to dig a hole," said she gravely. "Now, let's go somewhere else."

She arose to her feet, shaking the sand free from her skirts.

"I think, through these woods," she decided. "Can we get back to town this way?"

Receiving Orde's assurance, she turned at once down
the slope through the fringe of scrub spruces and juni-
pers into the tall woods. Here the air fell still. She remarked on how warm it seemed, and began to untie from
over her ears the narrow band of veil that held close
her hat.

"Yes," replied Orde. "The lumber-jacks say that the
woods are the poor man's overcoat."

She paused to savour this, her head on one side, her
arms upraised to the knot.

"Oh, I like that!" said she, continuing her task. In a
moment or so the veil hung free. She removed it and the
hat, and swung them both from one finger, and threw
back her head.

"Hear all the birds!" she said.

Softly she began to utter a cheeping noise between her
lips and teeth, low and plaintive. At once the volume of
bird-sounds about increased; the half-seen flashes became
more frequent. A second later the twigs were alive with
tiny warblers and creepers, flirting from branch to branch,
with larger, more circumspect chewinks, catbirds, and
finches hopping down from above, very silent, very grave.
In the depths of the thickets the shyer hermit and olive
thrushes and the oven birds revealed themselves ghost-like,
or as sea-growths lift into a half visibility through translucent shadows the colour of themselves. All were very intent, very earnest, very interested, each after his own manner, in the comradeship of the featherhood he imagined
to be uttering distressful cries. A few, like the chickadees,
quivered their wings, opened their little mouths, fluttered
down tiny but aggressive against the disaster. Others
hopped here and there restlessly, uttering plaintive, low-
toned cheeps. The shyest contented themselves by a discreet,
silent, and distant sympathy. Three or four freebooting
jays, attracted not so much by the supposed calls for help

as by curiosity, fluttered among the tops of the trees, uttering their harsh notes.

Finally, the girl ended her performance in a musical
laugh.

"Run away, Brighteyes," she called. "It's all right; nobody's damaged."

She waved her hand. As though at a signal, the host
she had evoked melted back into the shadows of the forest.
Only the chickadee, impudent as ever, retreated scolding
rather ostentatiously, and the jays, splendid in their ornate
blue, screamed opinions at each other from the tops of trees.

"How would you like to be a bird?" she inquired.

"Hadn't thought," replied Orde.

"Don't you ever indulge in vain and idle speculations?"
she inquired. "Never mind, don't answer. It's too much
to expect of a man."

She set herself in idle motion down the slope, swinging
the hat at the end of its veil, pausing to look or listen,
humming a little melody between her closed lips, throwing
her head back to breathe deep the warm air, revelling in
the woods sounds and woods odours and woods life with
entire self-abandonment. Orde followed her in silence. She
seemed to be quite without responsibility in regard to him;
and yet an occasional random remark thrown in his direction proved that he was not forgotten. Finally they emerged
from the beach woods.

They faced an open rolling country. As far as the eye
could reach were the old stumps of pine trees. Sometimes
they stood in place, burned and scarred, but attesting
mutely the abiding place of a spirit long since passed away.
Sometimes they had been uprooted and dragged to mark
the boundaries of fields, where they raised an abatis of
twisted roots to the sky.

The girl stopped short as she came face to face with
this open country. The inner uplift, that had lent to her

aspect the wide-eyed, careless joy of a child, faded. In its place came a new and serious gravity. She turned on him troubled eyes.

"You do this," she accused him quite simply.

For answer he motioned to the left where below them lay a wide and cultivated countryside—farmhouses surrounded by elms; compact wood lots of hardwood; crops and orchards, all fair and pleasant across the bosom of a fertile nature.

"And this," said he. "That valley was once nothing but a pine forest—and so was all the southern part of the State, the peach belt and the farms. And for that matter Indiana, too, and all the other forest States right out to the prairies. Where would we be now, if we *hadn't* done that?" he pointed across at the stump-covered hills.

Mischief had driven out the gravity from the girl's eyes. She had lowered her head slightly sidewise as though to conceal their expression from him.

"I was beginning to be afraid you'd say 'yes-indeed,'" said she.

Orde looked bewildered, then remembered the Incubus, and laughed.

"I haven't been very conversational," he acknowledged.

"Certainly *not!*" she said severely. "That would have been very disappointing. There has been nothing to say."

She turned and waved her hat at the beech woods falling sombre against the lowering sun.

"Good-bye," she said gravely, "and pleasant dreams to you. I hope those very saucy little birds won't keep you awake." She looked up at Orde. "He was rather nice to us this afternoon," she explained, "and it's always well to be polite to them anyway." She gazed steadily at Orde for signs of amusement. He resolutely held his face sympathetic.

"Now I think we'll go home," said she.

They made their way between the stumps to the edge of the sand-hill overlooking the village. With one accord they stopped. The low-slanting sun cast across the vista a sleepy light of evening.

"How would you like to live in a place like that all your life?" asked Orde.

"I don't know." She weighed her words carefully. "It would depend. The place isn't of so much importance, it seems to me. It's the life one is called to. It's whether one finds her soul's realm or not that a place is liveable or not. I can imagine entering my kingdom at a railway water-tank," she said quaintly, "or missing it entirely in a big city."

Orde looked out over the raw little village with a new interest.

"Of course I can see how a man's work can lie in a small place," said he; "but a woman is different."

"Why is a woman different?" she challenged. "What is her 'work,' as you call it; and why shouldn't it, as well as a man's, lie in a small place? What is work—outside of drudgery—unless it is correspondence of one's abilities to one's task?"

"But the compensations—" began Orde vaguely.

"Compensations?" she cried. "What do you mean? Here are the woods and fields, the river, the lake, the birds, and the breezes. We'll check them off against the theatre and balls. Books can be had here as well as anywhere. As to people: in a large city you meet a great many, and they're all busy, and unless you make an especial and particular effort—which you're not likely to—you'll see them only casually and once in a great while. In a small place you know fewer people; but you know them intimately." She broke off with a half-laugh. "I'm from New York," she stated humorously, "and you've magicked me into an eloquent defence of Podunk!" She laughed up at Orde quite frankly. "Giant Strides!" she challenged suddenly. She turned off the edge of the sand-hill, and began to plunge down its slope, leaning far back, her arms extended, increasing as much as possible the length of each step. Orde followed at full speed. When the bottom was reached, he steadied her to a halt. She shook herself, straightened her hat, and wound the veil around it. Her whole aspect seemed to have changed with the descent into the conventionality of the village street. The old, gentle though capable and self-contained reserve had returned. She moved beside Orde with dignity.

"I came down with Jane and Mrs. Hubbard to see Mr. Hubbard off on the boat for Milwaukee last night," she told him. "Of course we had to wait over Sunday. Mrs. Hubbard and Jane had to see some relative or other; but I preferred to take a walk."

"Where are you staying?" asked Orde.

"At the Bennetts'. Do you know where it is?"

"Yes," replied Orde.

They said little more until the Bennetts' gate was reached. Orde declined to come in.

"Good-night," she said. "I want to thank you. You did not once act as though you thought I was silly or crazy. And you didn't try, as all the rest of them would, to act silly too. You couldn't have done it; and you didn't try. Oh, you may have felt it—I know!" She smiled one of her quaint and quizzical smiles. "But men aren't built for foolishness. They have to leave that to us. You've been very nice this afternoon; and it's helped a lot. I'm good for quite a long stretch now. Good-night."

She nodded to him and left him tongue-tied by the gate.

Orde, however, walked back to the hotel in a black rage with himself over what he termed his imbecility. As he remembered it, he had made just one consecutive speech that afternoon.

" Joe," said he to Newmark, at the hotel office, " what's the plural form of Incubus? I dimly remember it isn't ' busses.' "

" Incubi," answered Newmark.

" Thanks," said Orde gloomily.

XIII

I HAVE Heinzman's contract all drawn," said New-mark the next morning, "and I think I'll go around with you to the office."

At the appointed time they found the little German await-ing them, a rotund smile of false good-nature illuminating his rosy face. Orde introduced his partner. Newmark im-mediately took charge of the interview.

"I have executed here the contract, and the bonds se-cured by Mr. Orde's and my shares of stock in the new company," he explained. "It is only necessary that you affix your signature and summon the required witnesses."

Heinzman reached his hands for the papers, beaming over his glasses at the two young men.

As he read, however, his smile vanished, and he looked up sharply.

"Vat is this?" he inquired, a new crispness in his voice. "You tolt me," he accused Orde, "dot you were not bre-pared to break out the rollways. You tolt me you would egspect me to do that for myself."

"Certainly," agreed Orde.

"Vell, why do you put in this?" demanded Heinzman, reading from the paper in his hand. "'In case said roll-ways belonging to said parties of the second part are not broken out by the time the drive has reached them, and in case on demand said parties of the second part do refuse or do not exercise due diligence in breaking out said roll-ways, the said parties of the first part shall themselves break out said rollways, and the said parties of the second part do hereby agree to reimburse said parties of the first part at the rate of a dollar per thousand board feet.' "

" That is merely to protect ourselves," struck in Newmark.

" But," exploded Heinzman, his face purpling, " a dollar a tousand is absurd! "

" Of course it is," agreed Newmark. " We expect it to be. But also we expect you to break out your own rollways in time. It is intended as a penalty in case you don't."

" I vill not stand for such foolishness," pounded Heinzman on the arm of his chair.

" Very well," said Newmark crisply, reaching for the contract.

But Heinzman clung to it.

" It is absurd," he repeated in a milder tone. " See, I vill strike it out." He did so with a few dashes of the pen.

" We have no intention," stated Newmark with decision, " of giving you the chance to hang up our drive."

Heinzman caught his breath like a child about to cry out.

" So that is what you think! " he shouted at them. " That's the sort of men you think we are! I'll show you you cannot come into honest men's offices to insoolt them by such insinuations! " He tore the contract in pieces and threw it in the waste basket. " Get oudt of here! " he cried.

Newmark arose as dry and precise as ever. Orde was going red and white by turns, and his hands twitched.

" Then I understand you to refuse our offer? " asked Newmark coolly.

" Refuse! Yes! You and your whole kapoodle! " yelled Heinzman.

He hopped down and followed them to the grill door, repeating over and over that he had been insulted. The clerks stared in amazement.

Once at the foot of the dark stairs and in the open street, Orde looked up at the sky with a deep breath of relief.

"Whew!" said he, "that was a terror! We've gone off the wrong foot that time."

Newmark looked at him with some amusement.

"You don't mean to say that fooled you!" he marvelled.

"What?" asked Orde.

"All that talk about insults, and the rest of the rubbish. He saw we had spotted his little scheme; and he had to retreat somehow. It was as plain as the nose on your face."

"You think so?" doubted Orde.

"I know so. If he was mad at all, it was only at being found out."

"Maybe," said Orde.

"We've got an enemy on our hands in any case," concluded Newmark, "and one we'll have to look out for. I don't know how he'll do it; but he'll try to make trouble on the river. Perhaps he'll try to block the stream by not breaking his rollways."

"One of the first things we'll do will be to boom through a channel where Mr. Man's rollways will be," said Orde.

A faint gleam of approval lit Newmark's eyes.

"I guess you'll be equal to the occasion," said he drily.

Before the afternoon train, there remained four hours. The partners at once hunted out the little one-story frame building near the river in which Johnson conducted his business.

Johnson received them with an evident reserve of suspicion.

"I see no use in it," said he, passing his hand over his hair "slicked" down in the lumber-jack fashion. "I can run me own widout help from any man."

"Which seems to settle that!" said Newmark to Orde after they had left.

"Oh, well, his drive is small; and he's behind us," Orde pointed out.

"True," said Newmark thoughtfully.

"Now," said Newmark, as they trudged back to their hotel to get lunch and their hand-bags. "I'll get to work at my part of it. This proposition of Heinzman's has given me an idea. I'm not going to try to sell this stock outside, but to the men who own timber along the river. Then they won't be objecting to the tolls; for if the company makes any profits, part will go to them."

"Good idea!" cried Orde.

"I'll take these contracts, to show we can do the business."

"All correct."

"And I'll see about incorporation. Also I'll look about and get a proper office and equipments, and get hold of a book-keeper. Of course we'll have to make this our headquarters."

"I suppose so," said Orde a little blankly. After an instant he laughed. "Do you know, I hadn't thought of that! We'll have to live here, won't we?"

"Also," went on Newmark calmly, "I'll buy the supplies to the best advantage I can, and see that they get here in good shape. I have our preliminary lists, and as fast as you think you need anything, send a requisition in to me, and I'll see to it."

"And I?" inquired Orde.

"You'll get right at the construction. Get the booms built and improve the river where it needs it. Begin to get your crew—I'm not going to tell you how; you know better than I do. Only get everything in shape for next spring's drive. You can start right off. We have my money to begin on."

Orde laughed and stretched his arms over his head.

"My! She's a nice big job, isn't she?" he cried joyously.

XIV

ORDE, in spite of his activities, managed to see Carroll Bishop twice during the ensuing week.

On his return home late Monday afternoon, Grandma Orde informed him with a shrewd twinkle that she wanted him surely at home the following evening.

"I've asked in three or four of the young people for a candy pull," said she.

"Who, mother?" asked Orde.

"Your crowd. The Smiths, Collinses, Jane Hubbard, and Her," said Grandma Orde, which probably went to show that she had in the meantime been making inquiries, and was satisfied with them.

"Do you suppose they'll care for candy pulling?" hazarded Orde a little doubtfully.

"You mean, will she?" countered Grandma. "Well, I hope for both your sakes she is not beyond a little old-fashioned fun."

So it proved. The young people straggled in at an early hour after supper—every one had supper in those days. Carroll Bishop and Jane arrived nearly the last. Orde stepped into the hall to help them with their wraps. He was surprised as he approached Miss Bishop to lift her cloak from her shoulders, to find that the top of her daintily poised head, with its soft, fine hair, came well below the level of his eyes. Somehow her poise, her slender grace of movement and of attitude, had lent her the impression of a stature she did not possess. To-night her eyes, while fathomless as ever, shone quietly in anticipation.

"Do you know," she told Orde delightedly, "I have never been to a real candy pull in my life. It was so good of your mother to ask me. What a dear she looks to-night. And is that your father? I'm going to speak to him."

She turned through the narrow door into the lighted, low-ceilinged parlour where the company were chatting busily. Orde mechanically followed her. He was arrested by the sound of Jane Hubbard's slow good-humoured voice behind him.

"Now, Jack," she drawled, "I agree with you perfectly; but that is *no* reason why I should be neglected entirely. Come and hang up my coat."

Full of remorse, Orde turned. Jane Hubbard stood accusingly in the middle of the hall, her plain, shrewd, good-humoured face smiling faintly. Orde met her frank wide eyes with some embarrassment.

"Here it is," said Jane, holding out the coat. "I don't much care whether you hang it up or not. I just wanted to call you back to wish you luck." Her slow smile widened, and her gray eyes met his still more knowingly.

Orde seized the coat and her hand at the same time.

"Jane, you're a trump," said he. "No wonder you're the most popular girl in town."

"Of course I am, Jack," she agreed indolently. She entered the parlour.

The candy pulling was a success. Of course everybody got burned a little and spattered a good deal; but that was to be expected. After the product had been broken and been piled on dishes, all trooped to the informal "back sitting-room," where an open fire invited to stories and games of the quieter sort. Some of the girls sat in chairs, though most joined the men on the hearth.

Carroll Bishop, however, seemed possessed of a spirit of restlessness. The place seemed to interest her. She wandered here and there in the room, looking now at the walnut-framed photograph of Uncle Jim Orde, now at the great pink conch shells either side the door, now at the marble-topped table with its square paper-weight of polished agate and its glass " bell," beneath which stood a very life-like robin. This " back sitting-room " contained little in the way of ornament. It was filled, on the contrary, with old comfortable chairs, and worn calf-backed books. The girl peered at the titles of these; but the gas-jets had been turned low in favour of the firelight, and she had to give over the effort to identify the volumes. Once she wandered close to Grandma Orde's cushioned wooden rocker, and passed her hand lightly over the old lady's shoulder.

" Do you mind if I look at things? " she asked. " It's so dear and sweet and old and different from our New York homes."

" Look all you want to, dearie," said Grandma Orde.

After a moment she passed into the dining-room. Here Orde found her, her hands linked in front of her.

" Oh, it *is* so quaint and delightful," she exhaled slowly. " This dear, dear old house with its low ceilings and its queer haphazard lines, and its deep windows, and its old pictures, and queer unexpected things that take your breath away."

" It is one of the oldest houses in town," said Orde, " and I suppose it is picturesque. But, you see, I was brought up here, so I'm used to it."

" Wait until you leave it," said she prophetically, " and live away from it. Then all these things will come back to you to make your heart ache for them."

They rambled about together, Orde's enthusiasm gradually kindling at the flame of her own. He showed her the marvellous and painstaking pencil sketch of Napoleon looking out over a maltese-cross sunset done by Aunt Martha at the age of ten. It hung framed in the upper hall.

"It has always been there, ever since I can remember," said Orde, "and it has seemed to belong there. I've never thought of it as good or bad, just as belonging."

"I know," she nodded.

In this spirit also they viewed the plaster statue of Washington in the lower hall, and the Roger's group in the parlour. The glass cabinet of "curiosities" interested her greatly—the carved ivory chessmen, the dried sea-weeds, the stone from Sugar Loaf Rock, the bit from the wreck of the *North Star,* the gold and silver shells, the glittering geodes and pyrites, the sandal-wood fan, and all the hundred and one knick-knacks it was then the custom to collect under glass. They even ventured part way up the creaky attic stairs, but it was too dark to enter that mysterious region.

"I hear the drip of water," she whispered, her finger on her lips.

"It's the tank," said Orde.

"And has it a Dark Place behind it?" she begged.

"That's just what it has," said he.

"And—tell me—are there real hair trunks with brass knobs on 'em?"

"Yes, mother has two or three."

"O-o-h!" she breathed softly. "Don't tell me what's in them. I want to believe in brocades and sashes. Do you know," she looked at him soberly, "I never had any dark places behind the tank, nor mysterious trunks, when I was a child."

"You might begin now," suggested Orde.

"Do you mean to insinuate I haven't grown up?" she mocked. "Thank you! Look *out!*" she cried suddenly, "the Boojum will catch us," and picking up her skirts she fairly flew down the narrow stairs. Orde could hear the light swish of her draperies down the hall, and then the pat of her feet on the stair carpet of the lower flight.

He followed rather dreamily. A glance into the sitting-room showed the group gathered close around the fire listening to Lem Collin's attempt at a ghost story. She was not there. He found her, then, in the parlour. She was kneeling on the floor before the glass cabinet of curiosities, and she had quite flattened her little nose against the pane. At his exclamation she looked up with a laugh.

" This is the proper altitude from which to view a cabinet of curiosities," said she, " and something tells me you ought to flatten your nose, too." She held out both hands to be helped up. " Oh, *what* a house for a child ! " she cried.

After the company had gone, Orde stood long by the front gate looking up into the infinite spaces. Somehow, and vaguely, he felt the night to be akin to her elusive spirit. Farther and farther his soul penetrated into its depths ; and yet other depths lay beyond, other mysteries, other unguessed realms. And yet its beauty was the simplicity of space and dark and the stars.

The next time he saw her was at her own house—or rather the house of the friend she visited. Orde went to call on Friday evening and was lucky enough to find the girls home and alone. After a decent interval Jane made an excuse and went out. They talked on a great variety of subjects, and with a considerable approach toward intimacy. Not until nearly time to go did Orde stumble upon the vital point of the evening. He had said something about a plan for the week following.

" But you forget that by that time I shall be gone," said she.

" Gone ! " he echoed blankly. " Where ? "

" Home," said she. " Don't you remember I am to go Sunday morning ? "

" I thought you were going to stay a month."

" I was, but I—certain things came up that made it necessary for me to leave sooner."

"I—I'm sorry you're going," stammered Orde.

"So am I," said she. "I've had a very nice time here."

"Then I won't see you again," said Orde, still groping for realisation. "I must go to Monrovia to-morrow. But I'll be down to see you off."

"Do come," said she.

"It's not to be for good?" he expostulated. "You'll be coming back."

She threw her hands palm out, with a pretty gesture of ignorance.

"That is in the lap of the gods," said she.

"Will you write me occasionally?" he begged.

"As to that—" she began—"I'm a very poor correspondent."

"But won't you write?" he insisted.

"I do not make it a custom to write to young men."

"Oh!" he cried, believing himself enlightened. "Will you answer if I write you?"

"That depends."

"On what?"

"On whether there is a reply to make."

"But may I write you?"

"I suppose I couldn't very well prevent you, if you were sure to put on a three-cent stamp."

"Do you want me to?" persisted Orde.

She began gently to laugh, quite to herself, as though enjoying a joke entirely within her own personal privilege.

"You are so direct and persistent and boy-like," said she presently. "Now if you'll be very good, and not whisper to the other little pupils, I'll tell you how they do such things usually." She sat up straight from the depths of her chair, her white, delicately tapering forearms resting lightly on her knees. "Young men desiring to communicate with young ladies do not ask them bluntly. They make some excuse, like sending a book, a magazine, a marked newspaper, or even a bit of desired information. At the same time, they send notes informing the girl of the fact. The girl is naturally expected to acknowledge the politeness. If she wishes the correspondence to continue, she asks a question, or in some other way leaves an opening. Do you see?"

"Yes, I see," said Orde, slightly crestfallen. "But that's a long time to wait. I like to feel settled about a thing. I wanted to know."

She dropped back against the cushioned slant of her easy chair, and laughed again.

"And so you just up and asked!" she teased.

"I beg your pardon if I was rude," he said humbly.

The laughter died slowly from her eyes.

"Don't," she said. "It would be asking pardon for being yourself. You wanted to know: so you asked. And I'm going to answer. I shall be very glad to correspond with you and tell you about my sort of things, if you happen to be interested in them. I warn you: they are not very exciting."

"They are yours," said he.

She half rose to bow in mock graciousness, caught herself, and sank back.

"No, I won't," she said, more than half to herself. She sat brooding for a moment; then suddenly her mood changed. She sprang up, shook her skirts free, and seated herself at the piano. To Orde, who had also arisen, she made a quaint grimace over her shoulder.

"Admire your handiwork!" she told him. "You are rapidly bringing me to 'tell the truth and shame the devil.' Oh, he must be dying of mortification this evening!" She struck a great crashing chord, holding the keys while the strings reverberated and echoed down slowly into silence again. "It isn't fair," she went on, "for you big simple men to disarm us. I don't care! I have my private opinion of such brute strength. *Je me moque!*"

She wrinkled her nose and narrowed her eyes. Then ruthlessly she drowned his reply in a torrent of music. Like mad she played, rocking her slender body back and forth along the key-board; holding rigid her fingers, her hands, and the muscles of her arms. The bass notes roared like the rumbling of thunder; the treble flashed like the dart of lightnings. Abruptly she muted the instrument. Silence fell as something that had been pent and suddenly released. She arose from the piano stool quite naturally, both hands at her hair.

"Aren't Mr. and Mrs. Hubbard dear old people?" said she.

"What is your address in New York?" demanded Orde.

She sank into a chair nearby with a pretty uplifted gesture of despair.

"I surrender!" she cried, and then she laughed until the tears started from her eyes and she had to brush them away with what seemed to Orde an absurd affair to call a handkerchief. "Oh, you are delicious!" she said at last. "Well, listen. I live at 12 West Ninth Street. Can you remember that?" Orde nodded. "And now any other questions the prisoner can reply to without incriminating herself, she is willing to answer." She folded her hands demurely in her lap.

Two days later Orde saw the train carry her away. He watched the rear car disappear between the downward slopes of two hills, and then finally the last smoke from the locomotive dissipate in the clear blue.

Declining Jane's kindly meant offer of a lift, he walked back to town.

XV

THE new firm plunged busily into its more pressing activities. Orde especially had an infinitude of details on his hands. The fat note-book in his side pocket filled rapidly with rough sketches, lists, and estimates. Constantly he interviewed men of all kinds—rivermen, mill men, contractors, boat builders, hardware dealers, pile-driver captains, builders, wholesale grocery men, cooks, axe-men, chore boys—all a little world in itself.

The signs of progress soon manifested themselves. Below Big Bend the pile-drivers were at work, the square masses of their hammers rising rapidly to the tops of the derricks, there to pause a moment before dropping swiftly to a dull *thump!* They were placing a long, compact row, which should be the outer bulwarks separating the sorting-booms from the channel of the river. Ashore the carpenters were knocking together a long, low structure for the cook-house and a larger building, destined to serve as bunk-house for the regular boom-crew. There would also be a blacksmith's forge, a storehouse, a tool and supply-house, a barn, and small separate shanties for the married men. Below more labourers with picks, shovels, axes, and scrapers were cutting out and levelling a road which would, when finished, meet the county road to town. The numerous bayous of great marsh were crossed by " float-bridges," lying flat on the surface of the water, which spurted up in rhythmical little jets under the impact of hoofs. Down stream eight miles, below the mills, and just beyond where the drawbridge crossed over to Monrovia, Duncan Mc-

Leod's shipyards clipped and sawed, and steamed and bent and bolted away at two tugboats, the machinery for which was already being stowed in the hold of a vessel lying at wharf in Chicago. In the storerooms of hardware firms porters carried and clerks checked off chains, strap iron, bolts, spikes, staples, band iron, bar iron, peavies, cant-hooks, pike-poles, sledge-hammers, blocks, ropes, and cables.

These things took time and attention to details; also a careful supervision. The spring increased, burst into leaf and bloom, and settled into summer. Orde was constantly on the move. As soon as low water came with midsummer, however, he arranged matters to run themselves as far as possible, left with Newmark minute instructions as to personal supervision, and himself departed to Redding. Here he joined a crew which Tom North had already collected, and betook himself to the head of the river.

He knew exactly what he intended to do. Far back on the head-waters he built a dam. The construction of it was crude, consisting merely of log cribs filled with stone and débris placed at intervals across the bed of the stream, against which slanted logs made a face. The gate operated simply, and could be raised to let loose an entire flood. And indeed this was the whole purpose of the dam. It created a reservoir from which could be freed new supplies of water to eke out the dropping spring freshets.

Having accomplished this formidable labour—for the trees had to be cut and hauled, the stone carted, and the earth shovelled—the crew next moved down a good ten miles to where the river dropped over a rapids rough and full of boulders. Here were built and placed a row of stone-filled log cribs in a double row down stream to define the channel and to hold the drive in it and away from the shallows near either bank. The profile of these cribs was that of a right-angled triangle, the slanting side up stream.

Booms chained between them helped deflect the drive from the shoals. Their more important office, however, was to give footing to the drivers.

For twenty-five miles then nothing of importance was undertaken. Two or three particularly bad boulders were split out by the explosion of powder charges; a number of snags and old trees were cut away and disposed of; the channel was carefully examined for obstructions of any kind whatever. Then the party came to the falls.

Here Orde purposed his most elaborate bit of rough engineering. The falls were only about fifteen feet high, but they fell straight down to a bed of sheer rock. This had been eaten by the eddies into pot-holes and crannies until a jagged irregular scoop-hollow had formed immediately underneath the fall. Naturally this implied a ledge below.

In flood time the water boiled and roared through this obstruction in a torrent. The saw logs, caught in the rush, plunged end on into the scoop-hollow, hit with a crash, and were spewed out below more or less battered, barked, and stripped. Sometimes, however, when the chance of the drive brought down a hundred logs together, they failed to shoot over the barrier of the ledge. Then followed a jam, a bad jam, difficult and dangerous to break. The falls had taken her usurious share of the lives the river annually demands as her toll.

This condition of affairs Orde had determined, if possible, to obviate. From the thirty-five or forty miles of river that lay above, and from its tributaries would come the bulk of the white and Norway pine for years to follow. At least two thirds of each drive Orde figured would come from above the fall.

"If," said he to North, "we could carry an apron on a slant from just under the crest and over the pot-holes, it would shoot both the water and the logs off a better angle."

"Sure," agreed North, "but you'll have fun placing

your apron with all that water running through. Why, it would drown us!"

"I've got a notion on that," said Orde. "First thing is to get the material together."

A hardwood forest topped the slope. Into this went the axe-men. The straightest trees they felled, trimmed, and dragged, down travoy trails they constructed, on sleds they built for the purpose, to the banks of the river. Here they bored the two holes through either end to receive the bolts when later they should be locked together side by side in their places. As fast as they were prepared, men with cant-hooks rolled them down the slope to a flat below the falls. They did these things swiftly and well, because they were part of the practised day's work, but they shook their heads at the falls.

- After the trees had been cut in sufficient number—there were seventy-five of them, each twenty-six feet long—Orde led the way back up stream a half mile to a shallows, where he commanded the construction of a number of ex-aggerated sawhorses with very widespread slanting legs. In the meantime the cook-wagon and the bed-wagon had evidently been making many trips to Sand Creek, fifteen miles away, as was attested by a large pile of heavy planks. When the sawhorses were completed, Orde directed the picks and shovels to be brought up.

At this point the river, as has been hinted, widened over shoals. The banks at either hand, too, were flat and com-paratively low. As is often the case in bends of rivers sub-ject to annual floods, the banks sloped back for some dis-tance into a lower black-ash swamp territory.

Orde set his men to digging a channel through this bank. It was no slight job, from one point of view, as the slope down into the swamp began only at a point forty or fifty feet inland; but on the other hand the earth was soft and free from rocks. When completed the channel gave passage to a rather feeble streamlet from the outer fringe of the river. The men were puzzled, but Orde, by the strange freak of his otherwise frank and open nature, as usual told nothing of his plans, even to Tom North.

" He can't expect to turn that river," said Tim Nolan, who was once more with the crew. " He'd have to dig a long ways below that level to catch the main current— and then some."

" Let him alone," advised North, puffing at his short pipe. " He's wiser than a tree full of owls."

Next Orde assigned two men to each of the queer-shaped sawhorses, and instructed them to place the horses in a row across the shallowest part of the river, and broadside to the stream. This was done. The men, half-way to their knees in the swift water, bore down heavily to keep their charges in place. Other men immediately began to lay the heavy planks side by side, perpendicular to and on the up-stream side of the horses. The weight of the water clamped them in place; big rocks and gravel shovelled on in quantity prevented the lower ends from rising; the wide slant of the legs directed the pressure so far downward that the horses were prevented from floating away. And slowly the bulk of the water, thus raised a good three feet above its former level, turned aside into the new channel and poured out to inundate the black-ash swamp beyond.

A good volume still poured over the top of the temporary dam and down to the fall; but it was by this expedient so far reduced that work became possible.

" Now, boys! " cried Orde. " Lively, while we've got the chance! "

By means of blocks and tackles and the team horses the twenty-six-foot logs were placed side by side, slanting from a point two feet below the rim of the fall to the ledge below. They were bolted together top and bottom through the four holes bored for that purpose. This was a confusing and wet business. Sufficient water still flowed in the natural channel of the river to dash in spray over the entire work. Men toiled, wet to the skin, their garments clinging to them, their eyes full of water, barely able to breathe, yet groping doggedly at it, and arriving at last. The weather was warm with the midsummer. They made a joke of the difficulty, and found inexhaustible humour in the fact that one of their number was an Immersion Baptist. When the task was finished, they pried the flash-boards from the improvised dam; piled them neatly beyond reach of high water; rescued the sawhorses and piled them also for a possible future use; blocked the temporary channel with a tree or so—and earth. The river, restored to its immemorial channel by these men who had so nonchalantly turned it aside, roared on, singing again the song it had until now sung uninterruptedly for centuries. Orde and his crew tramped back to the falls, and gazed on their handiwork with satisfaction. Instead of plunging over an edge into a turmoil of foam and eddies, now the water flowed smoothly, almost without a break, over an incline of thirty degrees.

"Logs'll slip over that slick as a gun barrel," said Tom North. "How long do you think she'll last?"

"Haven't an idea," replied Orde. "We may have to do it again next summer, but I don't think it. There's nothing but the smooth of the water to wear those logs until they begin to rot."

Quite cheerfully they took up their long, painstaking journey back down the river.

Travel down the river was at times very pleasant, and at times very disagreeable. The ground had now hardened so that a wanigan boat was unnecessary. Instead, the camp outfit was transported in waggons, which often had to journey far inland, to make extraordinary detours, but which always arrived somehow at the various camping places. Orde and his men, of course, took the river trail.

The river trail ran almost unbroken for over a hundred miles of meandering way. It climbed up the high banks at the points, it crossed the bluffs along their sheer edges, it descended to the thickets in the flats, it crossed the swamps on pole-trails, it skirted the great, solemn woods. Sometimes, in the lower reaches, its continuity was broken by a town, but always after it recovered from its confusion it led on with purpose unvarying. Never did it desert for long the river. The cool, green still reaches, or the tumbling of the white-water, were always within its sight, sometimes beneath its very tread. When occasionally it cut in across a very long bend, it always sent from itself a little tributary trail which traced all the curves, and returned at last to its parent, undoubtedly with a full report of its task. And the trail was beaten hard by the feet of countless men, who, like Orde and his crew, had taken grave, interested charge of the river from her birth to her final rest in the great expanses of the Lake. It is there to-day, although the life that brought it into being has been gone from it these many years.

In midsummer Orde found the river trail most unfamiliar in appearance. Hardly did he recognise it in some places. It possessed a wide, leisurely expansiveness, an indolent luxury, a lazy invitation born of broad green leaves, deep and mysterious shadows, the growth of ferns, docks, and the like cool in the shade of the forest, the shimmer of aspens and poplars through the heat, the green of tangling vines, the drone of insects, the low-voiced call of birds, the opulent splashing of sun-gold through the woods, quite lacking to the hard, tight season in which his river work was usually performed. What, in the early year, had been merely a whip of brush, now had become a screen through whose waving, shifting interstices he caught glimpses of the river flowing green and cool. What had been bare timber amongst whose twigs and branches the full daylight had shone unobstructed, now had clothed itself in foliage and leaned over to make black and mysterious the water that flowed beneath. Countless insects hovered over the polished surface of that water. Dragon-flies cruised about. Little birds swooped silently down and fluttered back, intent on their tiny prey. Water-bugs skated hither and thither in apparently purposeless diagonals. Once in a great while the black depths were stirred. A bass rolled lazily over, carrying with him his captured insect, leaving on the surface of the water concentric rings which widened and died away.

The trail led the crew through many minor labours, all of which consumed time. At Reed's Mill Orde entered into diplomatic negotiations with Old Man Reed, whom he found singularly amenable. The skirmish in the spring seemed to have taken all the fight out of him; or perhaps, more simply, Orde's attitude toward him at that time had won him over to the young man's side. At any rate, as soon as he understood that Orde was now in business for himself, he readily came to an agreement. Thereupon Orde's crew built a new sluiceway and gate far enough down to assure a good head in the pond above. Other dam owners farther down the stream also signed agreements having to do with supplying water over and above what the law required of them. Above one particularly shallow rapid Orde built a dam of his own.

All this took time, and the summer months slipped away. Orde had fallen into the wild life as into a habit. He lived on the river or the trail. His face took on a ruddier hue than ever; his clothes faded to a nondescript neutral colour of their own; his hair below his narrow felt hat bleached three shades. He did his work, and figured on his schemes, and smoked his pipe, and occasionally took little trips to the nearest town, where he spent the day at the hotel desks reading and answering his letters. The weather was generally very warm. Thunder-storms were not infrequent. Until the latter part of August, mosquitoes and black flies were bad.

About the middle of September the crew had worked down as far as Redding, leaving behind them a river tamed, groomed, and harnessed for their uses. Remained still the forty miles between Redding and the Lake to be improved. As, however, navigation for light draught vessels extended as far as that city, Orde here paid off his men. A few days' work with a pile driver would fence the principal shoals from the channel.

He stayed over night with his parents, and at once took the train for Monrovia. There he made his way immediately to the little office the new firm had rented. Newmark had just come down.

" Hullo, Joe," greeted Orde, his teeth flashing in contrast to the tan of his face. " I'm done. Anything new since you wrote last?"

Newmark had acquired his articles of incorporation and sold his stock. How many excursions, demonstrations, representations, and arguments that implied, only one who has undertaken the floating of a new and untried scheme can imagine. Perhaps his task had in it as much of difficulty as Orde's taming of the river. Certainly he carried it to as successful a conclusion. The bulk of the stock he sold to the log-owners themselves; the rest he scattered here and there and everywhere in small lots, as he was able. Some five hundred and thousand dollar blocks even went to Chicago. His own little fortune of twenty thousand he paid in for the shares that represented his half of the majority retained by himself and Orde. The latter gave a note at ten per cent for his proportion of the stock. Newmark then borrowed fifteen thousand more, giving as security a mortgage on the company's newly acquired property—the tugs, booms, buildings, and real estate. Thus was the financing determined. It left the company with obligations of fifteen hundred dollars a year in interest, expenses which would run heavily into the thousands, and an obligation to make good outside stock worth at par exactly forty-nine thousand dollars. In addition, Orde had charged against his account a burden of two thousand dollars a year interest on his personal debt. To offset these liabilities—outside the river improvements and equipments, which would hold little or no value in case of failure—the firm held contracts to deliver about one hundred million feet of logs. After some discussion the partners decided to allow themselves twenty-five hundred dollars apiece by way of salary.

"If we don't make any dividends at first," Orde pointed out, "I've got to keep even on my interest."

"You can't live on five hundred," objected Newmark.

"I'll be on the river and at the booms six months of the year," replied Orde, "and I can't spend much there."

"I'm satisfied," said Newmark thoughtfully, "I'm getting a little better than good interest on my own investment from the start. And in a few years after we've paid up, there'll be mighty big money in it."

He removed his glasses and tapped his palm with their edge.

"The only point that is at all risky to me," said he, "is that we have only one-season contracts. If for any reason we hang up the drive, or fail to deliver promptly, we're going to get left the year following. And then it's B-U-S-T, bust."

"Well, we'll just try not to hang her," replied Orde.

XVI

ORDE'S bank account, in spite of his laughing assertion to Newmark, contained some eleven hundred dollars. After a brief but comprehensive tour of inspection over all the works then forward, he drew a hundred of this and announced to Newmark that business would take him away for about two weeks.

"I have some private affairs to attend to before settling down to business for keeps," he told Newmark vaguely.

At Redding, whither he went to pack his little sole-leather trunk, he told Grandma Orde the same thing. She said nothing at the time, but later, when Grandpa Orde's slender figure had departed, very courteous, very erect, very dignified, with its old linen duster flapping around it, she came and stood by the man leaning over the trunk.

"Speak to her, Jack," said she quietly. "She cares for you."

Orde looked up in astonishment, but he did not pretend to deny the implied accusation as to his destination.

"Why, mother!" he cried. "She's only seen me three or four times! It's absurd—yet."

"I know," nodded Grandma Orde, wisely. "I know. But you mark my words; she cares for you."

She said nothing more, but stood looking while Orde folded and laid away, his head bent low in thought. Then she placed her hand for an instant on his shoulder and went away. The Ordes were not a demonstrative people.

The journey to New York was at that time very long and disagreeable, but Orde bore it with his accustomed stoicism. He had visited the metropolis before, so it was not unfamiliar to him. He was very glad, however, to get away from the dust and monotony of the railroad train. The September twilight was just falling. Through its dusk the street lamps were popping into illumination as the lamplighter made his rapid way. Orde boarded a horse-car and jingled away down Fourth Avenue. He was pleased at having arrived, and stretched his legs and filled his lungs twice with so evident an enjoyment that several people smiled.

His comfort was soon disturbed, however, by an influx of people boarding the car at Twenty-third Street. The seats were immediately filled, and late comers found themselves obliged to stand in the aisle. Among these were several women. The men nearest buried themselves in the papers after the almost universal metropolitan custom. Two or three arose to offer their seats, among them Orde. When, however, the latter had turned to indicate to one of the women the vacated seat, he discovered it occupied by a chubby and flashily dressed youth of the sort common enough in the vicinity of Fourteenth Street; impudent of eye, cynical of demeanour, and slightly contemptuous of everything unaccustomed. He had slipped in back of Orde when that young man arose, whether under the impression that Orde was about to get off the car or from sheer impudence, it would be impossible to say.

Orde stared at him, a little astonished.

"I intended that seat for this lady," said Orde, touching him on the shoulder.

The youth looked up coolly.

"You don't come that!" said he.

Orde wasted no time in discussion, which no doubt saved the necessity of a more serious disturbance. He reached

over suddenly, seized the youth by the collar, braced his
knee against the seat, and heaved the interloper so rapidly
to his feet that he all but plunged forward among the passengers sitting opposite.

" Your seat, madam," said Orde.

The woman, frightened, unwilling to become the participant of a scene of any sort, stood looking here and there.
Orde, comprehending her embarrassment, twisted his antagonist about, and, before he could recover his equilibrium sufficiently to offer resistance, propelled him rapidly
to the open door, the passengers hastily making way for
them.

" Now, my friend," said Orde, releasing his hold on the
other's collar, " don't do such things any more. They aren't
nice."

Trivial as the incident was, it served to draw Orde to
the particular notice of an elderly man leaning against the
rear rail. He was a very well-groomed man, dressed in
garments whose fit was evidently the product of the highest
art, well buttoned up, well brushed, well cared for in every
way. In his buttonhole he wore a pink carnation, and in
his gloved hand he carried a straight, gold-headed cane.
A silk hat covered his head, from beneath which showed a
slightly empurpled countenance, with bushy white eye-
brows, a white moustache, and a pair of rather bloodshot,
but kindly, blue eyes. In spite of his somewhat pudgy
rotundity, he carried himself quite erect, in a manner that
bespoke the retired military man.

" You have courage, sir," said this gentleman, inclining
his head gravely to Orde.

The young man laughed in his good-humoured fashion.

" Not much courage required to root out that kind of a
skunk," said he cheerfully.

" I refer to the courage of your convictions. The young
men of this generation seem to prefer to avoid public dis-

turbances. That breed is quite capable of making a row, calling the police, raising the deuce, and all that."

"What of it?" said Orde.

The elderly gentleman puffed out his cheeks.

"You are from the West, are you not?" he stated, rather than asked.

"We call it the East out there," said Orde. "It's Michigan."

"I should call that pretty far west," said the old gentleman.

Nothing more was said. After a block or two Orde descended on his way to a small hotel just off Broadway. The old gentleman saluted. Orde nodded good-humouredly. In his private soul he was a little amused at the old boy. To his view a man and clothes carried to their last refinement were contradictory terms.

Orde ate, dressed, and set out afoot in search of Miss Bishop's address. He arrived in front of the house a little past eight o'clock, and, after a moment's hesitation, mounted the steps and rang the bell.

The door swung silently back to frame an impassive man-servant dressed in livery. To Orde's inquiry he stated that Miss Bishop had gone out to the theatre. The young man left his name and a message of regret. At this the footman, with an irony so subtle as to be quite lost on Orde, demanded a card. Orde scribbled a line in his note book, tore it out, folded it, and left it. In it he stated his regret, his short residence in the city, and desired an early opportunity to call. Then he departed down the brownstone steps, totally unconscious of the contempt he had inspired in the heart of the liveried man behind him.

He retired early and arose early, as had become his habit. When he descended to the office the night clerk, who had not yet been relieved, handed him a note delivered the night before. Orde ripped it open eagerly.

" My Dear Mr. Orde:

" I was so sorry to miss you that evening because of a stupid play. Come around as early as you can to-morrow morning. I shall expect you.

" Sincerely yours,

" Carroll Bishop."

Orde glanced at the clock, which pointed to seven. He breakfasted, read the morning paper, finally started leisurely in the direction of West Ninth Street. He walked slowly, so as to consume more time, then at University Place was seized with a panic, and hurried rapidly to his destination. The door was answered by the same man who had opened the night before, but now, in some indefinable way, his calm, while flawless externally, seemed to have lifted to a mere surface, as though he might hastily have assumed his coat. To Orde's inquiry he stated with great brevity that Miss Bishop was not yet visible, and prepared to close the door.

" You are mistaken," said Orde, with equal brevity, and stepped inside. " I have an engagement with Miss Bishop. Tell her Mr. Orde is here."

The man departed in some doubt, leaving Orde standing in the gloomy hall. That young man, however, quite cheerfully parted the heavy curtains leading into a parlour, and sat down in a spindle-legged chair. At his entrance, a maid disappeared out another door, carrying with her the implements of dusting and brushing.

Orde looked around the room with some curiosity. It was long, narrow, and very high. Tall windows admitted light at one end. The illumination was, however, modified greatly by hangings of lace covering all the windows, supplemented by heavy draperies drawn back to either side. The embrasure was occupied by a small table, over which seemed to flutter a beautiful marble Psyche. A rubber plant, then as now the mark of the city and suburban dweller, sent aloft its spare, shiny leaves alongside a closed square piano. The lack of ornaments atop the latter bespoke the musician. Through the filtered gloom of the demi-light Orde surveyed with interest the excellent reproductions of the Old World masterpieces framed on the walls—" Madonnas " by Raphael, Murillo, and Perugino, the " Mona Lisa," and Botticelli's " Spring "—the three oil portraits occupying the large spaces ; the spindle-legged chairs and tables, the tea service in the corner, the tall bronze lamp by the piano, the neat little grate-hearth, with its mantel of marble ; the ormolu clock, all the decorous and decorated gentility which marked the irreproachable correctness of whoever had furnished the apartment. Dark and heavy hangings depended in front of a double door leading into another room beyond. Equally dark and heavy hangings had closed behind Orde as he entered. An absolute and shrouded stillness seemed to settle down upon him. The ormolu clock ticked steadily. Muffled sounds came at long intervals from behind the portières. Orde began to feel oppressed and subdued.

For quite three quarters of an hour he waited without hearing any other indications of life than the muffled sounds just remarked upon. Occasionally he shifted his position, but cautiously, as though he feared to awaken some one. The three oil portraits stared at him with all the reserved aloofness of their painted eyes. He began to doubt whether the man had announced him at all.

Then, breaking the stillness with almost startling abruptness, he heard a clear, high voice saying something at the top of the stairs outside. A rhythmical *swish* of skirts, punctuated by the light *pat-pat* of a girl tripping downstairs, brought him to his feet. A moment later the curtains parted and she entered, holding out her hand.

"Oh, I did keep you waiting such a long time!" she cried.

He stood holding her hand, suddenly unable to say a word, looking at her hungrily. A flood of emotion, of which he had had no prevision, swelled up within him to fill his throat. An almost irresistible impulse all but controlled him to crush her to him, to kiss her lips and her throat, to lose his fingers in the soft, shadowy fineness of her hair. The crest of the wave passed almost immediately, but it left him shaken. A faint colour deepened under the transparence of her skin; her fathomless black eyes widened ever so little; she released her hand.

"It was good of you to come so promptly," said she. "I'm so anxious to hear all about the dear people at Redding."

She settled gracefully in one of the little chairs. Orde sat down, once more master of himself, but still inclined to devour her with his gaze. She was dressed in a morning gown, all laces and ribbons and long, flowing lines. Her hair was done low on the back of her head and on the nape of her neck. The blood ebbed and flowed beneath her clear skin. A faint fragrance of cleanliness diffused itself about her—the cool, sweet fragrance of daintiness. They entered busily into conversation. Her attitudes were no longer relaxed and languidly graceful as in the easy chairs under the lamplight. She sat forward, her hands crossed on her lap, a fire smouldering deep beneath the cool surface lights of her eyes.

The sounds in the next room increased in volume, as though several people must have entered that apartment. In a moment or so the curtains to the hall parted to frame the servant.

"Mrs. Bishop wishes to know, miss," said that functionary, "if you're not coming to breakfast."

Orde sprang to his feet.

"Haven't you had your breakfast yet?" he cried, conscience stricken.

"Didn't you gather the fact that I'm just up?" she mocked him. "I assure you it doesn't matter. The family has just come down."

"But," cried Orde, "I wasn't here until nine o'clock. I thought, of course, you'd be around. I'm mighty sorry——"

"Oh, la la!" she cried, cutting him short. "What a pother about nothing. Don't you see—I'm ahead a whole hour of good talk."

"You see, you told me in your note to come early," said Orde.

"I forgot you were one of those dreadful outdoor men. You didn't see any worms, did you? Next time I'll tell you to come the day after."

Orde was for taking his leave, but this she would not have.

"You must meet my family," she negatived. "For if you're here for so short a time we want to see something of you. Come right out now."

Orde thereupon followed her down a narrow, dark hall, squeezed between the stairs and the wall, to a door that opened slantwise into a dining-room the exact counterpart in shape to the parlour at the other side of the house. Only in this case the morning sun and more diaphanous curtains lent an air of brightness, further enhanced by a wire stand of flowers in the bow-windows.

The centre of the room was occupied by a round table, about which were grouped several people of different ages. With her back to the bow-window sat a woman well beyond middle age, but with evidently some pretensions to youth. She was tall, desiccated, quick in movement. Dark rings below her eyes attested either a nervous disease, an hysterical temperament, or both. Immediately at her left sat a boy of about fourteen years of age, his face a curious contradiction between a naturally frank and open expression and a growing sullenness. Next him stood a vacant chair, evidently for Miss Bishop. Opposite lolled a young man, holding a newspaper in one hand and a coffee cup in the other. He was very handsome, with a drooping black moustache, dark eyes, under lashes almost too luxuriant, and a long, oval face, dark in complexion, and a trifle sardonic in expression. In the *vis-à-vis* to Mrs. Bishop, Orde was surprised to find his ex-military friend of the street car. Miss Bishop performed the necessary introductions, which each acknowledged after his fashion, but with an apparent indifference that dashed Orde, accustomed to a more Western cordiality. Mrs. Bishop held out a languidly graceful hand, the boy mumbled a greeting, the young man nodded lazily over his newspaper. Only General Bishop, recognising him, arose and grasped his hand, with a real, though rather fussy, warmth.

"My dear sir," he cried, "I am honoured to see you again. This, my dear," he addressed his wife, "is the young man I was telling you about—in the street car," he explained.

"How very interesting," said Mrs. Bishop, with evidently no comprehension and less interest.

Gerald Bishop cast an ironically amused glance across at Orde. The boy looked up at him quickly, the sullenness for a moment gone from his face.

Carroll Bishop appeared quite unconscious of an atmosphere which seemed to Orde strained, but sank into her place at the table and unfolded her napkin. The silent butler drew forward a chair for Orde, and stood looking impassively in Mrs. Bishop's direction.

"You will have some breakfast with us?" she inquired. "No? A cup of coffee, at least?"

She began to manipulate the coffee pot, without paying the slightest attention to Orde's disclaimer. The general puffed out his cheeks, and coughed a bit in embarrassment.

"A good cup of coffee is never amiss to an old campaigner," he said to Orde. "It's as good as a full meal in a pinch. I remember when I was a major in the Eleventh, down near the City of Mexico, in '48, the time Hardy's command was so nearly wiped out by that viaduct—" He half turned toward Orde, his face lighting up, his fingers reaching for the fork with which, after the custom of old soldiers, to trace the chart of his reminiscences.

Mrs. Bishop rattled her cup and saucer with an uncontrollably nervous jerk of her slender body. For some moments she had awaited a chance to get the general's attention. "Spare us, father," she said brusquely. "Will you have another cup of coffee?"

The old gentleman, arrested in mid-career, swallowed, looked a trifle bewildered, but subsided meekly.

"No, thank you, my dear," said he, and went furiously at his breakfast.

Orde, overwhelmed by embarrassment, discovered that none of the others had paid the incident the slightest attention. Only on the lips of Gerald Bishop he surprised a fine, detached smile.

At this moment the butler entered bearing the mail. Mrs. Bishop tore hers open rapidly, dropping the mangled envelopes at her side. The contents of one seemed to vex her.

"Oh!" she cried aloud. "That miserable Marie! She promised me to have it done to-day, and now she puts it off until Monday. It's too provoking!" She turned to Orde for sympathy. "Do you know *anything* more aggravating than to work and slave to the limit of endurance, and then have everything upset by the stupidity of some one else?"

Orde murmured an appropriate reply, to which Mrs.

Bishop paid no attention whatever. She started suddenly up from the table.

"I must see about it!" she cried. "I plainly see I shall have to do it myself. I *will* do it myself. I promised it for Sunday."

"You mustn't do another stitch, mother," put in Carroll Bishop decidedly. "You know what the doctor told you. You'll have yourself down sick."

"Well, see for yourself!" cried Mrs. Bishop. "That's what comes of leaving things to others! If I'd done it myself, it would have saved me all this bother and fuss, and it would have been done. And now I've got to do it anyway."

"My dear," put in the general, "perhaps Carroll can see Marie about it. In any case, there's nothing to work yourself up into such an excitement about."

"It's very easy for you to talk, isn't it?" cried Mrs. Bishop, turning on him. "I like the way you all sit around like lumps and do nothing, and then tell me how I ought to have done it. John, have the carriage around at once." She turned tensely to Orde. "I hope you'll excuse me," she said very briefly; "I have something very important to attend to."

Carroll had also risen. Orde held out his hand.

"I must be going," said he.

"Well," she conceded, "I suppose I'd better see if I can't help mother out. But you'll come in again. Come and dine with us this evening. Mother will be delighted."

As Mrs. Bishop had departed from the room, Orde had to take for granted the expression of this delight. He bowed to the other occupants of the table. The general was eating nervously. Gerald's eyes were fixed amusedly on Orde.

To Orde's surprise, he was almost immediately joined on the street by young Mr. Bishop, most correctly appointed.

"Going anywhere in particular?" he inquired. "Let's go up the avenue, then. Everybody will be out."

They turned up the great promenade, a tour of which was then, even more than now, considered obligatory on the gracefully idle. Neither said anything—Orde because he was too absorbed in the emotions this sudden revelation of Carroll's environment had aroused in him; Gerald, apparently, because he was too indifferent. Nevertheless it was the young exquisite who finally broke the silence.

" It was an altar cloth," said he suddenly.

" What? " asked Orde, rather bewildered.

" Mother is probably the most devout woman in New York," went on Gerald's even voice. " She is one of the hardest workers in the church. She keeps all the fast days, and attends all the services. Although she has no strength to speak of, she has just completed an elaborate embroidered altar cloth. The work she accomplished while on her knees. Often she spent five or six hours a day in that position. It was very devout, but against the doctor's orders, and she is at present much pulled down. Finally she gave way to persuasion to the extent of sending the embroidery out to be bound and corded. As a result, the altar cloth will not be done for next Sunday."

He delivered this statement in a voice absolutely colourless, without the faintest trace discernible of either approval or disapproval, without the slightest irony, yet Orde felt vaguely uncomfortable.

" It must have been annoying to her," he said gravely, " and I hope she will get it done in time. Perhaps Miss Bishop will be able to do it."

" That," said Gerald, " is Madison Square—or perhaps you know New York? My sister would, of course, be only too glad to finish the work, but I fear that my mother's peculiarly ardent temperament will now insist on her own accomplishment of the task. But perhaps you do not understand temperaments? "

" Very little, I'm afraid," confessed Orde.

They walked on for some distance farther.

"Your father was in the Mexican War?" said Orde, to change the trend of his own thoughts.

"He was a most distinguished officer. I believe he received the Medal of Honour for a part in the affair of the Molina del Rey."

"What command had he in the Civil War?" asked Orde. "I fooled around the outskirts of that a little myself."

"My father resigned from the army in '54," replied Gerald, with his cool, impersonal courtesy.

"That was too bad; just before the chance for more service," said Orde.

"Army life was incompatible with my mother's temperament," stated Gerald.

Orde said nothing more. It was Gerald's turn to end the pause.

"You are from Redding, of course," said he. "My sister is very enthusiastic about the place. You are in business there?"

Orde replied briefly, but, forced by the direct, cold, and polite cross-questioning of his companion, he gave the latter a succinct idea of the sort of operations in which he was interested.

"And you," he said at last; "I suppose you're either a broker or lawyer; most men are down here."

"I am neither one nor the other," stated Gerald. "I am possessed of a sufficient income from a legacy to make business unnecessary."

"I don't believe I'd care to—be idle," said Orde vaguely.

"There is plenty to occupy one's time," replied Gerald. "I have my clubs, my gymnasium, my horse, and my friends."

"Isn't there anything that particularly attracts you?" asked Orde.

The young man's languid eyes grew thoughtful, and he puffed more strongly on his cigarette.

"I should like," said he slowly, at last, "to enter the navy."

"Why don't you?" asked Orde bluntly.

"Certain family reasons make it inexpedient at present," said Gerald. "My mother is in a very nervous state; she depends on us, and any hint of our leaving her is sufficient to render her condition serious."

By this time the two young men were well uptown. On Gerald's initiative, they turned down a side street, and shortly came to a stop.

"That is my gymnasium," said Gerald, pointing to a building across the way. "Won't you come in with me? I am due now for my practice."

XVII

ORDE'S evening was a disappointment to him. Mrs. Bishop had, by Carroll's report, worked feverishly at the altar cloth all the afternoon. As a consequence, she had gone to bed with a bad headache. This state of affairs seemed to throw the entire family into a state of indecision. It was divided in mind as to what to do, the absolute inutility of any effort balancing strongly against a sense of what the invalid expected.

"I wonder if mother wouldn't like just a taste of this beef," speculated the general, moving fussily in his chair. "I believe somebody ought to take some up. She *might* want it."

The man departed with the plate, but returned a few moments later, impassive—but still with the plate.

"Has she got her hot-water bag?" asked the boy unexpectedly.

"Yes, Master Kendrick," replied the butler.

After a preoccupied silence the general again broke out: "Seems to me somebody ought to be up there with her."

"You know, father, that she can't stand any one in the room," said Carroll equably.

Toward the close of the meal, however, a distant bell tinkled faintly. Every one jumped as though guilty. Carroll said a hasty excuse and ran out. After ringing the bell, the invalid had evidently anticipated its answer by emerging from her room to the head of the stairs, for Orde caught the sharp tones of complaint, and overheard something about "take all night to eat a simple meal, when I'm lying here suffering."

At the end of an interval a maid appeared in the doorway to say that Miss Carroll sent word she would not be down again for a time, and did not care for any more dinner. This seemed to relieve the general's mind of responsibility. He assumed his little fussy air of cheerfulness, told several stories of the war, and finally, after Kendrick had left, brought out some whisky and water. He winked slyly at Orde.

"Can't do this before the youngsters, you know," he chirruped craftily.

Throughout the meal Gerald had sat back silent, a faint amusement in his eye. After dinner he arose, yawned, consulted his watch, and departed, pleading an engagement. Orde lingered some time, listening to the general, in the hope that Carroll would reappear. She did not, so finally he took his leave.

He trudged back to his hotel gloomily. The day had passed in a most unsatisfactory manner, according to his way of looking at it. Yet he had come more clearly to an understanding of the girl; her cheerfulness, her unselfishness, and, above all, the sweet, beautiful philosophy of life that must lie back, to render her so uncomplainingly the slave of the self-willed woman, yet without the indifferent cynicism of Gerald, the sullen, yet real, partisanship of Kendrick, or the general's week-kneed acquiescence.

The next morning he succeeded in making an arrangement by letter for an excursion to the newly projected Central Park. Promptly at two o'clock he was at the Bishops' house. To his inquiry the butler said that Mrs. Bishop had recovered from her indisposition, and that Miss Bishop would be down immediately. Orde had not long to wait for her. The *swish, pat-pat* of her joyous descent of the stairs brought him to his feet. She swept aside the portières, and stood between their folds, bidding him welcome.

"I'm so sorry about last night," said she, "but poor

mother does depend on me so at such times. Isn't it a gorgeous day to walk? It won't be much like *our* woods, will it? But it will be something. *Oh*, I'm so glad to get out!"

She was in one of her elfish moods, the languid grace of her sleepy-eyed moments forgotten. With a little cry of rapture she ran to the piano, and dashed into a gay, tinkling air with brilliancy and abandon. Her head, surmounted by a perky, high-peaked, narrow-brimmed hat, with a flaming red bird in front, glorified by the braid and "waterfall" of that day, bent forward and turned to flash an appeal for sympathy toward Orde.

"There, I feel more able to stay on earth!" she cried, springing to her feet. "Now I'll get on my gloves and we'll start."

She turned slowly before the mirror, examining quite frankly the hang of her skirt, the fit of her close-cut waist, the turn of the adorable round, low-cut collars that were then the mode.

"It pays to be particular; we are in New York," she answered, or parried, Orde's glance of admiration.

The gloves finally drawn on and buttoned, Orde held aside the portières, and she passed fairly under his uplifted hand. He wanted to drop his arm about her, this slender girl with her quaint dignity, her bird-like ways, her gentle, graceful, mysterious, feminine soul. The flame-red bird lent its colour to her cheeks; her eyes, black and fathomless, the pupils wide in this dim light, shone with two stars of delight.

But, as they moved toward the massive front doors, Mrs. Bishop came down the stairs behind them. She, too, was dressed for the street. She received Orde's greeting and congratulation over her improved health in rather an absent manner. Indeed, as soon as she could hurry this preliminary over, she plunged into what evidently she considered a more important matter.

"You aren't thinking of going out, are you?" she asked Carroll.

"I told you, mother; don't you remember? Mr. Orde and I are going to get a little air in the park."

"I'm sorry," said Mrs. Bishop, with great brevity and decision, "but I'm going to the rectory to help Mr. Merritt, and I shall want you to go too, to see about the silver."

"But, mother," expostulated Carroll, "wouldn't Marie do just as well?"

"You know very well she can't be trusted without direction."

"I *do* so want to go to the park," said Carroll wistfully.

Mrs. Bishop's thin, nervous figure jerked spasmodically.

"There is very little asked of you from morning until night," she said, with some asperity, "and I should think you'd have some slight consideration for the fact that I'm just up from a sick bed to spare me all you could. Besides which, you do very little for the church. I won't insist. Do exactly as you think best."

Carroll threw a pathetic glance at Orde.

"How soon are you going?" she asked her mother.

"In about ten minutes," replied Mrs. Bishop; "as soon as I've seen Honorine about the dinner." She seemed abruptly to realise that the amenities demanded something of her. "I'm sorry we must go so soon," she said briefly to Orde, "but of course church business— We shall hope to see you often."

Once more Orde held aside the curtains. The flame-bird drooped from the twilight of the hall into the dimness of the parlour. All the brightness seemed to have drained from the day, and all the joy of life seemed to have faded from the girl's soul. She sank into a chair, and tried pathetically to smile across at Orde.

"I'm such a baby about disappointments," said she.

"I know," he replied, very gently.

" And it's such a blue and gold day."

" I know," he repeated.

She twisted her glove in her lap, a bright spot of colour burning in each cheek.

" Mother is not well, and she has a great deal to try her. Poor mother! " she said softly, her head cast down.

" I know," said Orde in his gentle tones.

After a moment he arose to go. She remained seated, her head down.

" I'm sorry about this afternoon," said he cheerfully, " but it couldn't be helped, could it? Jane used to tell me about your harp playing. I'm going to come in to hear you this evening. May I? "

" Yes," she said, in a stifled voice, and held out her hand.

She sat quite still until she heard the front door close after him; then she ran to the curtains and looked after his sturdy, square figure, as it swung up the street.

" Well done; oh, well done, gentle heart! " she breathed after him. Then she went back to the piano.

But Orde's mouth, could she have seen it, was set in grim lines, and his feet, could she have heard them, rang on the pavement with quite superfluous vigour. He turned to the left, and, without pause, walked some ten or twelve miles.

The evening turned out very well, fortunately; Orde could not have stood much more. They had the parlour quite to themselves. Carroll took the cover from the tall harp, and, leaning her cheek against it, she played dreamily for a half hour. Her arms were bare, and as her fingers reached out lingeringly and caressingly to draw the pure, golden chords from the golden instrument, her soft bosom pressed against the broad sounding board. There is about the tones of a harp well played something luminous, like rich, warm sunlight. When the girl muted the strings at last, it seemed to Orde as though all at once the room had perceptibly darkened. He took his leave finally, his spirit soothed and restored.

Tranquillity was not for long, however. Orde's visits were, naturally, as frequent as possible. To them almost instantly Mrs. Bishop opposed the strong and intuitive jealousy of egotism. She had as yet no fears as to the young man's intentions, but instinctively she felt an influence that opposed her own supreme dominance. In consequence, Orde had much time to himself. Carroll and the rest of the family, with the possible exception of Gerald, shared the belief that the slightest real opposition to Mrs. Bishop would suffice to throw her into one of her "spells," a condition of alarming and possibly genuine collapse. "To drive mother into a spell" was an expression of the worst possible domestic crime. It accused the perpetrator—through Mrs. Bishop—of forgetting the state of affairs, of ingratitude for care and affection, of common inhumanity, and of impiety in rendering impossible of performance the multifarious church duties Mrs. Bishop had invented and assumed as so many particularly shining virtues. Orde soon discovered that Carroll went out in society very little for the simple reason that she could never give an unqualified acceptance to an invitation. At the last moment, when she had donned her street wraps and the carriage was at the door, she was liable to be called back, either to assist at some religious function, which, by its sacred character, was supposed to have precedence over everything, or to attend a nervous crisis, brought on by some member of the household, or by mere untoward circumstances. The girl always acquiesced most sweetly in these recurrent disappointments. And the very fact that she accepted few invitations gave Orde many more chances to see her, in spite of Mrs. Bishop's increasing exactions. He did not realise this fact, however, but ground his teeth and clung blind-eyed to his temper whenever the mother cut short his visits or annulled his engagements on some petty excuse of her own. He could almost believe these interruptions malicious, were it not that he soon discovered Mrs. Bishop well disposed toward him personally whenever he showed himself ready to meet her even quarter way on the topics that interested her—the church and her health.

In this manner the week passed. Orde saw as much as he could of Miss Bishop. The remainder of the time he spent walking the streets and reading in the club rooms to which Gerald's courtesy had given him access. Gerald himself seemed to be much occupied. Precisely at eleven every morning, however, he appeared at the gymnasium for his practice; and in this Orde dropped into the habit of joining him. When the young men first stripped in each other's presence, they eyed each other with a secret surprise. Gerald's slender and elegant body turned out to be smoothly and gracefully muscled on the long lines of the Flying Mercury. His bones were small, but his flesh was hard, and his skin healthy with the flow of blood beneath. Orde, on the other hand, had earned from the river the torso of an ancient athlete. The round, full arch of his chest was topped by a mass of clean-cut muscle; across his back, beneath the smooth skin, the muscles rippled and ridged and dimpled with every movement; the beautiful curve of the deltoids, from the point of the shoulder to the arm, met the other beautiful curve of the unflexed biceps and that fulness of the back arm so often lacking in a one-sided development; the surface of the abdomen showed the peculiar corrugation of the very strong man; the round, columnar neck arose massive.

" By Jove! " said Gerald, roused at last from his habitual apathy.

" What's the matter? " asked Orde, looking up from tying the rubber-soled shoes that Gerald had lent him.

" Murphy," called Gerald, " come here."

A very hairy, thick-set, bullet-headed man, the type of semi-professional "handlers," emerged from somewhere across the gymnasium.

"Do you think you could down this fellow?" asked Gerald.

Murphy looked Orde over critically.

"Who ye ringin' in on me?" he inquired.

"This is a friend of mine," said Gerald severely.

"Beg your pardon. The gentleman is well put up. How much experience has he had?"

"Ever box much?" Gerald asked Orde.

"Box?" Orde laughed. "Never had time for that sort of thing. Had the gloves on a few times."

"Where did you get your training, sir?" asked the handler.

"My training?" repeated Orde, puzzled. "Oh, I see! I was always pretty heavy, and I suppose the work on the river keeps a man in pretty good shape."

Gerald's languor had vanished, and a glint had appeared in his eye that would have reminded Orde of Miss Bishop's most mischievous mood could he have seen it.

"Put on the gloves with Murphy," he suggested, "will you? I'd like to see you two at it."

"Surely," agreed Orde good-naturedly. "I'm not much good at it, but I'd just as soon try." He was evidently not in the least afraid to meet the handler, though as evidently without much confidence in his own skill.

"All right; I'll be with you in a second," said Gerald, disappearing. In the anteroom he rung a bell, and to the boy who leisurely answered its summons he said rapidly:

"Run over to the club and find Mr. Winslow, Mr. Clark, and whoever else is in the smoking room, and tell them from me to come over to the gymnasium. Tell them there's some fun on."

Then he returned to the gymnasium floor, where Mur-

phy was answering Orde's questions as to the apparatus.
While the two men were pulling on the gloves, Gerald
managed a word apart with the trainer.

" Can you do him, Murph? " he whispered.

" Sure! " said the handler. " Them kind's always as slow
as dray-horses. They gets muscle-bound."

" Give it to him," said Gerald, " but don't kill him. He's
a friend of mine."

Then he stepped back, the same joy in his soul that in-
spires a riverman when he encounters a high-banker; a
hunter when he takes out a greenhorn, or a cowboy as he
watches the tenderfoot about to climb the bronco.

" Time! " said he.

The first round was sharp. When Gerald called the end,
Orde grinned at him cheerfully.

" Don't look like I was much at this game, does it? "
said he. " I wouldn't pull down many persimmons out of
that tree. Your confounded man's too lively; I couldn't hit
him with a shotgun."

Orde had stood like a rock, his feet planted to the floor,
while Murphy had circled around him hitting at will. Orde
hit back, but without landing. Nevertheless Murphy, when
questioned apart, did not seem satisfied.

" The man's pig-iron," said he. " I punched him plenty
hard enough, and it didn't seem to jar him."

The gallery at one end the running track had by now
half filled with interested spectators.

" Time! " called Gerald for round two.

This time Murphy went in more viciously, aiming and
measuring his blows accurately. Orde stood as before, a
humourous smile of self-depreciation on his face, hitting
back at the elusive Murphy, but without much effect, his
feet never stirring in their tracks. The handler used his best
tactics and landed almost at will, but without apparent damage. He grew ugly—finally lost his head.

"Well, if ye will have it!" he muttered, and aimed what was intended as a knockout blow.

Gerald uttered a half cry of warning as his practised eye caught Murphy's intention. The blow landed. Orde's head snapped back, but to the surprise of every one the punch had no other effect, and a quick exchange of infighting sent Murphy staggering back from the encounter. The smile had disappeared from Orde's face, and his eye had calmed.

"Look here," he called to Gerald, "I don't understand this game very well. At school we used 'taps.' Is a man supposed to hit hard?"

Gerald hesitated, then looked beyond Orde to the gallery. To a man it made frantic and silent demonstration.

"Of course you hit," he replied. "You can't hurt any one with those big gloves."

Orde turned back to his antagonist. The latter advanced once more, his bullet head sunk between his shoulders, his little eyes twinkling. Evidently Mr. Bishop's friend would now take the aggressive, and forward movement would deliver an extra force to the professional's blows.

Orde did not wait for Murphy, however. Like a tiger he sprang forward, hitting out fiercely, first with one hand then with the other. Murphy gave ground, blocked, ducked, exerted all a ring general's skill either to stop or avoid the rush. Orde followed him insistent. Several times he landed, but always when Murphy was on the retreat, so the blows had not much weight. Several times Murphy ducked in and planted a number of short-arm jabs at close range. The round ended almost immediately to a storm of applause from the galleries.

"What do you think of his being muscle-bound?" Gerald asked Murphy, as the latter flung himself panting on the wrestling mat for his rest.

"He's quick as chained lightning," acknowledged the

other grudgingly. " But I'll get him. He can't keep that
up; he'll be winded in half a minute."

Orde sat down on a roll of mat. His smile had quite
vanished, and he seemed to be awaiting eagerly the beginning of the next round.

" Time ! " called Gerald for the third.

Orde immediately sprang at his adversary, repeating the
headlong rush with which the previous round had ended.
Murphy blocked, ducked, and kept away, occasionally delivering a jolt as opportunity offered, awaiting the time
when Orde's weariness would leave him at the other's
mercy. That moment did not come. The young man ham-
mered away tirelessly, insistently, delivering a hurricane
of his two-handed blows, pressing relentlessly in as Murphy shifted and gave ground, his head up, his eyes steady,
oblivious to the return hammering the now desperate handler opposed to him. Two minutes passed without perceptible slackening in this terrific pace. The gallery was in an
uproar, and some of the members were piling down the
stairs to the floor. Perspiration stood out all over Murphy's
body. His blows failed of their effect, and some of Orde's
were landing. At length, bewildered more by the continu-
ance than the violence of the attack, he dropped his ring
tactics and closed in to straight slugging, blow against
blow, stand up, give and take.

As he saw his opponent stand, Orde uttered a sound of
satisfaction. He dropped slightly his right shoulder behind
his next blow. The glove crashed straight as a pile-driver
through Murphy's upraised hands to his face, which it met
with a smack. The trainer, lifted bodily from the ground,
was hurled through the air, to land doubled up against the
supports of a parallel bars. There he lay quite still, his
palms up, his head sunk forward.

Orde stared at him a moment in astonishment, as though
expecting him to arise. When, however, he perceived that

Murphy was in reality unconscious, he tore off the gloves and ran forward to kneel by the professional's side.

" I didn't suppose one punch like that would hurt him," he muttered to the men crowding around. " Especially with the gloves. Do you suppose he's killed? "

But already Murphy's arms were making aimless motions, and a deep breath raised his chest.

" He's just knocked out," reassured one of the men, examining the prostrate handler with a professional attention. " He'll be as good as ever in five minutes. Here," he commanded one of the gymnasium rubbers who had appeared, " lend a hand here with some water."

The clubmen crowded about, all talking at once.

" You're a wonder, my friend," said one.

" By Jove, he's hardly breathing fast after all that rushing," said a second.

" So you didn't think one punch like that would hurt him," quoted another with good-natured sarcasm.

" No," said Orde, simply. " I've hit men that hard before with my bare fist."

" Did they survive? "

" Surely."

" What kind of armour-plates were they, in heaven's name? "

Orde had recovered his balance and humour.

" Just plain ordinary rivermen," said he with a laugh.

" Gentlemen," struck in Gerald, " I want to introduce you to my friend." He performed the introductions. It was necessary for him to explain apart that Orde was in reality his friend, an amateur, a chance visitor in the city. All in all, the affair made quite a little stir, and went far to give Orde a standing with these sport-loving youths.

Finally Gerald and Orde were permitted to finish their gymnasium practice. Murphy had recovered, and came forward.

"You have a strong punch, sir, and you're a born natural fighter, sir," said he. "If you had a few lessons in boxing, sir, I'd put you against the best."

But later, when the young men were resting, each under his sheet after a rub-down, the true significance of the affair for Orde came out. Since the fight, Gerald's customary lassitude of manner seemed quite to have left him. His eye was bright, a colour mounted beneath the pale olive of his skin, the almost effeminate beauty of his countenance had animated. He looked across at Orde several times, hesitated, and at last decided to speak.

"Look here, Orde," said he, "I want to confess something to you. When you first came here three days ago, I had lots of fun with myself about you. You know your clothes aren't quite the thing, and I thought your manner was queer, and all that. I was a cad. I want to apologise. You're a man, and I like you better than any fellow I've met for a long time. And if there's any trouble—in the future—that is—oh, hang it, I'm on your side—you know what I mean!"

Orde smiled slowly.

"Bishop," was his unexpected reply, "you're not near so much of a dandy as you think you are."

XVIII

AFFAIRS went thus for a week. Orde was much at the Bishop residence, where he was cordially received by the general, where he gained an occasional half-hour with Carroll, and where he was almost ignored by Mrs. Bishop in her complete self-absorption. Indeed, it is to be doubted whether he attained any real individuality to that lady, who looked on all the world outside her family as useful or useless to the church.

In the course of the happy moments he had alone with Carroll, he arrived at a more intimate plane of conversation with her. He came to an understanding of her unquestioning acceptance of Mrs. Bishop's attitude. Carroll truly believed that none but herself could perform for her mother the various petty offices that lady demanded from her next of kin, and that her practical slavery was due by every consideration of filial affection. To Orde's occasional tentative suggestion that the service was of a sort better suited to a paid companion or even a housemaid, she answered quite seriously that it made mother nervous to have others about her, and that it was better to do these things than to throw her into a " spell." Orde chafed at first over seeing his precious opportunities thus filched from him; later he fretted because he perceived that Carroll was forced, however willingly, to labours beyond her strength, to irksome confinement, and to that intimate and wearing close association with the abnormal which in the long run is bound to deaden the spirit. He lost sight of his own grievance in the matter. With perhaps somewhat of exag-

geration he came mightily to desire for her more of the
open air, both of body and spirit. Often when tramping
back to his hotel he communed savagely with himself, turning the problem over and over in his mind until, like a
snowball, it had gathered to itself colossal proportions.

And in his hotel room he brooded over the state of affairs until his thoughts took a very gloomy tinge indeed.
To begin with, in spite of his mother's assurance, he had
no faith in his own cause. His acquaintance with Carroll was
but an affair of months, and their actual meetings comprised incredibly few days. Orde was naturally humble-
minded. It did not seem conceivable to him that he could
win her without a long courtship. And superadded was the
almost intolerable weight of Carroll's ideas as to her domestic duties. Although Orde held Mrs. Bishop's exactions in very slight esteem, and was most sceptical in
regard to the disasters that would follow their thwarting,
nevertheless he had to confess to himself that all Carroll's
training, life, the very purity and sweetness of her dis-
position lent the situation an iron reality for her. He became much discouraged.

Nevertheless, at the very moment when he had made up
his mind that it would be utterly useless even to indulge
in hope for some years to come, he spoke. It came about
suddenly, and entirely without premeditation.

The two had escaped for a breath of air late in the evening. Following the conventions, they merely strolled to the
end of the block and back, always within sight of the
house. Fifth Avenue was gay with illumination and the
prancing of horses returning uptown or down to the Washington Square district. In contrast the side street, with its
austere rows of brownstone houses, each with its area and
flight of steps, its spaced gas lamps, its deserted roadway,
seemed very still and quiet. Carroll was in a tired and pen-
sive mood. She held her head back, breathing deeply.

"It's only a little strip, but it's the stars," said she, looking up to the sky between the houses. "They're so quiet and calm and big."

She seemed to Orde for the first time like a little girl. The maturer complexities which we put on with years, with experience, and with the knowledge of life had for the moment fallen from her, leaving merely the simple soul of childhood gazing in its eternal wonder at the stars. A wave of tenderness lifted Orde from his feet. He leaned over, his breath coming quickly.

"Carroll!" he said.

She looked up at him, and shrank back.

"No, no! You mustn't," she cried. She did not pretend to misunderstand. The preliminaries seemed in some mysterious fashion to have been said long ago.

"It's life or death with me," he said.

"I must not," she cried, fluttering like a bird. "I promised myself long ago that I must always, *always* take care of mother."

"Please, please, dear," pleaded Orde. He had nothing more to say than this, just the simple incoherent symbols of pleading; but in such crises it is rather the soul than the tongue that speaks. His hand met hers and closed about it. It did not respond to his grasp, nor did it draw away, but lay limp and warm and helpless in his own.

She shook her head slowly.

"Don't you care for me, dear?" asked Orde very gently.

"I have no right to tell you that," answered she. "I have tried, oh, so hard, to keep you from saying this, for I knew I had no right to hear you."

Orde's heart leaped with a wild exultation.

"You do care for me!" he cried.

They had mounted the steps and stood just within the vestibule. Orde drew her toward him, but she repulsed him gently.

" No," she shook her head. " Please be very good to me.
I'm very weak."

" Carroll!" cried Orde. " Tell me that you love me!
Tell me that you'll marry me!"

" It would kill mother if I should leave her," she said
sadly.

" But you must marry me," pleaded Orde. " We are
made for each other. God meant us for each other."

" It would have to be after a great many years," she
said doubtfully.

She pulled the bell, which jangled faintly in the depths
of the house.

" Good-night," she said. " Come to me to-morrow. No,
you must not come in." She cut short Orde's insistence
and the eloquence that had just found its life by slipping
inside the half-open door and closing it after her.

Orde stood for a moment uncertain; then turned away
and walked up the street, his eyes so blinded by the greater
glory that he all but ran down an inoffensive passer-by.

At the hotel he wrote a long letter to his mother. The
first part was full of the exultation of his discovery. He
told of his good fortune quite as something just born, ut
terly forgetting his mother's predictions before he came
East. Then as the first effervescence died, a more gloomy
view of the situation came uppermost. To his heated imagination the deadlock seemed complete. Carroll's devotion to
what she considered her duty appeared unbreakable. In
the reaction Orde doubted whether he would have it otherwise. And then his fighting blood surged back to his heart.
All the eloquence, the arguments, the pleadings he should
have commanded earlier in the evening hurried belated to
their posts. After the manner of the young and imaginative when in the white fire of emotion, he began drama-
tising scenes between Carroll and himself. He saw them
plainly. He heard the sound of his own voice as he re-

hearsed the arguments which should break her resolution. A woman's duty to her own soul; her obligation toward the man she could make or mar by her love; her self-respect; the necessity of a break some time; the advantage of having the crisis over with now rather than later; a belief in the ultimate good even to Mrs. Bishop of throwing that lady more on her own resources; and so forth and so on down a list of arguments obvious enough or trivial enough, but all inspired by the soul of fervour, all ennobled by the spirit of truth that lies back of the major premise that a woman should cleave to a man, forsaking all others. Orde sat back in his chair, his eyes vacant, his pen all but falling from his hand. He did not finish the letter to his mother. After a while he went upstairs to his own room.

The fever of the argument coursed through his veins all that long night. Over and over again he rehearsed it in wearisome repetition until it had assumed a certain and almost invariable form. And when he had reached the end of his pleading he began it over again, until the daylight found him weary and fevered. He arose and dressed himself. He could eat no breakfast. By a tremendous effort of the will he restrained himself from going over to Ninth Street until the middle of the morning.

He entered the drawing-room to find her seated at the piano. His heart bounded, and for an instant he stood still, summoning his forces to the struggle for which he had so painfully gathered his ammunition. She did not look up as he approached until he stood almost at her shoulder. Then she turned to him and held out both her hands.

" It is no use, Jack," she said. " I care for you too much. I will marry you whenever you say."

XIX

ORDE left that evening early. This was at Carroll's request. She preferred herself to inform her family of the news.

"I don't know yet how mother is going to get along," said she. "Come back to-morrow afternoon and see them all."

The next morning Orde, having at last finished and despatched the letter to his mother, drifted up the avenue and into the club. As he passed the smoking room he caught sight of Gerald seated in an armchair by the window. He entered the room and took a seat opposite the young fellow.

Gerald held out his hand silently, which the other took.

"I'm glad to hear it," said Gerald at last. "Very glad. I told you I was on your side." He hesitated, then went on gravely: "Poor Carroll is having a hard time, though. I think it's worse than she expected. It's no worse than I expected. You are to be one of the family, so I am going to give you a piece of advice. It's something, naturally, I wouldn't speak of otherwise. But Carroll is my only sister, and I want her to be happy. I think you are the man to make her so, but I want you to avoid one mistake. Fight it out right now, and never give back the ground you win."

"I feel that," replied Orde quietly.

"Mother made father resign from the army; and while he's a dear old boy, he's never done anything since. She holds me—although I see through her—possibly because I'm weak or indifferent, possibly because I have a silly idea I can make a bad situation better by hanging around. She is rapidly turning Kendrick into a sullen little prig, because he believes implicitly all the grievances against the world and the individual she pours out to him. You see, I have no illusions concerning my family. Only Carroll has held to her freedom of soul, because that's the joyous, free, sweet nature of her, bless her! For the first time she's pitted her will against mother's, and it's a bad clash."

"Your mother objected?" asked Orde.

Gerald laughed a little bitterly. "It was very bad," said he. "You've grown horns, hoofs, and a tail overnight. There's nothing too criminal to have escaped your notice. I have been forbidden to consort with you. So has the general. The battle of last night had to do with your coming to the house at all. As it is not Carroll's house, naturally she has no right to insist."

"I shall not be permitted to see her?" cried Orde.

"I did not say that. Carroll announced then quite openly that she would see you outside. I fancy that was the crux of the matter. Don't you see? The whole affair shifted ground. Carroll has offered direct disobedience. Oh, she's a bully little fighter!" he finished in admiring accents. "You can't quite realise what she's doing for your sake; she's not only fighting mother, but her own heart."

Orde found a note at the hotel, asking him to be in Washington Square at half-past two.

Carroll met him with a bright smile.

"Things aren't quite right at home," she said. "It is a great shock to poor mother at first, and she feels very strongly. Oh, it isn't you, dear; it's the notion that I can care for anybody but her. You see, she's been used to the other idea so long that I suppose it seemed a part of the universe to her. She'll get used to it after a little, but it takes time."

Orde examined her face anxiously. Two bright red spots

burned on her cheeks; her eyes flashed with a nervous animation, and a faint shade had sketched itself beneath them.

"You had a hard time," he murmured, "you poor dear!"

She smiled up at him.

"We have to pay for the good things in life, don't we, dear? And they are worth it. Things will come right after a little. We must not be too impatient. Now, let's enjoy the day. The park isn't so bad, is it?"

At five o'clock Orde took her back to her doorstep, where he left her.

This went on for several days.

At the end of that time Orde could not conceal from himself that the strain was beginning to tell. Carroll's worried expression grew from day to day, while the animation that characterised her manner when freed from the restraint became more and more forced. She was as though dominated by some inner tensity, which she dared not relax even for a moment. To Orde's questionings she replied as evasively as she could, assuring him always that matters were going as well as she had expected; that mother was very difficult; that Orde must have patience, for things would surely come all right. She begged him to remain quiescent until she gave him the word; and she implored it so earnestly that Orde, though he chafed, was forced to await the turn of events. Every afternoon she met him, from two to five. The situation gave little opportunity for lovers' demonstrations. She seemed entirely absorbed by the inner stress of the struggle she was going through, so that hardly did she seem able to follow coherently even plans for the future. She appeared, however, to gain a mysterious refreshment from Orde's mere proximity; so gradually he, with that streak of almost feminine intuition which is the especial gift to lovers, came to the point of sitting quite silent with her, clasping her hand out of sight of the chance passer-by. When the time came to return, they arose and walked back to Ninth Street, still in silence. At the door they said good-bye. He kissed her quite soberly.

" I wish I could help, sweetheart," said he.

She shook her head at him.

" You do help," she replied.

From Gerald at the club, Orde sought more intimate news of what was going on. For several days, however, the young man absented himself from his usual haunts. It was only at the end of the week that Orde succeeded in finding him.

" No," Gerald answered his greeting, " I haven't been around much. I've been sticking pretty close home."

Little by little, Orde's eager questions drew out the truth of the situation. Mrs. Bishop had shut herself up in a blind and incredible obstinacy, whence she sallied with floods of complaints, tears, accusations, despairs, reproaches, vows, hysterics—all the battery of the woman misunderstood, but in which she refused to listen to a consecutive conversation. If Carroll undertook to say anything, the third word would start her mother off into one of her long and hysterical tirades. It was very wearing, and there seemed to be nothing gained from day to day. Her child had disobeyed her. And as a climax, she had assumed the impregnable position of a complete prostration, wherein she demanded the minute care of an invalid in the crisis of a disorder. She could bear no faintest ray of illumination, no lightest footfall. In a hushed twilight she lay, her eyes swathed, moaning feebly that her early dissolution at the hands of ingratitude was imminent. Thus she established a deadlock which was likely to continue indefinitely. The mere mention of the subject nearest Carroll's heart brought the feeble complaint:

" Do you want to kill me? "

The only scrap of victory to be snatched from this

stricken field was the fact that Carroll insisted on going
to meet her lover every afternoon. The invalid demanded
every moment of her time, either for personal attendance
or in fulfilment of numerous and exacting church duties.
An attempt, however, to encroach thus on the afternoon
hours met a stone wall of resolution on Carroll's part.

This was the situation Orde gathered from his talk with
Gerald. Though he fretted under the tyranny exacted, he
could see nothing which could relieve the situation save
his own withdrawal. He had already long over-stayed his
visit; important affairs connected with his work demanded
his attention, he had the comfort of Carroll's love assured;
and the lapse of time alone could be depended on to change
Mrs. Bishop's attitude, a consummation on which Carroll
seemed set. Although Orde felt all the lively dissatisfaction
natural to a newly accepted lover who had gained slight
opportunity for favours, for confidences, even for the making of plans, nevertheless he could see for the present nothing else to do.

The morning after he had reached this conclusion he
again met Gerald at the gymnasium. That young man, while
as imperturbable and languid in movement as ever, concealed an excitement. He explained nothing until the two,
after a shower and rub-down, were clothing themselves
leisurely in the empty couch-room.

" Orde," said Gerald suddenly, " I'm worried about Carroll."

Orde straightened his back and looked steadily at Gerald, but said nothing.

" Mother has commenced bothering her again. It wasn't
so bad as long as she stuck to daytime, but now she's taken
to prowling in a dozen times a night. I hear their voices
for an hour or so at a time. I'm afraid it's beginning to
wear on Carroll more than you realise."

" Thank you," said Orde briefly.

That afternoon with Carroll he took the affair firmly in hand.

"This thing has come to the point where it must stop," said he, "and I'm going to stop it. I have some rights in the matter of the health and comfort of the girl I love."

"What do you intend to do?" asked Carroll, frightened.

"I shall have it out with your mother," replied Orde.

"You mustn't do that," implored Carroll. "It would do absolutely no good, and would just result in a quarrel that could never be patched up."

"I don't know as I care particularly," said Orde.

"But I do. Think—she is my mother."

Orde stirred uneasily with a mental reservation as to selfishness, but said nothing.

"And think what it means to a girl to be married and go away from home finally without her parent's consent. It's the most beautiful and sacred thing in her life, and she wants it to be perfect. It's worth waiting and fighting a little for. After all, we are both young, and we have known each other such a very short time."

So she pleaded with him, bringing forward all the unanswerable arguments built by the long average experience of the world—arguments which Orde could not refute, but whose falsity to the situation he felt most keenly. He could not specify without betraying Gerald's confidence. Raging inwardly, he consented to a further armistice.

At his hotel he found a telegram. He did not open it until he had reached his own room. It was from home, urging his immediate return for the acceptance of some contracted work.

"To hell with the contracted work!" he muttered savagely, and calling a bell-boy, sent an answer very much to that effect. Then he plunged his hands into his pockets, stretched out his legs, and fell into a deep and gloomy meditation.

He was interrupted by a knock on the door.

" Come in! " he called, without turning his head.

He heard the door open and shut. After a moment he looked around. Kendrick Bishop stood watching him.

Orde lit the gas.

" Hello, Kendrick! " said he. " Sit down."

The boy made no reply. Orde looked at him curiously, and saw that he was suffering from an intense excitement. His frame trembled convulsively, his lips were white, his face went red and pale by turns. Evidently he had something to say, but could not yet trust his voice. Orde sat down and waited.

" You've got to let my mother alone," he managed to say finally.

" I have done nothing to your mother, Kendrick," said Orde kindly.

" You've brought her to the point of death," asserted Kendrick violently. " You're hounding her to her grave. You're turning those she loves best against her."

Orde thought to catch the echo of quotation in these words.

" Did your mother send you to me? " he asked.

" If we had any one else worth the name of man in the family, I wouldn't have to come," said Kendrick, almost in the manner of one repeating a lesson.

" What do you want me to do? " asked Orde after a moment of thought.

" Go away," cried Kendrick. " Stop this unmanly contest against a defenceless woman."

" I cannot do that," replied Orde quietly.

Kendrick's face assumed a livid pallor, and his eyes seemed to turn black with excitement. Trembling in every limb, but without hesitation, he advanced on Orde, drew a short riding-whip from beneath his coat, and slashed the young man across the face. Orde made an involuntary movement to arise, but sank back, and looked steadily at the boy. Once again Kendrick hit; raised his arm for the third time; hesitated. His lips writhed, and then, with a sob, he cast the little whip from him and burst from the room.

Orde sat without moving, while two red lines slowly defined themselves across his face. The theatrical quality of the scene and the turgid rhetorical bathos of the boy's speeches attested his youth and the unformed violence of his emotions. Did they also indicate a rehearsal, or had the boy merely been goaded to vague action by implicit belief in a woman's vagaries? Orde did not know, but the incident brought home to him, as nothing else could, the turmoil of that household.

" Poor youngster! " he concluded his reverie, and went to wash his face in hot water.

He had left Carroll that afternoon in a comparatively philosophical and hopeful frame of mind. The next day she came to him with hurried, nervous steps, her usually pale cheeks mounting danger signals of flaming red, her eyes swimming. When she greeted him she choked, and two of the tears overflowed. Quite unmindful of the nursemaids across the square, Orde put his arm comfortingly about her shoulder. She hid her face against his sleeve and began softly to cry.

Orde did not attempt as yet to draw from her the cause of this unusual agitation. A park bench stood between two dense bushes, screened from all directions save one. To this he led her. He comforted her as one comforts a child, stroking clumsily her hair, murmuring trivialities without meaning, letting her emotion relieve itself. After awhile she recovered somewhat her control of herself and sat up away from him, dabbing at her eyes with a handkerchief dampened into a tiny wad. But even after she had shaken her head vigorously at last, and smiled up at him rather tremulously in token that the storm was over, she would not tell him that anything definite had happened to bring on the outburst.

"I just needed you," she said, "that's all. It's just nothing but being a woman, I think. You'll get used to little things like that."

"This thing has got to quit!" said he grimly.

She said nothing, but reached up shyly and touched his face where Kendrick's whip had stung, and her eyes became very tender. A carriage rolled around Washington Arch, and, coming to a stand, discharged its single passenger on the pavement.

"Why, it's Gerald!" cried Carroll, surprised.

The young man, catching sight of them, picked his way daintily and leisurely toward them. He was, as usual, dressed with metriculous nicety, the carnation in his buttonhole, the gloss on his hat and shoes, the freshness on his gloves, the correct angle on his stick. His dark, long face with its romantic moustache, and its almost effeminate soft eyes, was as unemotional and wearied as ever. As he approached, he raised his stick slightly by way of salutation.

"I have brought," said he, "a carriage, and I wish you would both do me the favour to accompany me on a short excursion."

Taking their consent for granted, he signalled the vehicle, which rapidly approached.

The three—Carroll and Orde somewhat bewildered—took their seats. During a brief drive, Gerald made conversation on different topics, apparently quite indifferent as to whether or not his companions replied. After an interval the carriage drew up opposite a brown-stone dwelling on a side street. Gerald rang the bell, and a moment later the three were ushered by a discreet and elderly maid into a little square reception-room immediately off the hall. The maid withdrew.

Gerald carefully deposited his top hat on the floor, placed in it his gloves, and leaned his stick against its brim.

"I have brought you here, among other purposes, to hear from me a little brief wisdom drawn from experience and the observation of life," he began, addressing his expectant and curious guests. "That wisdom is briefly this: there comes a time in the affairs of every household when a man must assert himself as the ruler. In all the details he may depend on the woman's judgment, experience, and knowledge, but when it comes to the big crises, where life is deflected into one channel or the other, then, unless the man does the deciding, he is lost for ever, and his happiness, and the happiness of those who depend on him. This is abstruse, but I come to the particular application shortly.

"But moments of decision are always clouded by many considerations. The decision is sure to cut across much that is expedient, much that seems to be necessary, much that is dear. Carroll remembers the case of our own father. The general would have made a name for himself in the army; his wife demanded his retirement; he retired, and his career ended. That was the moment of his decision. It is very easy to say, in view of that simple statement, that the general was weak in yielding to his wife, but a consideration of the circumstances——"

"Why do you say all this?" interrupted Orde.

Gerald raised his hand.

"Believe me, it is necessary, as you will agree when you have heard me through. Mrs. Bishop was in poor health; the general in poor financial circumstances. The doctors said the Riviera. Mrs. Bishop's parents, who were wealthy, furnished the money for her sojourn in that climate. She could not bear to be separated from her husband. A refusal to resign then, a refusal to accept the financial aid offered, would have been cast against him as a reproach—he did not love his wife enough to sacrifice his pride, his ambition, his what-you-will. Nevertheless, that was his moment of decision.

"I could multiply instances, yet it would only accumulate needless proof. My point is that in these great moments a man can afford to take into consideration only the affair itself. Never must he think of anything but the simple elements of the problem—he must ignore whose toes are trodden upon, whose feelings are hurt, whose happiness is apparently marred. For note this: if a man does fearlessly the right thing, I am convinced that in the readjustment all these conflicting interests find themselves bettered instead of injured. You want a concrete instance? I believe firmly that if the general had kept to his army life, and made his wife conform to it, after the storm had passed she would have settled down to a happy existence. I cannot prove it—I believe it."

"This may be all very true, Gerald," said Orde, "but I fail to see why you have brought us to this strange house to tell it."

"In a moment," replied Gerald. "Have patience. Believing that thoroughly, I have come in the last twenty-four hours to a decision. That this happens not to affect my own immediate fortunes does not seem to me to invalidate my philosophy."

He carefully unbuttoned his frock coat, crossed his legs, produced a paper and a package from his inside pocket, and eyed the two before him.

"I have here," he went on suddenly, "marriage papers duly made out; in this package is a plain gold ring; in the next room is waiting, by prearrangement, a very good friend of mine in the clergy. Personally I am at your disposal."

He looked at them expectantly.

" The very thing!" "Oh, no!" cried Orde and Carroll in unison.

Nevertheless, in spite of this divergence of opinion, ten minutes later the three passed through the door into the back apartment—Carroll still hesitant, Orde in triumph, Gerald as correct and unemotional as ever.

In this back room they found waiting a young clergyman conversing easily with two young girls. At the sight of Carroll, these latter rushed forward and overwhelmed her with endearments. Carroll broke into a quickly suppressed sob and clasped them close to her.

" Oh, you dears!" she cried, " I'm so glad you're here!" She flashed a grateful look in Gerald's direction, and a moment later took occasion to press his arm and whisper:

" You've thought of everything! You're the dearest brother in the world!"

Gerald received this calmly, and set about organising the ceremony. In fifteen minutes the little party separated at the front door, amid a chatter of congratulations and good wishes. Mr. and Mrs. Orde entered the cab and drove away.

XX

O H, it *is* the best way, dear, after all!" cried Carroll, pressing close to her husband. "A few minutes ago I was all doubts and fears, but now I feel so safe and settled," she laughed happily. "It is as though I had belonged to you always, you old Rock of Gibraltar! and anything that happens now will come from the outside, and not from the inside, won't it, dear?"

"Yes, sweetheart," said Orde.

"Poor mother! I wonder how she'll take it."

"We'll soon know, anyway," replied Orde, a little grimly.

In the hallway of the Bishop house Orde kissed her.

"Be brave, sweetheart," said he, "but remember that now you're my wife."

She nodded at him gravely and disappeared.

Orde sat in the dim parlour for what seemed to be an interminable period. Occasionally the sounds of distant voices rose to his ear and died away again. The front door opened to admit some one, but Orde could not see who it was. Twice a scurrying of feet overhead seemed to indicate the bustle of excitement. The afternoon waned. A faint whiff of cooking, escaping through some carelessly open door, was borne to his nostrils. It grew dark, but the lamps remained unlighted. Finally he heard the rustle of the portières, and turned to see the dim form of the general standing there.

"Bad business! bad business!" muttered the old man. "It's very hard on me. Perhaps you did the right thing—

183

you must be good to her—but I cannot countenance this affair. It was most high-handed, sir!"

The portières fell again, and he disappeared.

Finally, after another interval, Carroll returned. She went immediately to the gas-fixture, which she lit. Orde then saw that she was sobbing violently. She came to him, and for a moment hid her face against his breast. He patted her hair, waiting for her to speak. After a little she controlled herself.

"How was it?" asked Orde, then.

She shivered.

"I never knew people could be so cruel," she complained in almost a bewildered manner. "Jack, we must go to-night. She—she has ordered me out of the house, and says she never wants to see my face again." She broke down for a second. "Oh, Jack! she can't mean that. I've always been a good daughter to her. And she's very bitter against Gerald. Oh! I told her it wasn't his fault, but she won't listen. She sent for that odious Mr. Merritt—her rector, you know—and he supported her. I believe he's angry because we did not go to him. Could you believe such a thing! And she's shut herself up in her air of high virtue, and underneath it she's, oh, so angry!"

"Well, it's natural she should be upset," comforted Orde. "Don't think too much of what she does now. Later she'll get over it."

Carroll shivered again.

"You don't know, dear, and I'm not going to tell you. Why," she cried, "she told me that you and I were in a conspiracy to drive her to her grave so we could get her money!"

"She must be a little crazy," said Orde, still pacifically.

"Come, help me," said Carroll. "I must get my things."

"Can't you just pack a bag and leave the rest until to-morrow? It's about hungry time."

She Came to Him and for a Moment Hid Her Face Against His Breast

" She says I must take every stitch belonging to me to-night."

They packed trunks until late that night, quite alone. Gerald had departed promptly after breaking the news, probably without realising to what a pass affairs would come. A frightened servant, evidently in disobedience of orders and in fear of destruction, brought them a tray of food, which she put down on a small table and hastily fled. In a room down the hall they could hear the murmur of voices where Mrs. Bishop received spiritual consolation from her adviser. When the trunks were packed, Orde sent for a baggage waggon. Carroll went silently from place to place, saying farewell to such of her treasures as she had made up her mind to leave. Orde scribbled a note to Gerald, requesting him to pack up the miscellanies and send them to Michigan by freight. The baggage man and Orde carried the trunks downstairs. No one appeared. Carroll and Orde walked together to the hotel. Next morning an interview with Gerald confirmed them in their resolution of immediate departure.

" She is set in her opposition now, and at present she believes firmly that her influence will separate you. Such a state of mind cannot be changed in an hour."

" And you? " asked Carroll.

" Oh, I," he shrugged, " will go on as usual. I have my interests."

" I wish you would come out in our part of the country," ventured Orde.

Gerald smiled his fine smile.

" Good-bye," said he. " Going to a train is useless, and a bore to everybody."

Carroll threw herself on his neck in an access of passionate weeping.

" You *will* write and tell me of everything, won't you? " she begged.

"Of course. There now, good-bye."

Orde followed him into the hall.

"It would be quite useless to attempt another interview?" he inquired.

Gerald made a little mouth.

"I am in the same predicament as yourselves," said he, "and have since nine this morning taken up my quarters at the club. Please do not tell Carroll; it would only pain her."

At the station, just before they passed in to the train, the general appeared.

"There, there!" he fussed. "If your mother should hear of my being here, it would be a very bad business, very bad. This is very sad; but—well, good-bye, dear; and you, sir, be good to her. And write your daddy, Carroll. He'll be lonesome for you." He blew his nose very loudly and wiped his glasses. "Now, run along, run along," he hurried them. "Let us not have any scenes. Here, my dear, open this envelope when you are well started. It may help cheer the journey. Not a word!"

He hurried them through the gate, paying no heed to what they were trying to say. Then he steamed away and bustled into a cab without once looking back.

When the train had passed the Harlem River and was swaying its uneven way across the open country, Carroll opened the envelope. It contained a check for a thousand dollars.

"Dear old daddy!" she murmured. "Our only wedding present!"

"You are the capitalist of the family," said Orde. "You don't know how poor a man you've married. I haven't much more than the proverbial silver watch and bad nickel."

She reached out to press his hand in reassurance. He compared it humorously with his own.

"What a homely, knotted, tanned old thing it is by yours," said he.

"It's a strong hand," she replied soberly, "it's a dear hand." Suddenly she snatched it up and pressed it for a fleeting instant against her cheek, looking at him half ashamed.

XXI

THE winter months were spent at Monrovia, where Orde and his wife lived for a time at the hotel. This was somewhat expensive, but Orde was not quite ready to decide on a home, and he developed unexpected opposition to living at Redding in the Orde homestead.

"No, I've been thinking about it," he told Grandma Orde. "A young couple should start out on their own responsibility. I know you'd be glad to have us, but I think it's better the other way. Besides, I must be at Monrovia a good deal of the time, and I want Carroll with me. She can make you a good long visit in the spring, when I have to go up river."

To this Grandma Orde, being a wise old lady, had to nod her assent, although she would much have liked her son near her.

At Monrovia, then, they took up their quarters. Carroll soon became acquainted with the life of the place. Monrovia, like most towns of its sort and size, consisted of an upper stratum of mill owners and lumber operators, possessed of considerable wealth, some cultivation, and definite social ideas; a gawky, countrified, middle estate of storekeepers, catering both to the farm and local trade; and the lumber mill operatives, generally of Holland extraction, who dwelt in simple unpainted board shanties. The class first mentioned comprised a small coterie, among whom Carroll soon found two or three congenials—Edith Fuller, wife of the young cashier in the bank; Valerie Cathcart, whose husband had been killed in the Civil War;

Clara Taylor, wife of the leading young lawyer of the village; and, strangely enough, Mina Heinzman, the sixteen-year-old daughter of old Heinzman, the lumberman. Nothing was more indicative of the absolute divorce of business and social life than the unbroken evenness of Carroll's friendship for the younger girl. Though later the old German and Orde locked in serious struggle on the river, they continued to meet socially quite as usual; and the daughter of one and the wife of the other never suspected anything out of the ordinary. This impersonality of struggle has always been characteristic of the pioneer business man's good-nature.

Newmark received the news of his partner's sudden marriage without evincing any surprise, but with a sardonic gleam in one corner of his eye. He called promptly, conversed politely for a half hour, and then took his leave.

"How do you like him?" asked Orde, when he had gone.

"He looks like a very shrewd man," replied Carroll, picking her words for fear of saying the wrong thing.

Orde laughed.

"You don't like him," he stated.

"I don't dislike him," said Carroll. "I've not a thing against him. But we could never be in the slightest degree sympathetic. He and I don't—don't——"

"Don't jibe," Orde finished for her. "I didn't much think you would. Joe never was much of a society bug."

It was on the tip of Carroll's tongue to reply that "society bugs" were not the only sort she could appreciate, but she refrained. She had begun to realise the extent of her influence over her husband's opinion.

Newmark did not live at the hotel. Early in the fall he had rented a small one-story house situated just off Main Street, set well back from the sidewalk among clumps of oleanders. Into this he retired as a snail into its shell. At first he took his meals at the hotel, but later he imported an impassive, secretive man-servant, who took charge of him completely. Neither master nor man made any friends, and in fact rebuffed all advances. One Sunday, Carroll and Orde, out for a walk, passed this quaint little place, with its picket fence.

"Let's go in and return Joe's call," suggested Orde.

Their knock at the door brought the calm valet.

"Mr. Newmark is h'out, sir," said he. "Yes, sir, I'll tell him that you called."

They turned away. As they sauntered down the little brick-laid walk, Carroll suddenly pressed close to her husband's arm.

"Jack," she begged, "I want a little house like that, for our very own."

"We can't afford it, sweetheart."

"Not to own," she explained, "just to rent. It will be next best to having a home of our own."

"We'd have to have a girl, dear," said Orde, "and we can't even afford that, yet."

"A girl!" cried Carroll indignantly. "For us two!"

"You couldn't do the housework and the cooking," said Orde. "You've never done such a thing in your life, and I won't have my little girl slaving."

"It won't be slaving, it will be fun—just like play-housekeeping," protested Carroll. "And I've got to learn some time. I was brought up most absurdly, and I realise it now."

"We'll see," said Orde vaguely.

The subject was dropped for the time being. Later Carroll brought it up again. She was armed with several sheets of hotel stationery, covered with figures showing how much cheaper it would be to keep house than to board.

"You certainly make out a strong case—on paper," laughed Orde. "If you buy a rooster and a hen, and she raises two broods, at the end of a year you'll have twenty-six; and if they all breed—even allowing half roosters—you'll have over three hundred; and if they all breed, you'll have about thirty-five hundred; and if——"

"Stop! stop!" cried Carroll, covering her ears.

"All right," agreed Orde equably, "but that's the way it figures. Funny the earth isn't overrun with chickens, isn't it?"

She thrust her tables of figures into her desk drawer.

"You're just making fun of me always," she said reproachfully.

Two days later Orde took her one block up the street to look at a tiny little house tucked on a fifty-foot lot beneath the shadow of the church.

"It's mighty little," said he. "I'll have to go out in the hall to change my collar, and we couldn't have more than two people at a time to call on us."

"It's a dear!" said she, "and I'm not so e-nor-mous myself, whatever *you* may be."

They ended by renting the little house, and Carroll took charge of it delightedly. What difficulties she overcame, and what laughable and cryable mistakes she made only those who have encountered a like situation could realise. She learned fast, however, and took a real pride in her tiny box of a home. A piano was, of course, out of the question, but the great golden harp occupied one corner, or rather one side, of the parlour. Standing thus enshrouded in its covering, it rather resembled an august and tremendous veiled deity. To Carroll's great delight, Orde used solemnly to go down on all fours and knock his forehead thrice on the floor before it when he entered the house at evening. When the very cold weather came and they had to light the base-burner stove, which Orde stoutly maintained occupied all the other half of the parlour, the harp's delicate constitution necessitated its stand-

ing in the hall. Nevertheless, Carroll had great comfort
from it. While Orde was away at the office, she whispered
through its mellow strings her great happiness, the dreams
for her young motherhood which would come in the summer, the vague and lingering pain over the hapless but
beloved ones she had left behind her in her other life. Then
she arose refreshed, and went about the simple duties of
her tiny domain.

The winter was severe. All the world was white. The
piles of snow along the sidewalks grew until Carroll could
hardly look over them. Great fierce winds swept in from
the lake. Sometimes Orde and his wife drove two miles
to the top of the sand hills, where first they had met in
this their present home, and looked out beyond the tumbled
shore ice to the steel-gray, angry waters. The wind pricked
their faces, and, going home, the sleigh-bells jingled, the
snowballs from the horses' hoofs hit against the dash, the
cold air seared the inside of their nostrils. When Orde
helped Carroll from beneath the warm buffalo robes, she
held up to him a face glowing with colour, framed in the
soft fluffy fur of a hood.

" You darling ! " he cried, and stooped to kiss her smooth,
cold cheek.

When he had returned from the stable around the corner, he found the lit lamp throwing its modified light and
shade over the little round table. He shook down the base-
burner vigorously, thrust several billets of wood in its
door, and turned to meet her eyes across the table.

" Kind of fun being married, isn't it ? " said he.

" Kind of," she admitted, nodding gravely.

The business of the firm was by now about in shape.
All the boom arrangements had been made ; the two tugs
were in the water and their machinery installed ; supplies
and equipments were stored away ; the foremen of the crews
engaged, and the crews themselves pretty well picked out.

And Looked Out Beyond the Tumbled Shore Ice to the Steel-Gray
Angry Waters

Only there needed to build the wanigan, and to cart in the supplies for the upper river works before the spring break-up and the almost complete disappearance of the roads. Therefore, Orde had the good fortune of unusual leisure to enjoy these first months with his bride. They entered together the Unexplored Country, and found it more wonderful than they had dreamed. Almost before they knew it, January and February had flown.

"We must pack up, sweetheart," said Orde.

"It's only yesterday that we came," she cried regretfully.

They took the train for Redding, were installed in the gable room, explored together for three days the delights of the old-fashioned house, the spicy joys of Grandma Orde's and Amanda's cookery, the almost adoring adulation of the old folks. Then Orde packed his "turkey," assumed his woods clothes, and marched off down the street carrying his bag on his back.

"He looks like an old tramp in that rig," said Grandma Orde, closing the storm door.

"He looks like a conqueror of wildernesses!" cried Carroll, straining her eyes after his vanishing figure. Suddenly she darted after him, calling in her high, bird-like tones. He turned and came back to her. She clasped him by the shoulders, reluctant to let him go.

"Good-bye," she said at last. "You'll take better care of my sweetheart than you ever did of Jack Orde, won't you, dear?"

XXII

ORDE had reconnoitred the river as a general reconnoitres his antagonist, and had made his dispositions as the general•disposes of his army, his commissary, his reserves. At this point five men could keep the river clear; at that rapid it would require twenty; there a dozen would suffice for ordinary contingencies, and yet an emergency might call for thirty—those thirty must not be beyond reach. In his mind's eye he apportioned the sections of the upper river. Among the remoter wildernesses every section must have its driving camp. The crews of each, whether few or many, would be expected to keep clear and running their own " beats " on the river. As fast as the rear crew should overtake these divisions, either it would absorb them or the members of them would be thrown forward beyond the lowermost beat, to take charge of a new division down stream. When the settled farm country or the little towns were reached, many of the driving camps would become unnecessary; the men could be boarded out at farms lying in their beats. A continual advance would progress toward the Lake, the drive crews passing and repassing each other like pigeons in the sown fields. Each of these sections would be in charge of a foreman, whose responsibility ceased with the delivery of the logs to the men next below. A walking boss would trudge continually the river trail, or ride the logs down stream, holding the correlation of these many units. Orde himself would drive up and down the river, overseeing the whole plan of campaign, throwing the camps forward, concentrating his forces here, spreading them elsewhere, keeping accurately in mind the entire situation so that he could say with full confidence: "Open Dam Number One for three hours at nine o'clock; Dam Number Two for two hours and a half at ten thirty," and so on down the line; sure that the flood waters thus released would arrive at the right moment, would supplement each other, and would so space themselves as to accomplish the most work with the least waste. In that one point more than in any other showed the expert. The water was his ammunition, a definite and limited quantity of it. To "get the logs out with the water" was the last word of praise to be said for the river driver. The more logs, the greater the glory.

Thus it can readily be seen, this matter was rather a campaign than a mere labour, requiring the men, the munitions, the organisation, the tactical ability, the strategy, the resourcefulness, the boldness, and the executive genius of a military commander.

To all these things, and to the distribution of supplies and implements among the various camps, Orde had attended. The wanigan for the rear crew was built. The foremen and walking boss had been picked out. Everything was in readiness. Orde was satisfied with the situation except that he found himself rather short-handed. He had counted on three hundred men for his crews, but scrape and scratch as he would, he was unable to gather over two hundred and fifty. This matter was not so serious, however, as later, when the woods camps should break up, he would be able to pick up more workmen.

"They won't be rivermen like my old crew, though," said Orde regretfully to Tom North, the walking boss. "I'd like to steal a few from some of those Muskegon outfits."

Until the logs should be well adrift, Orde had resolved to boss the rear crew himself.

As the rear was naturally the farthest up stream, Orde
had taken also the contract to break the rollways belonging to Carlin, which in the season's work would be piled
up on the bank. Thus he could get to work immediately at
the break-up, and without waiting for some one else. The
seven or eight million feet of lumber comprised in Carlin's
drive would keep the men below busy until the other owners, farther down and up the tributaries, should also have
put their season's cut afloat.

The ice went out early, to Orde's satisfaction. As soon
as the river ran clear in its lower reaches he took his rear
crew in to Carlin's rollways.

This crew was forty in number, and had been picked
from the best—a hard-bitten, tough band of veterans,
weather beaten, scarred in numerous fights or by the backwoods scourge of small-pox, compact, muscular, fearless,
loyal, cynically aloof from those not of their cult, out-
spoken and free to criticise—in short, men to do great
things under the strong leader, and to mutiny at the end
of three days under the weak. They piled off the train at
Sawyer's, stamped their feet on the board platform of the
station, shouldered their " turkeys," and straggled off down
the tote-road. It was an eighteen-mile walk in. The ground
had loosened its frost. The footing was ankle-deep in mud
and snow-water.

Next morning, bright and early, the breaking of the rollways began. During the winter the logs had been hauled
down ice roads to the river, where they were " banked "
in piles twenty, and even thirty, feet in height. The bed
of the stream itself was filled with them for a mile, save
in a narrow channel left down through the middle to
allow for some flow of water; the banks were piled with
them, side on, ready to roll down at the urging of the
men.

First of all, the entire crew set itself, by means of its

peavies, to rolling the lower logs into the current, where they were rapidly borne away. As the waters were now at flood, this was a quick and easy labour. Occasionally some tiers would be stuck together by ice, in which case considerable prying and heaving was necessary in order to crack them apart. But forty men, all busily at work, soon had the river full. Orde detailed some six or eight to drop below in order that the river might run clear to the next section, where the next crew would take up the task. These men, quite simply, walked to the edges of the rollway, rolled a log apiece into the water, stepped aboard, leaned against their peavies, and were swept away by the swift current. The logs on which they stood whirled in the eddies, caromed against other timbers, slackened speed, shot away; never did the riders alter their poses of easy equilibrium. From time to time one propelled his craft ashore by hooking to and pushing against other logs. There he stood on some prominent point, leaning his chin contemplatively against the thick shaft of his peavy, watching the endless procession of the logs drifting by. Apparently he was idle, but in reality his eyes missed no shift of the ordered ranks. When a slight hitch or pause, a subtle change in the pattern of the brown carpet caught his attention, he sprang into life. Balancing his peavy across his body, he made his way by short dashes to the point of threatened congestion. There, working vigorously, swept down stream with the mass, he pulled, hauled, and heaved, forcing the heavy, reluctant timbers from the cohesion that threatened trouble later. Oblivious to his surroundings, he wrenched and pried desperately. The banks of the river drifted by. Point succeeded point, as though withdrawn up stream by some invisible manipulator. The river appeared stationary, the banks in motion. Finally he heard at his elbow the voice of the man stationed below him, who had run out from his own point.

"Hullo, Bill," he replied to this man, "you old slough hog! Tie into this!"

"All the time!" agreed Bill cheerfully.

In a few moments the danger was averted, the logs ran free. The rivermen thereupon made their uncertain way back to shore, where they took the river trail up stream again to their respective posts.

At noon they ate lunches they had brought with them in little canvas bags, snatched before they left the rollways from a supply handy by the cook. In the meantime the main crew were squatting in the lea of the brush, devouring a hot meal which had been carried to them in wooden boxes strapped to the backs of the chore boys. Down the river and up its tributaries other crews, both in the employ of Newmark & Orde and of others, were also pausing from their cold and dangerous toil. The river, refreshed after its long winter, bent its mighty back to the great annual burden laid upon it.

By the end of the second day the logs actually in the bed of the stream had been shaken loose, and a large proportion of them had floated entirely from sight. It now became necessary to break down the rollways piled along the tops of the banks.

The evening of this day, however, Orde received a visit from Jim Denning, the foreman of the next section below, bringing with him Charlie, the cook of Daly's last year's drive. Leaving him by the larger fire, Jim Denning drew his principal one side.

"This fellow drifted in to-night two days late after a drunk, and he tells an almighty queer story," said he. "He says a crew of bad men from the Saginaw, sixty strong, have been sent in by Heinzman. He says Heinzman hired them to come over not to work, but just to fight and annoy us."

"That so?" said Orde. "Well, where are they?"

Leaned Against Their Peavies and Were Swept Away by the Swift Current

"Don't know. But he sticks by his story, and tells it pretty straight."

"Bring him over, and let's hear it," said Orde.

"Hullo, Charlie!" he greeted the cook when the latter stood before him. "What's this yarn Jim's telling me?"

"It's straight, Mr. Orde," said the cook. "There's a big crew brought in from the Saginaw waters to do you up. They're supposed to be over here to run his drive, but really they're goin' to fight and raise hell. For why would he want sixty men to break out them little rollways of his'n up at the headwaters?"

"Is that where they've gone?" asked Orde like a flash.

"Yes, sir. And he only owns a 'forty' up there, and it ain't more'n half cut, anyway."

"I didn't know he owned any."

"Yes, sir. He bought that little Johnson piece last winter. I been workin' up there with a little two-horse crew since January. We didn't put up more'n a couple hundred thousand."

"Is he breaking out his rollways below?" Orde asked Denning.

"No, sir," struck in Charlie, "he ain't."

"How do you happen to be so wise?" inquired Orde. "Seems to me you know about as much as old man Solomon."

"Well," explained Charlie, "you see it's like this. When I got back from the woods last week, I just sort of happened into McNeill's place. I wasn't drinkin' a drop!" he cried virtuously, in answer to Orde's smile.

"Of course not," said Orde. "I was just thinking of the last time we were in there together."

"That's just it!" cried Charlie. "They was always sore at you about that. Well, I was lyin' on one of those there benches back of the 'Merican flags in the dance hall 'cause I was very sleepy, when in blew old man Heinzman and

McNeill himself. I just lay low for black ducks and heard their talk. They took a look around, but didn't see no one, so they opened her up wide."

" What did you hear?" asked Orde.

" Well, McNeill he agreed to get a gang of bad ones from the Saginaw to run in on the river, and I heard Heinzman tell him to send 'em in to headwaters. And McNeill said, ' That's all right about the cash, Mr. Heinzman, but I been figgerin' on gettin' even with Orde for some myself.' "

" Is that all?" inquired Orde.

" That's about all," confessed Charlie.

" How do you know he didn't hire them to carry down his drive for him? He'd need sixty men for his lower rollways, and maybe they weren't all to go to headwaters?" asked Orde by way of testing Charlie's beliefs.

" He's payin' them four dollars a day," replied Charlie simply. " Now, who'd pay that fer just river work?"

Orde nodded at Jim Denning.

" Hold on, Charlie," said he. " Why are you giving all this away if you were working for Heinzman?"

" I'm working for you now," replied Charlie with dignity. " And, besides, you helped me out once yourself."

" I guess it's a straight tip all right," said Orde to Denning, when the cook had resumed his place by the fire.

" That's what I thought. That's why I brought him up."

" If that crew's been sent in there, it means only one thing at that end of the line," said Orde.

" Sure. They're sent up to waste out the water in the reservoir and hang this end of the drive," replied Denning.

" Correct," said Orde. " The old skunk knows his own rollways are so far down stream that he's safe, flood water or no flood water."

A pause ensued, during which the two smoked vigorously.

" What are you going to do about it? " asked Denning at last.

" What would you do? " countered Orde.

" Well," said Denning slowly, and with a certain grim joy, " I don't bet those Saginaw river-pigs are any more two-fisted than the boys on this river. I'd go up and clean 'em out."

" Won't do," negatived Orde briefly. " In the first place, as you know very well, we're short-handed now, and we can't spare the men from the work. In the second place, we'd hang up sure, then; to go up in that wilderness, fifty miles from civilisation, would mean a first-class row of too big a size to handle. Won't do! "

" Suppose you get a lawyer," suggested Denning sarcastically.

Orde laughed with great good-humour.

" Where'd our water be by the time he got an injunction for us? "

He fell into a brown study, during which his pipe went out.

" Jim," he said finally, " it isn't a fair game. I don't know what to do. Delay will hang us; taking men off the work will hang us. I've just got to go up there myself and see what can be done by talking to them."

" Talking to them! " Denning snorted. " You might as well whistle down the draught-pipe of hell! If they're just up there for a row, there'll be whisky in camp; and you can bet McNeill's got some of 'em instructed on *your* account. They'll kill you, sure! "

" I agree with you it's risky," replied Orde. " I'm scared; I'm willing to admit it. But I don't see what else to do. Of course he's got no rights, but what the hell good does that do us after our water is gone? And Jim, my son, if we hang this drive, I'll be buried so deep I never will dig out. No; I've got to go. You can stay up here in charge of the rear until I get back. Send word by Charlie who's to boss your division while you're gone."

XXIII

ORDE tramped back to Sawyer's early next morning, hitched into the light buckboard the excellent team with which later, when the drive should spread out, he would make his longest jumps, and drove to headwaters. He arrived in sight of the dam about three o'clock. At the edge of the clearing he pulled up to survey the scene.

A group of three small log-cabins marked the Johnson, and later the Heinzman, camp. From the chimneys a smoke arose. Twenty or thirty rivermen lounged about the sunny side of the largest structure. They had evidently just arrived, for some of their "turkeys" were still piled outside the door. Orde clucked to his horses, and the spidery wheels of the buckboard swung lightly over the wet hummocks of the clearing, to come to a stop opposite the men. Orde leaned forward against his knees.

"Hullo, boys!" said he cheerfully.

No one replied, though two or three nodded surlily. Orde looked them over with some interest.

They were a dirty, unkempt, unshaven, hard-looking lot, with bloodshot eyes, a flicker of the dare-devil in expression, beyond the first youth, hardened into an enduring toughness of fibre—bad men from the Saginaw, in truth, and, unless Orde was mistaken, men just off a drunk, and therefore especially dangerous; men eager to fight at the drop of the hat, or sooner, to be accommodating, and ready to employ in their assaults all the formidable and terrifying weapons of the rough-and-tumble; reckless, hard, irreverent, blasphemous, to be gained over by no words, fair or foul; absolutely scornful of any and all institutions imposed on them by any other but the few men whom they acknowledged as their leaders. And to master these men's respect there needed either superlative strength, superlative recklessness, or superlative skill.

"Who's your boss?" asked Orde.

"The Rough Red," growled one of the men without moving.

Orde had heard of this man, of his personality and his deeds. Like Silver Jack of the Muskegon, his exploits had been celebrated in song. A big, broad-faced man, with a red beard, they had told him, with little, flickering eyes, a huge voice that bellowed through the woods in a torrent of commands and imprecations, strong as a bull, and savage as a wild beast. A hint of his quality will suffice from the many stories circulated about him. It was said that while jobbing for Morrison & Daly, in some of that firm's Saginaw Valley holdings, the Rough Red had discovered that a horse had gone lame. He called the driver of that team before him, seized an iron starting bar, and with it broke the man's leg. "Try th' lameness yourself, Barney Mallan," said he. To appeal to the charity of such a man would be utterly useless. Orde saw this point. He picked up his reins and spoke to his team.

But before the horses had taken three steps, a huge riverman had planted himself squarely in the way. The others rising, slowly surrounded the rig.

"I don't know what you're up here for," growled the man at the horses' heads, "but you wanted to see the boss, and I guess you'd better see him."

"I intend to see him," said Orde sharply. "Get out of the way and let me hitch my team."

He drove deliberately ahead, forcing the man to step aside, and stopped his horses by a stub. He tied them there

and descended, to lean his back also against the log walls
of the little house.

After a few moments a huge form appeared above the
river bank at some forty rods' distance.

"Yonder he comes now," vouchsafed the man nearest
Orde.

Orde made out the great square figure of the boss, his
soft hat, his flaming red beard, his dingy mackinaw coat,
his dingy black-and-white checked flannel shirt, his dingy
blue trousers tucked into high socks, and, instead of driving boots, his ordinary lumberman's rubbers. As a spot of
colour, he wore a flaming red knit sash, with tassels. Before he had approached near enough to be plainly distin-
guishable, he began to bellow at the men, commanding
them, with a mighty array of oaths, to wake up and get
the sluice-gate open. In a moment or so he had disappeared
behind some bushes that intervened in his approach to the
house. His course through them could be traced by the top
of his cap, which just showed above them. In a moment
he thrust through the brush and stood before Orde.

For a moment he stared at the young man, and then,
with a wild Irish yell, leaped upon him. Orde, caught un-
awares and in an awkward position, was hardly able even
to struggle against the gigantic riverman. Indeed, before
he had recovered his faculties to the point of offering
determined resistance, he was pinned back against the wall
by his shoulders, and the Rough Red's face was within
two feet of his own.

"And how are ye, ye ould darlint?" shouted the latter,
with a roll of oaths.

"Why, Jimmy Bourke!" cried Orde, and burst into a
laugh.

The Rough Red jerked him to his feet, delivered a bear
hug that nearly crushed his ribs, and pounded him mightily on the back.

" You ould snoozer! " he bellowed. " Where the blankety blank in blank did you come from? Byes," he shouted to the men, " it's me ould boss on th' Au Sable six year back— that time, ye mind, whin we had th' ice jam! Glory be! but I'm glad to see ye! "

Orde was still laughing.

" I didn't know you'd turned into the Rough Red, Jimmy," said he. " I don't believe we were either of us old enough for whiskers then, were we? "

The Rough Red grinned.

" Thrue for ye! " said he. " And what have ye been doing all these years? "

" That's just it, Jimmy," said Orde, drawing the giant one side, out of ear-shot. " All my eggs are in one basket, and it's a mean trick of you to hire out for filthy lucre to kick that basket."

" What do ye mane? " asked the Rough Red, fixing his twinkling little eyes on Orde.

" You don't mean to tell me," countered Orde, glancing down at the other's rubber-shod feet, " that this crew has been sent up here just to break out those measly little rollways? "

" Thim? " said the Rough Red. " Thim? Hell, *no*! Thim's my bodyguard. They can lick their weight in wild cats, and I'd loike well to see the gang of highbankers that infists this river thry to pry thim out. We weren't sint here to wurrk; we were sint here to foight."

" Fight? Why? " asked Orde.

" Oh, I dunno," replied the Rough Red easily. " Me boss and the blank of a blank blanked blank that's attimptin' to droive this river has some sort of a row."

" Jimmy," said Orde, " didn't you know that I am the gentleman last mentioned? "

" What! "

" I'm driving this river, and that's my dam-keeper you've

"And How Are Ye, Ye Ould Darlint?"

got hid away somewhere here, and that's my water you're planning to waste!"

"What?" repeated the Rough Red, but in a different tone of voice.

"That's right," said Orde.

In a tone of vast astonishment, the Rough Red mentioned his probable deserts in the future life.

"Luk here, Jack," said he after a moment, "here's a crew of white-water birlers that ye can't beat nowheres. What do you want us to do? We're now gettin' four dollars a day *an'* board from that murderin' ould villain, Heinzman, *so we can afford to wurrk for you cheap*."

Orde hesitated.

"Oh, please do now, darlint!" wheedled the Rough Red, his little eyes agleam with mischief. "Sind us some oakum and pitch and we'll caulk yure wanigan for ye. Or maybe some more peavies, and we'll hilp ye on yure rollways. And till us, afore ye go, how ye want this dam, and that's the way she'll be. Come, now, dear! and ain't ye short-handed now?"

Orde slapped his knee and laughed.

"This is sure one hell of a joke!" he cried.

"And ain't it now?" said the Rough Red, smiling with as much ingratiation as he was able.

"I'll take you boys on," said Orde at last, "at the usual wages—dollar and a half for the jam, three for the rear. I doubt if you'll see much of Heinzman's money when this leaks out."

XXIV

THUS Orde, by the sheer good luck that sometimes favours men engaged in large enterprises, not only frustrated a plan likely to bring failure to his interests, but filled up his crews. It may be remarked here, as well as later, that the "terrors of the Saginaw" stayed with the drive to its finish, and proved reliable and tractable in every particular. Orde scattered them judiciously, so there was no friction with the local men. The Rough Red he retained on the rear.

Here the breaking of the rollways had reached a stage more exciting both to onlooker and participant than the mere opening of the river channel. Huge stacks of logs piled sidewise to the bank lined the stream for miles. When the lowermost log on the river side was teased and pried out, the upper tiers were apt to cascade down with a roar, a crash, and a splash. The man who had done the prying had to be very quick-eyed, very cool, and very agile to avoid being buried under the tons of timber that rushed down on him. Only the most reliable men were permitted at this initial breaking down. Afterwards the crew rolled in what logs remained.

The Rough Red's enormous strength, dare-devil spirit, and nimbleness of body made him invaluable at this dangerous work. Orde, too, often took a hand in some of the more ticklish situations. In old days, before he had attained the position of responsibility that raised the value of his time beyond manual work, he had been one of the best men on the river at breaking bank rollways. A slim, graceful, handsome boy of twenty, known as "Rollway Charlie," also distinguished himself by the quickness and certainty of his work. Often the men standing near lost sight of him entirely in the spray, the confusion, the blur of the breaking rollways, until it seemed certain he must have perished. Nevertheless, always he appeared at right or left, sometimes even on a log astream, nonchalant, smiling, escaped easily from the destructive power he had loosed. Once in the stream the logs ran their appointed course, watched by the men who herded them on their way. And below, from the tributaries, from the other rollways a never-ending procession of recruits joined this great brown army on its way to the lake, until for miles and miles the river was almost a solid mass of logs.

The crews on the various beats now had their hands full to keep the logs running. The slightest check at any one point meant a jam, for there was no way of stopping the unending procession. The logs behind floated gently against the obstruction and came to rest. The brown mass thickened. As far as the eye could reach the surface of the water was concealed. And then, as the slow pressure developed from the three or four miles of logs forced against each other by the pushing of the current, the breast of the jam began to rise. Timbers up-ended, crossed, interlocked, slid one over the other, mounted higher and higher in the formidable game of jack-straws the loss of which spelled death to the players.

Immediately, and with feverish activity, the men nearest at hand attacked the work. Logs on top they tumbled and rolled into the current below. Men beneath the breast tugged and pried in search of the key logs causing all the trouble. Others "flattened out the wings," hoping to get a " draw " around the ends. As the stoppage of the drive indicated to the men up and down stream that a jam had formed, they gathered at the scene—those from above over the logs, those from below up the river trail.

Rarely, unless in case of unusual complications, did it take more than a few hours at most to break the jam. The breast of it went out with a rush. More slowly the wings sucked in. Reluctantly the mass floating on the surface for miles up stream stirred, silently moved forward. For a few minutes it was necessary to watch carefully until the flow onward steadied itself, until the congestion had spaced and ordered as before. Then the men moved back to their posts; the drive was resumed. At night the river was necessarily left to its own devices. Rivermen, with the touch of super-stition inseparably connected with such affairs, believe implicitly that "logs run free at night." Certainly, though it might be expected that each morning would reveal a big jam to break, such was rarely the case. The logs had usually stopped, to be sure, but generally in so peaceful a situation as easily to be started on by a few minutes' work. Probably this was because they tended to come to rest in the slow, still reaches of the river, through which, in day-time, they would be urged by the rivermen.

Jams on the river, contrary to general belief, are of very common occurrence. Throughout the length of the drive there were probably three or four hang-ups a day. Each of these had to be broken, and in the breaking was danger. The smallest misstep, the least slowness in reading the signs of the break, the slightest lack of promptness in acting on the hint or of agility in leaping from one to the other of the plunging timbers, the faintest flicker from rigid attention to the antagonist crouching on the spring, would mean instant death to the delinquent. Thus it was literally true that each one of these men was called upon almost daily to wager his personal skill against his destruction.

In the meantime the rear was "sacking" its way as fast as possible, moving camp with the wanigan whenever necessary, working very hard and very cold and very long. In its work, however, beyond the breaking of the rollways, was little of the spectacular.

Orde, after the rear was well started, patrolled the length of the drive in his light buckboard. He had a first-class team of young horses—high-spirited, somewhat fractious, but capable on a pinch of their hundred miles in a day. He handled them well over the rough corduroys and swamp roads. From jam to rear and back again he travelled, pausing on the river banks to converse earnestly with one of the foremen, surveying the situation with the bird's-eye view of the general. At times he remained at one camp for several days watching the trend of the work. The improvements made during the preceding summer gave him the greatest satisfaction, especially the apron at the falls.

" We'd have had a dozen bad jams here before now with all these logs in the river," said he to Tim Nolan, who was in charge of that beat.

" And as it is," said Tim, " we've had but the one little wing jam."

The piers to define the channel along certain shallows also saved the rear crew much labour in the matter of stranded logs. Everything was very satisfactory. Even old man Reed held to his chastened attitude, and made no trouble. In fact, he seemed glad to turn an honest penny by boarding the small crew in charge of sluicing the logs.

No trouble was experienced until Heinzman's rollways were reached. Here Orde had, as he had promised his partner, boomed a free channel to prevent Heinzman from filling up the entire river-bed with his rollways. When the jam of the drive had descended the river as far as this, Orde found that Heinzman had not yet begun to break out. Hardly had Orde's first crew passed, however, when Heinzman's men began to break down the logs into the drive. Long before the rear had caught up, all Heinzman's drive was in the water, inextricably mingled with the sixty or eighty million feet Orde had in charge.

The situation was plain. All Heinzman now had to do was to retain a small crew, which should follow after the rear in order to sack what logs the latter should leave stranded. This amounted practically to nothing. As it was impossible in so great a mass of timbers, and in the haste of a pressing labour, to distinguish or discriminate against any single brand, Heinzman was in a fair way to get his logs sent down stream with practically no expense.

" Vell, my boy," remarked the German quite frankly to Orde as they met on the road one day, " looks like I got you dis time, eh? "

Orde laughed, also with entire good-humour.

" If you mean your logs are going down with ours, why I guess you have. But you paste this in your hat: you're going to keep awful busy, and it's going to cost you something yet to get 'em down."

To Newmark, on one of his occasional visits to the camps, Orde detailed the situation.

" It doesn't amount to much," said he, " except that it complicates matters. We'll make him scratch gravel, if we have to sit up nights and work overtime to do it. We can't injure him or leave his logs, but we can annoy him a lot."

The state of affairs was perfectly well known to the men, and the entire river entered into the spirit of the contest. The drivers kept a sharp lookout for Ⓗ logs, and whenever possible thrust them aside into eddies and backwaters. This, of course, merely made work for the sackers Heinzman had left above the rear. Soon they were in charge of a very fair little drive of their own. Their lot was not enviable. Indeed, only the pressure of work prevented some of the more aggressive of Orde's rear—among whom could be numbered the Rough Red—from going back and "cleaning out" this impertinent band of hangers-on. One day two of the latter, conducting the jam of the miniature drive astern, came within reach of the Rough Red. The latter had lingered in hopes of rescuing his peavy, which had gone overboard. To lose one's peavy is, among rivermen, the most mortifying disgrace. Consequently, the Rough Red was in a fit mood for trouble. He attacked the two single-handed. A desperate battle ensued, which lasted upward of an hour. The two rivermen punched, kicked, and battered the Rough Red in a manner to tear his clothes, deprive him to some extent of red whiskers, bloody his face, cut his shoulder, and knock loose two teeth. The Rough Red, more than the equal of either man singly, had reciprocated in kind. Orde, driving in toward the rear from a detour to avoid a swamp, heard, and descended from his buckboard. Tying his horses to trees, he made his way through the brush to the scene of conflict. So winded and wearied were the belligerents by now that he had no difficulty in separating them. He surveyed their wrecks with a sardonic half smile.

"I call this a draw," said he finally. His attitude became threatening as the two up-river men, recovering somewhat, showed ugly symptoms. "Git!" he commanded. "Scat! I guess you don't know me. I'm Jack Orde. Jimmy and I together could do a dozen of you." He menaced them until, muttering, they had turned away.

"Well, Jimmy," said he humorously, "you look as if you'd been run through a thrashing machine."

"Those fellers make me sick!" growled the Rough Red. Orde looked him over again.

"You look sick," said he.

When the buckboard drew into camp, Orde sent Bourke away to repair damages while he called the cookee to help unpack several heavy boxes of hardware. They proved to contain about thirty small hatchets, well sharpened, and each with a leather guard. When the rear crew had come in that night, Orde distributed the hatchets.

"Boys," said he, "while you're on the work, I want you all to keep a watch-out for these Ⓗ logs, and whenever you strike one I want you to blaze it plainly, so there won't be any mistake about it."

"What for?" asked one of the Saginaw men as he received his hatchet.

But the riverman who squatted next nudged him with his elbow.

"The less questions you ask Jack, the more answers you'll get. Just do what you're told to on this river and you'll see fun sure."

Three days later the rear crew ran into the head of the pond above Reed's dam. To every one's surprise, Orde called a halt on the work and announced a holiday.

Now, holidays are unknown on drive. Barely is time allowed for eating and sleeping. Nevertheless, all that day the men lay about in complete idleness, smoking, talking, sleeping in the warm sun. The river, silenced by the closed sluice-gates, slept also. The pond filled with logs. From above, the current, aided by a fair wind, was driving down still other logs—the forerunners of the little drive astern. At sight of these, some of the men grumbled. "We're losin' what we made," said they. "We left them logs, and sorted 'em out once already."

Orde sent a couple of axe-men to blaze the newcomers. A little before sundown he ordered the sluice-gates of the dam opened.

"Night work," said the men to one another. They knew, of course, that in sluicing logs, the gate must be open a couple of hours before the sluicing begins in order to fill the river-bed below. Logs run ahead faster than the water spreads.

Sure enough, after supper Orde suddenly appeared among them, the well-known devil of mischief dancing in his eyes and broadening his good-natured face.

"Get organised, boys," said he briskly. "We've got to get this pond all sluiced before morning, and there's enough of us here to hustle it right along."

The men took their places. Orde moved here and there, giving his directions.

"Sluice through everything but the Ⓗ logs," he commanded. "Work them off to the left and leave them."

Twilight, then dark, fell. After a few moments the moon, then just past its full, rose behind the new-budding trees. The sluicing, under the impetus of a big crew, went rapidly.

"I bet there's mighty near a million an hour going through there," speculated Orde, watching the smooth, swift, but burdened waters of the chute.

And in this work the men distinguished easily the new white blaze-marks on Heinzman's logs; so they were able without hesitation to shunt them one side into the smoother water, as Orde had commanded.

About two o'clock the last log shot through.

"Now, boys," said Orde, "tear out the booms."

The chute to the dam was approached, as has been earlier explained, by two rows of booms arranged in a V, or funnel, the apex of which emptied into the sluice-way, and the wide, projecting arms of which embraced the width of the stream. The logs, floating down the pond, were thus concentrated toward the sluice. Also, the rivermen, walking back and forth the length of the booms, were able easily to keep the drive moving.

Now, however, Orde unchained these boom logs. The men pushed them ashore. There as many as could find room on either side the boom-poles clamped in their peavies, and, using these implements as handles, carried the booms some

distance back into the woods. Then everybody tramped
back and forth, round and about, to confuse the trail. Orde
was like a mischievous boy at a school prank. When the
last timber had been concealed, he lifted up his deep voice
in a roar of joy, in which the crew joined.

" Now let's turn in for a little sleep," said he.

This situation, perhaps a little cloudy in the reader's
mind, would have cleared could he have looked out over
the dam pond the following morning. The blazed logs belonging to Heinzman, drifting slowly, had sucked down
into the corner toward the power canal where, caught
against the grating, they had jammed. These logs would
have to be floated singly, and pushed one by one against
the current across the pond and into the influence of the
sluice-gate. Some of them would be hard to come at.

" I guess that will keep them busy for a day or two,"
commented Orde, as he followed the rear down to where
it was sacking below the dam.

This, as Orde had said, would be sufficiently annoying
to Heinzman, but would have little real effect on the main
issue, which was that the German was getting down his
logs with a crew of less than a dozen men. Nevertheless,
Orde, in a vast spirit of fun, took delight in inventing and
executing practical jokes of the general sort just described.
For instance, at one spot where he had boomed the deeper
channel from the rocks on either side, he shunted as many
of Heinzman's logs as came by handily through an opening he had made in the booms. There they grounded on the
shallows—more work for the men following. Many of the
logs in charge of the latter, however, catching the free
current, overtook the rear, so that the number of the Ⓗ
logs in the drive was not materially diminished.

At first, as has been hinted, these various tactics had little
effect. One day, however, the chore boy, who had been over
to Spruce Rapids after mail, reported that an additional

crew of twenty had been sent in to Heinzman's drive. This was gratifying.

"We're making him scratch gravel, boys, anyway," said Orde.

The men entered into the spirit of the thing. In fact, their enthusiasm was almost too exuberant. Orde had constantly to negative new and ingenious schemes.

"No, boys," said he, "I want to keep on the right side of the law. We may need it later."

Meanwhile the entire length of the river was busy and excited. Heinzman's logs were all blazed inside a week. The men passed the hatchets along the line, and slim chance did a marked log have of rescue once the poor thing fell into difficulties. With the strange and interesting tendency rivermen and woodsmen have of personifying the elements of their daily work, the men addressed the helpless timbers in tones of contempt.

"Thought you'd ride that rock, you —— —— ——," said they, "and got left, did you? Well, lie there and be —— to you!"

And if chance offered, and time was not pressing, the riverman would give his helpless victim a jerk or so into a more difficult position. Times of rising water—when the sluice-gates above had been opened—were the most prolific of opportunities. Logs rarely jam on rising water, for the simple reason that constantly the surface area of the river is increasing, thus tending to separate the logs. On the other hand, falling water, tending to crowd the drive closer together, is especially prolific of trouble. Therefore, on flood water the watchers scattered along the stretches of the river had little to do—save strand Heinzman's logs for him. And when flood water had passed, some of those logs were certainly high and dry.

Up to a certain point this was all very well. Orde took pains not to countenance it officially, and caused word to

be passed about, that while he did not expect his men to
help drive Heinzman's logs, they must not go out of their
way to strand them.

" If things get too bad, he'll have spies down here to
collect evidence on us," said Orde, " and he'll jug some
of us for interference with his property. We don't own
the river."

" How about them booms? " asked the Rough Red.

" I did own them," explained Orde, " and I had a right
to take them up when I had finished with them."

This hint was enough. The men did not cease from a
labour that tickled them mightily, but they adopted a code
of signals. Strangers were not uncommon. Spectators came
out often from the little towns and from the farms round-
about. When one of these appeared the riverman nearest
raised a long falsetto cry. This was taken up by his next
neighbour and passed on. In a few minutes all that section
of the drive knew that it would be wise to " lie low." And
inside of two weeks Orde had the great satisfaction of
learning that Heinzman was working—and working hard
—a crew of fifty men.

" A pretty fair crew, even if he was taking out his whole
drive," commented Orde.

The gods of luck seemed to be with the new enterprise.
Although Orde had, of course, taken the utmost pains to
foresee every contingency possible to guard against, nevertheless, as always when dealing with Nature's larger forces,
he anticipated some of those gigantic obstacles which continually render uncertain wilderness work. Nothing of the
kind happened. There formed none of the tremendous
white-water jams that pile up several million feet of logs,
tax every resource of men, horses, and explosives, and require a week or so to break. No men were killed, and only
two injured. No unexpected floods swept away works on
which the drive depended. The water held out to carry the

last stick of timber over the shallowest rapids. Weather conditions were phenomenal—and perfect. All up and down the river the work went with that vim and dash that is in itself an assurance of success. The Heinzman affair, which under auspices of evil augury might have become a serious menace to the success of the young undertaking, now served merely to add a spice of humour to the situation. Among the men gained currency a half-affectionate belief in " Orde's luck."

After this happy fashion the drive went, until at last it entered the broad, deep, and navigable stretches of the river from Redding to the lake. Here, barring the accident of an extraordinary flood, the troubles were over. On the broad, placid bosom of the stream the logs would float. A crew, following, would do the easy work of sacking what logs would strand or eddy in the lazy current; would roll into the faster waters the component parts of what were by courtesy called jams, but which were in reality pile-ups of a few hundred logs on sand bars mid-stream; and in the growing tepid warmth of summer would tramp pleasantly along the river trail. Of course, a dry year would make necessary a larger crew and more labour; of course, a big flood might sweep the logs past all defences into the lake for an irretrievable loss. But such floods come once in a century, and even the dryest of dry years could not now hang the drive. As Orde sat in his buckboard, ready to go into town for a first glimpse of Carroll in more than two months, he gazed with an immense satisfaction over the broad river moving brown and glacier-like as though the logs that covered it were viscid and composed all its substance. The enterprise was practically assured of success.

For a while now Orde was to have a breathing spell. A large number of men were here laid off. The remainder, under the direction of Jim Denning, would require little

or no actual supervision. Until the jam should have reached
the distributing booms above Monrovia, the affair was very
simple. Before he left, however, he called Denning to him.

"Jim," said he, "I'll be down to see you through the
sluiceways at Redding, of course. But now that you have
a good, still stretch of river, I want you to have the boys
let up on sacking out those (H) logs. And I want you to
include in our drive all the Heinzman logs from above
you possibly can. If you can fix it, let their drive drift
down into ours."

"Then we'll have to drive their logs for them," objected
Denning.

"Sure," rejoined Orde, "but it's easy driving; and if
that crew of his hasn't much to do, perhaps he'll lay most
of them off here at Redding."

Denning looked at his principal for a moment, then a
slow grin overspread his face. Without comment he turned
back to camp, and Orde took up his reins.

XXV

"OH, I'm so *glad* to get you back!" cried Carroll over and over again, as she clung to him. "I don't live while you're away. And every drop of rain that patters on the roof chills my heart, because I think of it as chilling you; and every creak of this old house at night brings me up broad awake, because I hear in it the crash of those cruel great timbers. Oh, oh, *oh*! I'm so glad to get you! You're the light of my life; you're my whole life itself!"—she smiled at him from her perch on his knee —"I'm silly, am I not?" she said. "Dear heart, don't leave me again."

"I've got to support an extravagant wife, you know," Orde reminded her gravely.

"I know, of course," she breathed, bending lightly to him. "You have your work in the world to do, and I would not have it otherwise. It is great work—wonderful work—I've been asking questions."

Orde laughed.

"It's work, just like any other. And it's hard work," said he.

She shook her head at him slowly, a mysterious smile on her lips. Without explaining her thought, she slipped from his knee and glided across to the tall golden harp, which had been brought from Monrovia. The light and diaphanous silk of her loose peignoir floated about her, defining the maturing grace of her figure. Abruptly she struck a great crashing chord.

Then, with an abandon of ecstasy she plunged into one

of those wild and sea-blown saga-like rhapsodies of the
Hungarians, full of the wind in rigging, the storm in the
pines, of shrieking, vast forces hurtling unchained through
a resounding and infinite space, as though deep down in
primeval nature the powers of the world had been loosed.
Back and forth, here and there, erratic and swift and sudden as lightning the theme played breathless. It fell.

" What is that? " gasped Orde, surprised to find himself
tense, his blood rioting, his soul stirred.

She ran to him to hide her face in his neck.

" Oh, it's you, you, you! " she cried.

He held her to him closely until her excitement had died.

" Do you think it is good to get quite so nervous, sweetheart? " he asked gently, then. " Remember———"

" Oh, I do, I do! " she broke in earnestly. " Every moment of my waking and sleeping hours I remember him.
Always I keep his little soul before me as a light on a
shrine. But to-night—oh! to-night I could laugh and shout
aloud like the people in the Bible, with clapping of hands."
She snuggled herself close to Orde with a little murmur
of happiness. " I think of all the beautiful things," she
whispered, " and of the noble things, and of the great
things. He is going to be sturdy, like his father; a wonderful boy, a boy all of fire———"

" Like his mother," said Orde.

She smiled up at him. " I want him just like you, dear,"
she pleaded.

XXVI

THREE days later the jam of the drive reached the dam at Redding. Orde took Carroll downtown in the buckboard. There a seat by the dam-watcher's little house was given her, back of the brick factory buildings next the power canal, whence for hours she watched the slow onward movement of the sullen brown timbers, the smooth, polished-steel rush of the waters through the chute, the graceful certain movements of the rivermen. Some of the latter were brought up by Orde and introduced. They were very awkward, and somewhat embarrassed, but they all looked her straight in the eye, and Carroll felt somehow that back of their diffidence they were quite dispassionately appraising her. After a few gracious speeches on her part and monosyllabic responses on theirs, they blundered away. In spite of the scant communication, these interviews left something of a friendly feeling on both sides.

"I like your Jim Denning," she told Orde; "he's a nice, clean-cut fellow. And Mr. Bourke," she laughed. "Isn't he funny with his fierce red beard and his little eyes? But he simply adores you."

Orde laughed at the idea of the Rough Red's adoring anybody.

"It's so," she insisted, "and I like him for it—only I wish he were a little cleaner."

She thought the feats of "log-riding" little less than wonderful, and you may be sure the knowledge of her presence did not discourage spectacular display. Finally,

Johnny Challan, uttering a loud whoop, leaped aboard a log and went through the chute standing bolt upright. By a marvel of agility, he kept his balance through the white-water below, and emerged finally into the lower waters still proudly upright, and dry above the knees.

Carroll had arisen, the better to see.

"Why," she cried aloud, "it's marvellous! Circus riding is nothing to it!"

"No, ma'am," replied a gigantic riverman who was working near at hand, "that ain't nothin'. Ordinary, how-ever, we travel that way on the river. At night we have the cookee pass us out each a goose-ha'r piller, and lay down for the night."

Carroll looked at him in reproof. He grinned slowly.

"Don't git worried about me, ma'am," said he, "I'm hopeless. For twenty year now I been wearin' crape on my hat in memory of my departed virtues."

After the rear had dropped down river from Redding, Carroll and Orde returned to their deserted little box of a house at Monrovia.

Orde breathed deep of a new satisfaction in walking again the streets of this little sandy, sawdust-paved, shanty-fied town, with its yellow hills and its wide blue river and its glimpse of the lake far in the offing. It had never meant anything to him before. Now he enjoyed every brick and board of it; he trod the broken, aromatic shingles of the roadway with pleasure; he tramped up the broad stairs and down the dark hall of the block with anticipation; he breathed the compounded office odour of ledgers, cocoa matting, and old cigar smoke in a long, reminiscent whiff; he took his seat at his roll-top desk, enchanted to be again in these homely though familiar surroundings.

"Hanged if I know what's struck me," he mused. "Never experienced any remarkable joy before in getting back to this sort of truck."

Then, with a warm glow at the heart, the realisation was brought to him. This was home, and over yonder, under the shadow of the heaven-pointing spire, a slip of a girl was waiting for him.

He tried to tell her this when next he saw her.

" I felt that I ought to make you a little shrine, and burn candles to you, the way the Catholics do——"

" To the Mater Dolorosa? " she mocked.

He looked at her dark eyes so full of the sweetness of content, at her sensitive lips with the quaintly upturned corners, and he thought of what her home life had been and of the real sorrow that even yet must smoulder somewhere down in the deeps of her being.

" No," said he slowly, " not that. I think my shrine will be dedicated to Our Lady of the Joyous Soul."

The rest of the week Orde was absent up the river, superintending in a general way the latter progress of the drive, looking into the needs of the crews, arranging for supplies. The mills were all working now, busily cutting into the residue of last season's logs. Soon they would need more.

At the booms everything was in readiness to receive the jam. The long swing arm slanting across the river channel was attached to its winch which would operate it. When shut it would close the main channel and shunt into the booms the logs floating in the river. There, penned at last by the piles driven in a row and held together at the top by bolted timbers, they would lie quiet. Men armed with pike-poles would then take up the work of distribution according to the brands stamped on the ends. Each brand had its own separate " sorting pens," the lower end leading again into the open river. From these each owner's property was rafted and towed to his private booms at his mill below.

Orde spent the day before the jam appeared in constructing what he called a " boomerang."

"Invention of my own," he explained to Newmark. "Secret invention just yet. I'm going to hold up the drive in the main river until we have things bunched, then I'm going to throw a big crew down here by the swing. Heinzman anticipates, of course, that I'll run the entire drive into the booms and do all my sorting there. Naturally, if I turn his logs loose into the river as fast as I run across them, he will be able to pick them up one at a time, for he'll only get them occasionally. If I keep them until everything else is sorted, only Heinzman's logs will remain; and as we have no right to hold logs, we'll have to turn them loose through the lower sorting booms, where he can be ready to raft them. In that way he gets them all right without paying us a cent. See?"

"Yes, I see," said Newmark.

"Well," said Orde, with a laugh, "here is where I fool him. I'm going to rush the drive into the booms all at once, but I'm going to sort out Heinzman's logs at these openings near the entrance and turn them into the main channel."

"What good will that do?" asked Newmark sceptically. "He gets them sorted just the same, doesn't he?"

"The current's fairly strong," Orde pointed out, "and the river's almighty wide. When you spring seven or eight million feet on a man, all at once and unexpected, and he with no crew to handle them, he's going to keep almighty busy. And if he don't stop them this side his mill, he'll have to raft and tow them back; and if he don't stop 'em this side the lake, he may as well kiss them all good-bye—except those that drift into the bayous and inlets and marshes, and other ungodly places."

"I see," said Newmark drily.

"But don't say a word anywhere," warned Orde. "Secrecy is the watchword of success with this merry little joke."

The boomerang worked like a charm. The men had been grumbling at an apparently peaceful yielding of the point at issue, and would have sacked out many of the blazed logs if Orde had not held them rigidly to it. Now their spirits flamed into joy again. The sorting went like clockwork. Orde, in personal charge, watched that through the different openings in his " boomerang " the Ⓗ logs were shunted into the river. Shortly the channel was full of logs floating merrily away down the little blue wavelets. After a while Orde handed over his job to Tom North.

"Can't stand it any longer, boys," said he. " I've got to go down and see how the Dutchman is making it."

" Come back and tell us! " yelled one of the crew.

" You bet I will! " Orde shouted back.

He drove the team and buckboard down the marsh road to Heinzman's mill. There he found evidences of the wildest excitement. The mill had been closed down, and all the men turned in to rescue logs. Boats plied in all directions. A tug darted back and forth. Constantly the number of floating logs augmented, however. Many had already gone by.

" If you think you're busy now," said Orde to himself with a chuckle, " just wait until you begin to get *logs*."

He watched for a few moments in silence.

" What's he doing with that tug? " thought he. " O-ho! He's stringing booms across the river to hold the whole outfit."

He laughed aloud, turned his team about, and drove frantically back to the booms. Every few moments he chuckled. His eyes danced. Hardly could he wait to get there. Once at the camp, he leaped from the buckboard, with a shout to the stableman, and ran rapidly out over the booms to where the sorting of Ⓗ logs was going merrily forward.

" He's shut down his mill," shouted Orde, " and he's got all that gang of highbankers out, and every old rum-blossom in Monrovia, and I bet if you say ' logs ' to him, he'd chase his tail in circles."

" Want this job? " North asked him.

" No," said Orde, suddenly fallen solemn, " haven't time. I'm going to take Marsh and the *Sprite* and go to town. Old Heinzman," he added as an afterthought, " is stringing booms across the river—obstructing navigation."

He ran down the length of the whole boom to where lay the two tugs.

" Marsh," he called when still some distance away, " got up steam? "

There appeared a short, square, blue-clad man, with hard brown cheeks, a heavy bleached flaxen moustache, and eyes steady, unwavering, and as blue as the sky.

" Up in two minutes," he answered, and descended from the pilot house to shout down a low door leading from the deck into the engine room.

" Harvey," he commanded, " fire her up! "

A tall, good-natured negro reached the upper half of his body from the low door to seize an armful of the slabs piled along the narrow deck. Ten minutes later the *Sprite*, a cloud of white smoke pouring from her funnel, was careening down the stretch of the river.

Captain Marsh guided his energetic charge among the logs floating in the stream with the marvellous second instinct of the expert tugboat man. A whirl of the wheel to the right, a turn to the left—the craft heeled strongly under the forcing of her powerful rudder to avoid by an arm's-length some timbers fairly flung aside by the wash. The displacement of the rapid running seemed almost to press the water above the level of the deck on either side and about ten feet from the gunwale. As the low marshes and cat-tails flew past, Orde noted with satisfaction that many of the logs, urged one side by the breeze, had found lodgment among the reeds and in the bayous and inlets.

One at a time, and painfully, these would have to be salvaged.

In a short time the mills' tall smokestacks loomed in sight. The logs thickened until it was with difficulty that Captain Marsh could thread his way among them at all. Shortly Orde, standing by the wheel in the pilot-house, could see down the stretches of the river a crowd of men working antlike.

"They've got 'em stopped," commented Orde. "Look at that gang working from boats! They haven't a dozen 'cork boots' among 'em."

"What do you want me to do?" asked Captain Marsh.

"This is a navigable river, isn't it?" replied Orde. "Run through!"

Marsh rang for half-speed and began to nose his way gently through the loosely floating logs. Soon the tug had reached the scene of activity, and headed straight for the slender line of booms hitched end to end and stretching quite across the river.

"I'm afraid we'll just ride over them if we hit them too slow," suggested Marsh.

Orde looked at his watch.

"We'll be late for the mail unless we hurry," said he.

Marsh whirled the spokes of his wheel over and rang the engine-room bell. The water churned white behind, the tug careened.

"Vat you do! Stop!" cried Heinzman from one of the boats.

Orde stuck his head from the pilot-house door.

"You're obstructing navigation!" he yelled. "I've got to go to town to buy a postage-stamp."

The prow of the tug, accurately aimed by Marsh, hit square in the junction of two of the booms. Immediately the water was agitated on both sides and for a hundred feet or so by the pressure of the long poles sidewise. There ensued a moment of strain; then the links snapped, and the *Sprite* plunged joyously through the opening. The booms, swept aside by the current, floated to either shore. The river was open.

Orde, his head still out the door, looked back.

"Slow down, Marsh," said he. "Let's see the show."

Already the logs caught by the booms had taken their motion and had swept past the opening. Although the lonesome tug Heinzman had on the work immediately picked up one end of the broken boom, and with it started out into the river, she found difficulty in making headway against the sweep of the logs. After a long struggle she reached the middle of the river, where she was able to hold her own.

"Wonder what next?" speculated Orde. "How are they going to get the other end of the booms out from the other bank?"

Captain Marsh had reversed the *Sprite*. The tug lay nearly motionless amidstream, her propeller slowly revolving.

Up river all the small boats gathered in a line, connected one to the other by a rope. The tug passed over to them the cable attached to the boom. Evidently the combined efforts of the rowboats were counted on to hold the half-boom across the current while the tug brought out the other half. When the tug dropped the cable, Orde laughed.

"Nobody but a Dutchman would have thought of that!" he cried. "Now for the fun!"

Immediately the weight fell on the small boats, they were dragged irresistibly backward. Even from a distance the three men on the *Sprite* could make out the white-water as the oars splashed and churned and frantically caught crabs in a vain effort to hold their own. Marsh lowered his telescope, the tears streaming down his face.

"It's better than a goat fight," said he.

Futilely protesting, the rowboats were dragged backward, turned as a whip is snapped, and strung out along the bank below.

"They'll have to have two tugs before they can close the break that way," commented Orde.

"Sure thing," replied Captain Marsh.

But at that moment a black smoke rolled up over the marshes, and shortly around the bend from above came the *Lucy Belle*.

The *Lucy Belle* was the main excuse for calling the river navigable. She made trips as often as she could between Redding and Monrovia. In luck, she could cover the forty miles in a day. It was no unusual thing, however, for the *Lucy Belle* to hang up indefinitely on some one of the numerous shifting sand bars. For that reason she carried more imperishable freight than passengers. In appearance she was two-storied, with twin smokestacks, an iron Indian on her top, and a "splutter-behind" paddle-wheel.

"There comes his help," said Orde. "Old Simpson would stop to pick up a bogus three-cent piece."

Sure enough, on hail from one of the rowboats, the *Lucy Belle* slowed down and stopped. After a short conference, she steamed clumsily over to get hold of one end of the booms. The tug took the other. In time, and by dint of much splashing, some collisions, and several attempts, the ends of the booms were united.

By this time, however, nearly all the logs had escaped. The tug, towing a string of rowboats, set out in pursuit.

The *Sprite* continued on her way until beyond sight. Then she slowed down again. The *Lucy Belle* churned around the bend, and turned in toward the tug.

"She's going to speak us," marvelled Orde. "I wonder what the dickens she wants."

"Tug ahoy!" bellowed a red-faced individual from the upper deck. He was dressed in blue and brass buttons,

carried a telescope in one hand, and was liberally festooned
with gold braid and embroidered anchors.

"Answer him," Orde commanded Marsh.

"Hullo there, commodore! what is it?" replied the tug
captain.

The red-faced figure glared down for a moment.

"They want a tug up there at Heinzman's. Can you
go?"

"Sure!" cried Marsh, choking.

The *Lucy Belle* sheered off magnificently.

"What do you think of that?" Marsh asked Orde.

"The commodore always acts as if that old raft was
a sixty-gun frigate," was Orde's non-committal answer.
"Head up stream again."

Heinzman saw the *Sprite* coming, and rowed out frantically, splashing at every stroke and yelling with every
breath.

"Don't you go through there! Vait a minute! Stop, I
tell you!"

"Hold up!" said Orde to Marsh.

Heinzman rowed alongside, dropped his oars and mopped
his brow.

"Vat you do?" he demanded heatedly.

"I forgot the money to buy my stamp with," said Orde
sweetly. "I'm going back to get it."

"Not through my pooms!" cried Heinzman.

"Mr. Heinzman," said Orde severely, "you are obstructing a navigable stream. I am doing business, and I cannot
be interfered with."

"But my logs!" cried the unhappy mill man.

"I have nothing to do with your logs. You are driving
your own logs," Orde reminded him.

Heinzman vituperated and pounded the gunwale.

"Go ahead, Marsh!" said Orde.

The tug gathered way. Soon Heinzman was forced to

let go. For a second time the chains were snapped. Orde and Marsh looked back over the churning wake left by the *Sprite*. The severed ends of the booms were swinging back toward either shore. Between them floated a rowboat. In the rowboat gesticulated a pudgy man. The river was well sprinkled with logs. Evidently the sorting was going on well.

"May as well go back to the works," said Orde. "He won't string them together again to-day—not if he waits for that tug he sent Simpson for."

Accordingly, they returned to the booms, where work was suspended while Orde detailed to an appreciative audience the happenings below. This tickled the men immensely.

"Why, we hain't sorted out more'n a million feet of his logs," cried Rollway Charlie. "He hain't *seen* no logs yet!"

They turned with new enthusiasm to the work of shunting Ⓗ logs into the channel.

In ten minutes, however, the stableman picked his way out over the booms with a message for Orde.

"Mr. Heinzman's ashore, and wants to see you," said he.

Orde and Jim Denning exchanged glances.

"'Coon's come down," said the latter.

Orde found the mill man pacing restlessly up and down before a steaming pair of horses. Newmark, perched on a stump, was surveying him sardonically and chewing the end of an unlighted cigar.

"Here you poth are!" burst out Heinzman, when Orde stepped ashore. "Now, this must stop. I must not lose my logs! Vat is your proposition?"

Newmark broke in quickly before Orde could speak.

"I've told Mr. Heinzman," said he, "that we would sort and deliver the rest of his logs for two dollars a thousand."

"That will be about it," agreed Orde.

"But," exploded Heinzman, "that is as much as you agreet to drive and deliffer my whole cut!"

"Precisely," said Newmark.

"Put I haf all the eggspence of driving the logs myself. Why shoult I pay you for doing what I haf alretty paid to haf done?"

Orde chuckled.

"Heinzman," said he, "I told you I'd make you scratch gravel. Now it's time to talk business. You thought you were boring with a mighty auger, but it's time to revise. We aren't forced to bother with your logs, and you're lucky to get out so easy. If I turn your whole drive into the river, you'll lose more than half of it outright, and it'll cost you a heap to salvage the rest. And what's more, I'll turn 'em in before you can get hold of a pile-driver. I'll sort night and day," he bluffed, "and by to-morrow morning you won't have a stick of timber above my booms." He laughed again. "You want to get down to business almighty sudden."

When finally Heinzman had driven sadly away, and the whole drive, Ⓗ logs included, was pouring into the main boom, Orde stretched his arms over his head in a luxury of satisfaction.

"That just about settles that campaign," he said to Newmark.

"Oh, no, it doesn't," replied the latter decidedly.

"Why?" asked Orde, surprised. "You don't imagine he'll do anything more?"

"No, but I will," said Newmark.

XXVII

EARLY in the fall the baby was born. It proved to be a boy. Orde, nervous as a cat after the ordeal of doing nothing, tiptoed into the darkened room. He found his wife weak and pale, her dark hair framing her face, a new look of rapt inner contemplation rendering even more mysterious her always fathomless eyes. To Orde she seemed fragile, aloof, enshrined among her laces and dainty ribbons. Hardly dared he touch her when she held her hand out to him weakly, but fell on his knees beside the bed and buried his face in the clothes. She placed a gentle hand caressingly on his head.

So they remained for some time. Finally he raised his eyes. She held her lips to him. He kissed them.

"It seems sort of make-believe even yet, sweetheart," she smiled at him whimsically, "that we have a real, live baby all of our own."

"Like other people," said Orde.

"Not like other people at all!" she disclaimed, with a show of indignation.

Grandma Orde brought the newcomer in for Orde's inspection. He looked gravely down on the puckered, discoloured bit of humanity with some feeling of disappointment, and perhaps a faint uneasiness. After a moment he voiced the latter.

"Is—do you think—that is—" he hesitated, "does the doctor say he's going to be all right?"

"All right!" cried Grandma Orde indignantly. "I'd like to know if he isn't all right now! What in the world do you expect of a new-born baby?"

But Carroll was laughing softly to herself on the bed. She held out her arms for the baby, and cuddled it close to her breast.

"He's a little darling," she crooned, "and he's going to grow up big and strong, just like his daddy." She put her cheek against the sleeping babe's and looked up side-wise at the two standing above her. "But I know how you feel," she said to her husband. "When they first showed him to me, I thought he looked like a peanut a thousand years old."

Grandma Orde fairly snorted with indignation.

"Come to your old grandmother, who appreciates you!" she cried, possessing herself of the infant. "He's a beauti-ful baby; one of the best-looking new-born babies I ever saw!"

Orde escaped to the open air. He had to go to the office to attend to some details of the business. With every step his elation increased. At the office he threw open his desk with a slam. Newmark jumped nervously and frowned. Orde's big, open, and brusque manners bothered him as they would have bothered a cat.

"Got a son and heir over at my place," called Orde in his big voice. "This old firm's got to rustle now, I tell you."

"Congratulate you, I'm sure," said Newmark rather shortly. "Mrs. Orde is doing well, I hope?"

"Fine, fine!" cried Orde.

Newmark dropped the subject and plunged into a busi-ness matter. Orde's attention, however, was flighty. After a little while he closed his desk with another bang.

"No use!" said he. "Got to make it a vacation. I'm going to run over to see how the family is."

Strangely enough, the young couple had not discussed before the question of a name. One evening at twilight, when Orde was perched at the foot of the bed, Carroll brought up the subject.

"He ought to be named for you," she began timidly. "I know that, Jack, and I'd love to have another Jack Orde in the family; but, dear, I've been thinking about father. He's a poor, forlorn old man, who doesn't get much out of life. And it would please him so—oh, more than you can imagine such a thing could please anybody!"

She looked up at him doubtfully. Orde said nothing, but walked around the bed to where the baby lay in his little cradle. He leaned over and took the infant up in his gingerly awkward fashion.

"How are you to-day, Bobby Orde?" he inquired of the blinking mite.

XXVIII

THE first season of the Boom Company was most successful. Its prospects for the future were bright. The drive had been delivered to its various owners at a price below what it had cost them severally, and without the necessary attendant bother. Therefore, the loggers were only too willing to renew their contracts for another year. This did not satisfy Newmark, however.

"What we want," he told Orde, "is a charter giving us exclusive rights on the river, and authorising us to ask toll. I'm going to try and get one out of the legislature."

He departed for Lansing as soon as the Assembly opened, and almost immediately became lost in one of those fierce struggles of politics not less bitter because concealed. Heinzman was already on the ground.

Newmark had the shadow of right on his side, for he applied for the charter on the basis of the river improvements already put in by his firm. Heinzman, however, possessed much political influence, a deep knowledge of the subterranean workings of plot and counterplot, and a "barrel." Although armed with an apparently incontestable legal right, Newmark soon found himself fighting on the defensive. Heinzman wanted the improvements already existing condemned and sold as a public utility to the highest bidder. He offered further guarantees as to future improvements. In addition were other and more potent arguments proffered behind closed doors. Many cases resolved themselves into a bald question of cash. Others demanded diplomacy. Jobs, fat contracts, business favours, influence

were all flung out freely—bribes as absolute as though
stamped with the dollar mark. Newspapers all over the
State were pressed into service. These, bought up by Heinzman and his prospective partners in a lucrative business,
spoke virtuously of private piracy of what are now called
public utilities, the exploiting of the people's natural
wealths, and all the rest of a specious reasoning the more con-
vincing in that it was in many other cases only too true.
The independent journals, uninformed of the rights of the
case, either remained silent on the matter, or groped in a
puzzled and undecided manner on both sides.

Against this secret but effective organisation Newmark
most unexpectedly found himself pitted. He had anticipated being absent but a week; he became involved in an
affair of months.

With decision he applied himself to the problem. He
took rooms at the hotel, sent for Orde, and began at once to
set in motion the machinery of opposition. The refreshed
resources of the company were strained to the breaking-
point in order to raise money for this new campaign opening before it. Orde, returning to Lansing after a trip de-
voted to the carrying out of Newmark's directions as to
finances, was dismayed at the tangle of strategy and cross-
strategy, innuendo, vague and formless cobweb forces by
which he was surrounded. He could make nothing of them.
They brushed his face, he felt their influence, yet he could
place his finger on no tangible and comprehensible solidity.
Among these delicate and complicated cross-currents Newmark moved silent, cold, secret. He seemed to understand
them, to play with them, to manipulate them as elements
of the game. Above them was the hollow shock of the
ostensible battle—the speeches, the loud talk in lobbies, the
newspaper virtue, indignation, accusations; but the real
struggle was here in the furtive ways, in whispered words
delivered hastily aside, in hotel halls on the way to and

from the stairs, behind closed doors of rooms without open transoms.

Orde in comic despair acknowledged that it was all "too deep for him." Nevertheless, it was soon borne in on him that the new company was struggling for its very right to existence. It had been doing that from the first; but now, to Orde the fight, the existence, had a new importance. The company up to this point had been a scheme merely, an experiment that might win or lose. Now, with the history of a drive behind it, it had become a living entity. Orde would have fought against its dissolution as he would have fought against a murder. Yet he had practically to stand one side, watching Newmark's slender, gray-clad, tense figure gliding here and there, more silent, more reserved, more watchful every day.

The fight endured through most of the first half of the session. When finally it became evident to Heinzman that Newmark would win, he made the issue of toll rates the ditch of his last resistance, trying to force legal charges so low as to eat up the profits. At the last, however, the bill passed the board. The company had its charter.

At what price only Newmark could have told. He had fought with the tense earnestness of the nervous temperament that fights to win without count of the cost. The firm was established, but it was as heavily in debt as its credit would stand. Newmark himself, though as calm and reserved and precise as ever, seemed to have turned gray, and one of his eyelids had acquired a slight nervous twitch which persisted for some months. He took his seat at the desk, however, as calmly as ever. In three days the scandalised howls of bribery and corruption had given place in the newspapers to some other sensation.

"Joe," said Orde to his partner, "how about all this talk? Is there really anything in it? You haven't gone in for that business, have you?"

Newmark stretched his arms wearily.

"Press bought up," he replied. "I know for a fact that old Stanford got five hundred dollars from some of the Heinzman interests. I could have swung him back for an extra hundred, but it wasn't worth while. They howl bribery at us to distract attention from their own performances."

With this evasive reply Orde contented himself. Whether it satisfied him or whether he was loath to pursue the subject further it would be impossible to say.

"It's cost us plenty, anyway," he said, after a moment. "The proposition's got a load on it. It will take us a long time to get out of debt. The river driving won't pay quite so big as we thought it would," he concluded, with a rueful little laugh.

"It will pay plenty well enough," replied Newmark decidedly, "and it gives us a vantage point to work from. You don't suppose we are going to quit at river driving, do you? We want to look around for some timber of our own; there's where the big money is. And perhaps we can buy a schooner or two and go into the carrying trade—the country's alive with opportunity. Newmark & Orde means something to these fellows now. We can have anything we want, if we just reach out for it."

His thin figure, ordinarily slightly askew, had straightened; his steel-gray, impersonal eyes had lit up behind the bowed glasses and were seeing things beyond the wall at which they gazed. Orde looked up at him with a sudden admiration.

"You're the brains of this concern," said he.

"We'll get on," replied Newmark, the fire dying from his eyes.

XXIX

IN the course of the next eight years Newmark & Orde floated high on that flood of apparent prosperity that attends a business well conceived and passably well managed. The Boom and Driving Company made money, of course, for with the margin of fifty per cent or thereabouts necessitated by the temporary value of the improvements, good years could hardly fail to bring good returns. This, it will be remembered, was a stock company. With the profits from that business the two men embarked on a separate copartnership. They made money at this, too, but the burden of debt necessitated by new ventures, constantly weighted by the heavy interest demanded at that time, kept affairs on the ragged edge.

In addition, both Orde and Newmark were more inclined to extension of interests than to " playing safe." The assets gained in one venture were promptly pledged to another. The ramifications of debt, property, mortgages, and expectations overlapped each other in a cobweb of interests.

Orde lived at ease in a new house of some size surrounded by grounds. He kept two servants: a blooded team of horses drew the successor to the original buckboard. Newmark owned a sail yacht of five or six tons, in which, quite solitary, he took his only pleasure. Both were considered men of substance and property, as indeed they were. Only, they risked dollars to gain thousands. A succession of bad years, a panic-contraction of money markets, any one of a dozen possible, though not probable, contingencies

242

would render it difficult to meet the obligations which constantly came due, and which Newmark kept busy devising ways and means of meeting. If things went well—and it may be remarked that legitimately they should—Newmark & Orde would some day be rated among the millionaire firms. If things went ill, bankruptcy could not be avoided. There was no middle ground. Nor were Orde and his partner unique in this; practically every firm then developing or exploiting the natural resources of the country found itself in the same case.

Immediately after the granting of the charter to drive the river the partners had offered them an opportunity of acquiring about thirty million feet of timber remaining from Morrison & Daly's original holdings. That firm was very anxious to begin development on a large scale of its Beeson Lake properties in the Saginaw waters. Daly proposed to Orde that he take over the remnant, and having confidence in the young man's abilities, agreed to let him have it on long-time notes. After several consultations with Newmark, Orde finally completed the purchase. Below the booms they erected a mill, the machinery for which they had also bought of Daly, at Redding. The following winter Orde spent in the woods. By spring he had banked, ready to drive, about six million feet.

For some years these two sorts of activity gave the partners about all they could attend to. As soon as the drive had passed Redding, Orde left it in charge of one of his foremen while he divided his time between the booms and the mill. Late in the year his woods trips began, the tours of inspection, of surveying for new roads, the inevitable preparation for the long winter campaigns in the forest.* As soon as the spring thaws began, once more the drive demanded his attention. And in marketing the lumber, manipulating the firm's financial affairs, collecting its dues,

* See *The Blazed Trail* for descriptions of woods work.

paying its bills, making its purchases, and keeping oiled
the intricate bearing points of its office machinery, Newmark was busy—and invaluable.

At the end of the fifth year the opportunity came,
through a combination of a bad debt and a man's death,
to get possession of two lake schooners. Orde at once suggested the contract for a steam barge. Towing was then
in its infancy. The bulk of lake traffic was by means of
individual sailing ships—a method uncertain as to time.
Orde thought that a steam barge could be built powerful
enough not only to carry its own hold and deck loads,
but to tow after it the two schooners. In this manner
the crews could be reduced, and an approximate date
of delivery could be guaranteed. Newmark agreed with
him. Thus the firm, in accordance with his prophecy,
went into the carrying trade, for the vessels more than
sufficed for its own needs. The freighting of lumber
added much to the income, and the carrying of machinery and other heavy freight on the return trip grew every
year.

But by far the most important acquisition was that of
the northern peninsula timber. Most operators called the
white pine along and back from the river inexhaustible.
Orde did not believe this. He saw the time, not far distant,
when the world would be compelled to look elsewhere for
its lumber supply, and he turned his eyes to the almost
unknown North. After a long investigation through agents,
and a month's land-looking on his own account, he located
and purchased three hundred million feet. This was to be
paid for, as usual, mostly by the firm's notes secured by
its other property. It would become available only in the
future, but Orde believed, as indeed the event justified, this
future would prove to be not so distant as most people
supposed.

As these interests widened, Orde became more and more

immersed in them. He was forced to be away all of every day, and more than the bulk of every year. Nevertheless, his home life did not suffer for it.

To Carroll he was always the same big, hearty, whole-souled boy she had first learned to love. She had all his confidence. If this did not extend into business affairs, it was because Orde had always tried to get away from them when at home. At first Carroll had attempted to keep in the current of her husband's activities, but as the latter broadened in scope and became more complex, she perceived that their explanation wearied him. She grew out of the habit of asking him about them. Soon their rapid advance had carried them quite beyond her horizon. To her, also, as to most women, the word "business" connoted nothing but a turmoil and a mystery.

In all other things they were to each other what they had been from the first. No more children had come to them. Bobby, however, had turned out a sturdy, honest little fellow, with more than a streak of his mother's charm and intuition. His future was the subject of all Orde's plans.

"I want to give him all the chance there is," he explained to Carroll. "A boy ought to start where his father left off, and not have to do the same thing all over again. But being a rich man's son isn't much of a job."

"Why don't you let him continue your business?" smiled Carroll, secretly amused at the idea of the small person before them ever doing anything.

"By the time Bobby's grown up this business will all be closed out," replied Orde seriously.

He continued to look at his minute son with puckered brow, until Carroll smoothed out the wrinkles with the tips of her fingers.

"Of course, having only a few minutes to decide," she

mocked, " perhaps we'd better make up our minds right now to have him a street-car driver."

" Yes! " agreed Bobby unexpectedly, and with emphasis.

Three years after this conversation, which would have made Bobby just eight, Orde came back before six of a summer evening, his face alight with satisfaction.

" Hullo, bub! " he cried to Bobby, tossing him to his shoulder. " How's the kid? "

They went out together, while awaiting dinner, to see the new setter puppy in the woodshed.

" Named him yet? " asked Orde.

" Duke," said Bobby.

Orde surveyed the animal gravely.

" Seems like a good name," said he.

After dinner the two adjourned to the library, where they sat together in the " big chair," and Bobby, squirmed a little sidewise in order the better to see, watched the smoke from his father's cigar as it eddied and curled in the air.

" Tell a story," he commanded finally.

" Well," acquiesced Orde, " there was once a man who had a cow——"

" Once upon a time," corrected Bobby.

He listened for a moment or so.

" I don't like that story," he then announced. " Tell the story about the bears."

" But this is a new story," protested Orde, " and you've heard about the bears so many times."

" Bears," insisted Bobby.

" Well, once upon a time there were three bears—a big bear and a middle-sized bear and a little bear—" began Orde obediently.

Bobby, with a sigh of rapture and content, curled up in a snug, warm little ball. The twilight darkened.

" Blind-man's holiday!" warned Carroll behind them so suddenly that they both jumped. " And the sand man's been at somebody, I know!"

She bore him away to bed. Orde sat smoking in the darkness, staring straight ahead of him into the future. He believed he had found the opportunity—twenty years distant—for which he had been looking so long.

XXX

AFTER a time Carroll descended the stairs, chuckling. "Jack," she called into the sitting-room, "come out on the porch. What do you suppose the young man did to-night?"

"Give it up," replied Orde promptly. "No good guessing when it's a question of that youngster's performances. What was it?"

"He said his ' Now I lay me,' and asked blessings on you and me, and the grandpas and grandmas, and Auntie Kate, as usual. Then he stopped. ' What else?' I reminded him. ' And,' he finished with a rush, ' make-Bobby-a-good-boy-and-give-him-plenty-of-bread-'n-butter-'n-apple-sauce!'"

They laughed delightedly over this, clinging together like two children. Then they stepped out on the little porch and looked into the fathomless night. The sky was full of stars, aloof and calm, but waiting breathless on the edge of action, attending the word of command or the celestial vision, or whatever it is for which stars seem to wait. Along the street the dense velvet shade of the maples threw the sidewalks into impenetrable blackness. Sounds carried clearly. From the Welton's, down the street, came the tinkle of a mandolin and an occasional low laugh from the group of young people that nightly frequented the front steps. Tree toads chirped in unison or fell abruptly silent as though by signal. All up and down the rows of houses whirred the low monotone of the lawn sprinklers, and the aroma of their wetness was borne cool and refreshing through the tepid air.

Orde and his wife sat together on the top step. He slipped his arm about her. They said nothing, but breathed deep of the quiet happiness that filled their lives.

The gate latch clicked and two shadowy figures defined themselves approaching up the concrete walk.

" Hullo! " called Orde cheerfully into the darkness.

" Hullo! " a man's voice instantly responded.

" Taylor and Clara," said Orde to Carroll with satisfaction. " Just the man I wanted to see."

The lawyer and his wife mounted the steps. He was a quick, energetic, spare man, with lean cheeks, a bristling, clipped moustache, and a slight stoop to his shoulders. She was small, piquant, almost child-like, with a dainty upturned nose, a large and lustrous eye, a constant, bird-like animation of manner—the Folly of artists, the adorable, lovable, harmless Folly standing tiptoe on a complaisant world.

" Just the man I wanted to see," repeated Orde, as the two approached.

Clara Taylor stopped short and considered him for a moment.

" Let us away," she said seriously to Carroll. " My prophetic soul tells me they are going to talk business, and if any more business is talked in my presence, I shall *expire* ! "

Both men laughed, but Orde explained apologetically:

" Well, you know, Mrs. Taylor, these are my especially busy days for the firm, and I have to work my private affairs in when I can."

" I thought Frank was very solicitous about my getting out in the air," cried Clara. " Come, Carroll, let's wander down the street and see Mina Heinzman."

The two interlocked arms and sauntered along the walk. Both men lit cigars and sat on the top step of the porch.

" Look here, Taylor," broke in Orde abruptly, " you told

me the other day you had fifteen or twenty thousand you wanted to place somewhere."

"Yes," replied Taylor.

"Well, I believe I have just the proposition."

"What is it?"

"California pine," replied Orde.

"California pine?" repeated Taylor, after a slight pause. "Why California? That's a long way off. And there's no market, is there? Why way out there?"

"It's cheap," replied Orde succinctly. "I don't say it will be good for immediate returns, nor even for returns in the near future, but in twenty or thirty years it ought to pay big on a small investment made now."

Taylor shook his head doubtfully.

"I don't see how you figure it," he objected. "We have more timber than we can use in the East. Why should we go several thousand miles west for the same thing?"

"When our timber gives out, then we'll *have* to go west," said Orde.

Taylor laughed.

"Laugh all you please," rejoined Orde, "but I tell you Michigan and Wisconsin pine is doomed. Twenty or thirty years from now there won't be any white pine for sale."

"Nonsense!" objected Taylor. "You're talking wild. We haven't even begun on the upper peninsula. After that there's Minnesota. And I haven't observed that we're quite out of timber on the river, or the Muskegon, or the Saginaw, or the Grand, or the Cheboygan—why, Great Scott! man, our children's children's children may be thinking of investing in California timber, but that's about soon enough."

"All right," said Orde quietly. "Well, what do you think of Indiana as a good field for timber investment?"

"Indiana!" cried Taylor, amazed. "Why, there's no timber there; it's a prairie."

"There used to be. And all the southern Michigan farm belt was timbered, and around here. We have our stumps to show for it, but there are no evidences at all farther south. You'd have hard work, for instance, to persuade a stranger that Van Buren County was once forest."

"Was it?" asked Taylor doubtfully.

"It was. You take your map and see how much area has been cut already, and how much remains. That'll open your eyes. And remember all that has been done by crude methods for a relatively small demand. The demand increases as the country grows and methods improve. It would not surprise me if some day thirty or forty millions would constitute an average cut.* 'Michigan pine exhaustless!'—those fellows make me sick!"

"Sounds a little more reasonable," said Taylor slowly.

"It'll sound a lot more reasonable in five or ten years," insisted Orde, "and then you'll see the big men rushing out into that Oregon and California country. But now a man can get practically the pick of the coast. There are only a few big concerns out there."

"Why is it that no one——"

"Because," Orde cut him short, "the big things are for the fellow who can see far enough ahead."

"What kind of a proposition have you?" asked Taylor after a pause.

"I can get ten thousand acres at an average price of eight dollars an acre," replied Orde.

"Acres? What does that mean in timber?"

"On this particular tract it means about four hundred million feet."

"That's about twenty cents a thousand."

Orde nodded.

"And of course you couldn't operate for a long time?"

* At the present day some firms cut as high as 150,000,000 feet.

"Not for twenty, maybe thirty, years," replied Orde calmly.

"There's your interest on your money, and taxes, and the risk of fire and——"

"Of course, of course," agreed Orde impatiently, "but you're getting your stumpage for twenty cents or a little more, and in thirty years it will be worth as high as a dollar and a half." *

"What!" cried Taylor.

"That is my opinion," said Orde.

Taylor relapsed into thought.

"Look here, Orde," he broke out finally, "how old are you?"

"Thirty-eight. Why?"

"How much timber have you in Michigan?"

"About ten million that we've picked up on the river since the Daly purchase and three hundred million in the northern peninsula."

"Which will take you twenty years to cut, and make you a million dollars or so?"

"Hope so."

"Then why this investment thirty years ahead?"

"It's for Bobby," explained Orde simply. "A man likes to have his son continue on in his business. I can't do it here, but there I can. It would take fifty years to cut that pine, and that will give Bobby a steady income and a steady business."

"Bobby will be well enough off, anyway. He won't have to go into business."

Orde's brow puckered.

"I know a man—Bobby is going to work. A man is not a success in life unless he does something, and Bobby is going to be a success. Why, Taylor," he chuckled, "the

* At the present time (1908) sugar pine such as Orde described would cost $3.50 to $4.

little rascal fills the wood-box for a cent a time, and that's all the pocket-money he gets. He's saving now to buy a thousand-dollar boat. I've agreed to pool in half. At his present rate of income, I'm safe for about sixty years yet."

"How soon are you going to close this deal?" asked Taylor, rising as he caught sight of two figures coming up the walk.

"I have an option until November 1," replied Orde. "If you can't make it, I guess I can swing it myself. By the way, keep this dark."

Taylor nodded, and the two turned to defend themselves as best they could against Clara's laughing attack.

XXXI

ORDE had said nothing to Newmark concerning this purposed new investment, nor did he intend doing so.

"It is for Bobby," he told himself, "and I want Bobby, and no one else, to run it. Joe would want to take charge, naturally. Taylor won't. He knows nothing of the business."

He walked downtown next morning busily formulating his scheme. At the office he found Newmark already seated at his desk, a pile of letters in front of him. Upon Orde's boisterous greeting his nerves crisped slightly, but of this there was no outward sign beyond a tightening of his hands on the letter he was reading. Behind his eye-glasses his blue, cynical eyes twinkled like frost crystals. As always, he was immaculately dressed in neat gray clothes, and carried in one corner of his mouth an unlighted cigar.

"Joe," said Orde, spinning a chair to Newmark's roll-top desk and speaking in a low tone, "just how do we stand on that upper peninsula stumpage?"

"What do you mean? How much of it is there? You know that as well as I do—about three hundred million."

"No; I mean financially."

"We've made two payments of seventy-five thousand each, and have still two to make of the same amount."

"What could we borrow on it?"

"We don't want to borrow anything on it," returned Newmark in a flash.

"Perhaps not; but if we should?"

"We might raise fifty or seventy-five thousand, I suppose."

"Joe," said Orde, "I want to raise about seventy-five thousand dollars on my share in this concern, if it can be done."

"What's up?" inquired Newmark keenly.

"It's a private matter."

Newmark said nothing, but for some time thought busily, his light blue eyes narrowed to a slit.

"I'll have to figure on it a while," said he at last, and turned back to his mail. All day he worked hard, with only a fifteen-minute intermission for a lunch which was brought up from the hotel below. At six o'clock he slammed shut the desk. He descended the stairs with Orde, from whom he parted at their foot, and walked precisely away, his tall, thin figure held rigid and slightly askew, his pale eyes slitted behind his eye-glasses, the unlighted cigar in one corner of his straight lips. To the occasional passerby he bowed coldly and with formality. At the corner below he bore to the left, and after a short walk entered the small one-story house set well back from the sidewalk among the clumps of oleanders. Here he turned into a study, quietly and richly furnished ten years in advance of the taste then prevalent in Monrovia, where he sank into a deep-cushioned chair and lit the much-chewed cigar. For some moments he lay back with his eyes shut. Then he opened them to look with approval on the dark walnut book-cases, the framed prints and etchings, the bronzed student's lamp on the square table desk, the rugs on the polished floor. He picked up a magazine, into which he dipped for ten minutes.

The door opened noiselessly behind him.

"Mr. Newmark, sir," came a respectful voice, "it is just short of seven."

"Very well," replied Newmark, without looking around.

The man withdrew as softly as he had come. After a moment, Newmark replaced the magazine on the table, yawned, threw aside the cigar, of which he had smoked but an inch, and passed from his study into his bedroom across the hall. This contained an exquisite Colonial four-poster, with a lowboy and dresser to match, and was papered and carpeted in accordance with these, its chief ornaments. Newmark bathed in the adjoining bathroom, shaved carefully between the two wax lights which were his whim, and dressed in what were then known as " swallow-tail " clothes. Probably he was the only man in Monrovia at that moment so apparelled. Then calmly, and with all the deliberation of one under fire of a hundred eyes, he proceeded to the dining-room, where waited the man who had a short time before reminded him of the hour. He was a solemn, dignified man, whose like was not to be found elsewhere this side the city. He, too, wore the " swallow-tail," but its buttons were of gilt.

Newmark seated himself in a leather-upholstered mahogany chair before a small, round, mahogany table. The room was illuminated only by four wax candles with red shades. They threw into relief the polish of mahogany, the glitter of glass, the shine of silver, but into darkness the detail of massive sideboard, dull panelling, and the two or three dark-toned sporting prints on the wall.

" You may serve dinner, Mallock," said Newmark.

He ate deliberately and with enjoyment the meal, exquisitely prepared and exquisitely presented to him. With it he drank a single glass of Burgundy—a deed that would, in the eyes of Monrovia, have condemned him as certainly as driving a horse on Sunday or playing cards for a stake. Afterward he returned to the study, whither Mallock brought coffee. He lit another cigar, opened a drawer in his desk, extracted therefrom some bank-books and small personal account books. From these he figured all the evening. His cigar went out, but he did not notice that, and chewed away quite contentedly on the dead butt. When he had finished, his cold eye exhibited a gleam of satisfaction. He had resolved on a course of action. At ten o'clock he went to bed.

Next morning Mallock closed the door behind him promptly upon the stroke of eight. It was strange that not one living soul but Mallock had ever entered Newmark's abode. Curiosity had at first brought a few callers; but these were always met by the imperturbable servant with so plausible a reason for his master's absence that the visitors had departed without a suspicion that they had been deliberately excluded. And as Newmark made no friends and excited little interest, the attempts to cultivate him gradually ceased.

"Orde," said Newmark, as the former entered the office, "I think I can arrange this matter."

Orde drew up a chair.

"I talked last evening with a man from Detroit named Thayer, who thinks he may advance seventy-five thousand dollars on a mortgage on our northern peninsula stumpage. For that, of course, we will give the firm's note with interest at ten per cent. I will turn this over to you."

"That's—" began Orde.

"Hold on," interrupted Newmark. "As collateral security you will deposit for me your stock in the Boom Company, indorsed in blank. If you do not pay the full amount of the firm's note to Thayer, then the stock will be turned in to me."

"I see," said Orde.

"Now, don't misunderstand me," said Newmark drily. "This is your own affair, and I do not urge it on you. If we raise as much as seventy-five thousand dollars on that upper peninsula stumpage, it will be all it can stand, for next year we must make a third payment on it. If you take that money, it is of course proper that you pay the interest on it."

"Certainly," said Orde.

"And if there's any possibility of the foreclosure of the mortgage, it is only right that you run all the risk of loss —not myself."

"Certainly," repeated Orde.

"From another point of view," went on Newmark, "you are practically mortgaging your interest in the Boom Company for seventy-five thousand dollars. That would make, on the usual basis of a mortgage, your share worth above two hundred thousand—and four hundred thousand is a high valuation of our property."

"That looks more than decent on your part," said Orde.

"Of course, it's none of my business what you intend to do with this," went on Newmark, "but unless you're *sure* you can meet these notes, I should strongly advise against it."

"The same remark applies to any mortgage," rejoined Orde.

"Exactly."

"For how long a time could I get this?" asked Orde at length.

"I couldn't promise it for longer than five years," replied Newmark.

"That would make about fifteen thousand a year?"

"And interest."

"Certainly—and interest. Well, I don't see why I can't carry that easily on our present showing and prospects."

"If nothing untoward happens," insisted Newmark, determined to put forward all objections possible.

"It's not much risk," said Orde hopefully. "There's nothing surer than lumber. We'll pay the notes easily enough as we cut, and the Boom Company's on velvet now. What do our earnings figure, anyway?"

"We're driving one hundred and fifty million at a profit of about sixty cents a thousand," said Newmark.

"That's ninety thousand dollars—in five years, four hundred and fifty thousand," said Orde, sucking his pencil.

"We ought to clean up five dollars a thousand on our mill."

"That's about a hundred thousand on what we've got left."

"And that little barge business nets us about twelve or fifteen thousand a year."

"For the five years about sixty thousand more. Let's see—that's a total of say six hundred thousand dollars in five years."

"We will have to take up in that time," said Newmark, who seemed to have the statistics at his finger-tips, "the two payments on our timber, the note on the First National, the Commercial note, the remaining liabilities on the Boom Company—about three hundred thousand all told, counting the interest."

Orde crumpled the paper and threw it into the waste basket.

"Correct," said he. "Good enough. I ought to get along on a margin like that."

He went over to his own desk, where he again set to figuring on his pad. The results he eyed a little doubtfully. Each year he must pay in interest the sum of seven thousand five hundred dollars. Each year he would have to count on a proportionate saving of fifteen thousand dollars toward payment of the notes. In addition, he must live.

"The Orde family is going to be mighty hard up," said he, whistling humorously.

But Orde was by nature and training sanguine and fond of big risks.

"Never mind; it's for Bobby," said he to himself. "And maybe the rate of interest will go down. And I'll be able to borrow on the California tract if anything does go wrong."

He put on his hat, thrust a bundle of papers into his pocket, and stepped across the hall into Taylor's office.

The lawyer he found tipped back in his revolving chair, reading a printed brief.

"Frank," began Orde immediately, "I came to see you about that California timber matter."

Taylor laid down the brief and removed his eye-glasses, with which he began immediately to tap the fingers of his left hand.

"Sit down, Jack," said he. "I'm glad you came in. I was going to try to see you some time to-day. I've been thinking the matter over very carefully since the other day, and I've come to the conclusion that it is too steep for me. I don't doubt the investment a bit, but the returns are too far off. Fifteen thousand means a lot more to me than it does to you, and I've got to think of the immediate future. I hope you weren't counting on me——"

"Oh, that's all right," broke in Orde. "As I told you, I can swing the thing myself, and only mentioned it to you on the off chance you might want to invest. Now, what I want is this——" he proceeded to outline carefully the agreement between himself and Newmark while the lawyer took notes and occasionally interjected a question.

"All right," said the latter, when the details had been mastered. "I'll draw the necessary notes and papers."

"Now," went on Orde, producing the bundle of papers from his pocket, "here's the abstract of title. I wish you'd look it over. It's a long one, but not complicated, as near as I can make out. Trace seems to have acquired this tract mostly from the original homesteaders and the like, who, of course, take title direct from the government. But naturally there are a heap of them, and I want you to look it over to be sure everything's shipshape."

" All right," agreed Taylor, reaching for the papers.

" One other thing," concluded Orde, uncrossing his legs. " I want this investment to get no further than the office door. You see, this is for Bobby, and I've given a lot of thought to that sort of thing; and nothing spoils a man sooner than to imagine the thing's all cut and dried for him, and nothing keeps him going like the thought that he's got to rustle his own opportunities. You and I know that. Bobby's going to have the best education possible; he's going to learn to be a lumberman by practical experience, and that practical experience he'll get with other people. No working for his dad in Bobby's, I can tell you. When he gets through college, I'll get him a little job clerking with some good firm, and he'll have a chance to show what is in him and to learn the business from the ground up, the way a man ought to. Of course, I'll make arrangements that he has a real chance. Then, when he's worked into the harness a little, the old man will take him out and show him the fine big sugar pine and say to him, ' There, my boy, there's your opportunity, and you've earned it. How does *Orde & Son* sound to you?' What do you think of it, Frank?"

Taylor nodded several times.

" I believe you're on the right track, and I'll help you all I can," said he briefly.

" So, of course, I want to keep the thing dead secret," continued Orde. " You're the only man who knows anything about it. I'm not even going to buy directly under my own name. I'm going to incorporate myself," he said, with a grin. " You know how those things will get out, and how they always get back to the wrong people."

" Count on me," Taylor assured him.

As Orde walked home that evening, after a hot day, his mind was full of speculation as to the immediate future. He had a local reputation for wealth, and no one knew better than himself how important it is for a man in debt to keep up appearances. Nevertheless, decided retrenchment would be necessary. After Bobby had gone to bed, he explained this to his wife.

"What's the matter?" she asked quickly. "Is the firm losing money?"

"No," replied Orde, "it's a matter of reinvestment." He hesitated. "It's a dead secret, which I don't want to get out, but I'm thinking of buying some western timber for Bobby when he grows up."

Carroll laughed softly.

"You so relieve my mind," she smiled at him. "I was afraid you'd decided on the street-car-driver idea. Why, sweetheart, you know perfectly well we could go back to the little house next the church and be as happy as larks."

XXXII

IN the meantime Newmark had closed his desk, picked his hat from the nail, and marched precisely down the street to Heinzman's office. He found the little German in. Newmark demanded a private interview, and without preliminary plunged into the business that had brought him. He had long since taken Heinzman's measure, as, indeed, he had taken the measure of every other man with whom he did or was likely to do business.

"Heinzman," said he abruptly, "my partner wants to raise seventy-five thousand dollars for his personal use. I have agreed to get him that money from the firm."

Heinzman sat immovable, his round eyes blinking behind his big spectacles.

"Proceed," said he shrewdly.

"As security in case he cannot pay the notes the firm will have to give, he has signed an agreement to turn over to me his undivided one-half interest in our enterprises."

"Vell? You vant to borrow dot money of me?" asked Heinzman. "I could not raise it."

"I know that perfectly well," replied Newmark coolly. "You are going to have difficulty meeting your July notes, as it is."

Heinzman hardly seemed to breathe, but a flicker of red blazed in his eye.

"Proceed," he repeated non-committally, after a moment.

"I intend," went on Newmark, "to furnish this money myself. It must, however, seem to be loaned by another. I want you to lend this money on mortgage."

"What for?" asked Heinzman.

"For a one tenth of Orde's share in case he does not meet those notes."

"But he vill meet the notes," objected Heinzman. "You are a prosperous concern. I know somethings of *your* business, also."

"He thinks he will," rejoined Newmark grimly. "I will merely point out to you that his entire income is from the firm, and that from this income he must save twenty-odd thousand a year."

"If the firm has hard luck—" said Heinzman.

"Exactly," finished Newmark.

"Vy you come to me?" demanded Heinzman at length.

"Well, I'm offering you a chance to get even with Orde. I don't imagine you love him?"

"Vat's de matter mit my gettin' efen with you, too?" cried Heinzman. "Ain't you beat me out at Lansing?"

Newmark smiled coldly under his clipped moustache.

"I'm offering you the chance of making anywhere from thirty to fifty thousand dollars."

"Perhaps. And suppose this liddle scheme don't work out?"

"And," pursued Newmark calmly, "I'll carry you over in your present obligations." He suddenly hit the arm of his chair with his clenched fist. "Heinzman, if you don't make those July payments, what's to become of you? Where's your timber and your mills and your new house —and that pretty daughter of yours?"

Heinzman winced visibly.

"I vill get an extension of time," said he feebly.

"Will you?" countered Newmark.

The two men looked each other in the eye for a moment.

"Vell, maybe," laughed Heinzman uneasily. "It looks to me like a winner."

" All right, then," said Newmark briskly. " I'll make out
a mortgage at ten per cent for you, and you'll lend the
money on it. At the proper time, if things happen that way,
you will foreclose. That's all you have to do with it. Then,
when the timber land comes to you under the foreclose,
you will reconvey an undivided nine-tenths' interest—for
proper consideration, of course, and without recording the
deed."

Heinzman laughed with assumed lightness.

" Suppose I fool you," said he. " I guess I joost keep
it for mineself."

Newmark looked at him coldly.

" I wouldn't," he advised. " You may remember the
member from Lapeer County in that charter fight? And
the five hundred dollars for his vote? Try it on, and see
how much evidence I can bring up. It's called bribery in
this State, and means penitentiary usually."

" You don't take a joke," complained Heinzman.

Newmark arose.

" It's understood, then?" he asked.

" How so I know you play fair?" asked the German.

" You don't. It's a case where we have to depend more
or less on each other. But I don't see what you stand to
lose—and anyway you'll get carried over those July payments," Newmark reminded him.

Heinzman was plainly uneasy and slightly afraid of these
new waters in which he swam.

" If you reduce the firm's profits, he iss going to sus-
pect," he admonished.

" Who said anything about reducing the firm's profits?"
said Newmark impatiently. " If it does work out that way,
we'll win a big thing; if it does not, we'll lose nothing."

He nodded to Heinzman and left the office. His demeanour was as dry and precise as ever. No expression
illuminated his impassive countenance. If he felt the slight-

est uneasiness over having practically delivered his inten tions to the keeping of another, he did not show it. For one thing, an accomplice was absolutely essential. And, too, he held the German by his strongest passions—his avarice, his dread of bankruptcy, his pride, and his fear of the penitentiary. As he entered the office of his own firm, his eye fell on Orde's bulky form seated at the desk. He paused involuntarily, and a slight shiver shook his frame from head to foot—the dainty, instinctive repulsion of a cat for a large robustious dog. Instantly controlling himself, he stepped forward.

"I've made the loan," he announced.

Orde looked up with interest.

"The banks wouldn't touch northern peninsula," said Newmark steadily, "so I had to go to private individuals."

"So you said. Don't care who deals it out," laughed Orde.

"Thayer backed out, so finally I got the whole amount from Heinzman," Newmark announced.

"Didn't know the old Dutchman was that well off," said Orde, after a slight pause.

"Can't tell about those secretive old fellows," said Newmark.

Orde hesitated.

"I didn't know he was friendly enough to lend us money."

"Business is business," replied Newmark.

XXXIII

THERE exists the legend of an eastern despot who, wishing to rid himself of a courtier, armed the man and shut him in a dark room. The victim knew he was to fight something, but whence it was to come, when, or of what nature he was unable to guess. In the event, while groping tense for an enemy, he fell under the fatal fumes of noxious gases.

From the moment Orde completed the secret purchase of the California timber lands from Trace, he became an unwitting participant in one of the strangest duels known to business history. Newmark opposed to him all the subtleties, all the ruses and expedients to which his position lent itself. Orde, sublimely unconscious, deployed the magnificent resources of strength, energy, organisation, and combative spirit that animated his pioneer's soul. The occult manœuvrings of Newmark called out fresh exertions on the part of Orde.

Newmark worked under this disadvantage: he had carefully to avoid the slightest appearance of an attitude inimical to the firm's very best prosperity. A breath of suspicion would destroy his plans. If the smallest untoward incident should ever bring it clearly before Orde that Newmark might have an interest in reducing profits, he could not fail to tread out the logic of the latter's devious ways. For this reason Newmark could not as yet fight even in the twilight. He did not dare make bad sales, awkward transactions. In spite of his best efforts, he could not succeed, without the aid of chance, in striking a blow from which Orde could not recover. The profits of the first year were not quite up to the usual standard, but they sufficed. Newmark's finesse cut in two the firm's income of the second year. Orde roused himself. With his old-time energy of resource, he hurried the woods work until an especially big cut gave promise of recouping the losses of the year before. Newmark found himself struggling against a force greater than he had imagined it to be. Blinded and bound, it nevertheless made head against his policy. Newmark was forced to a temporary quiescence. He held himself watchful, intent, awaiting the opportunity which chance should bring.

Chance seemed by no means in haste. The end of the fourth year found Newmark puzzled. Orde had paid regularly the interest on his notes. How much he had been able to save toward the redemption of the notes themselves his partner was unable to decide. It depended entirely on how much the Ordes had disbursed in living expenses, whether or not Orde had any private debts, and whether or not he had private resources. In the meantime Newmark contented himself with tying up the firm's assets in such a manner as to render it impossible to raise money on its property when the time should come.

What Orde regarded as a series of petty annoyances had made the problem of paying for the California timber a matter of greater difficulty than he had supposed it would be. A pressure whose points of support he could not place was closing slowly on him. Against this pressure he exerted himself. It made him a trifle uneasy, but it did not worry him. The margin of safety was not as broad as he had reckoned, but it existed. And in any case, if worse came to worst, he could always mortgage the California timber for enough to make up the difference—and more. Against this expedient, however, he opposed a sentimental obstinacy. It was Bobby's, and he objected to encumbering it. In fact, Orde was capable of a prolonged and bitter struggle to avoid doing so. Nevertheless, it was there—an asset. A loan on its security would, with what he had set aside, more than pay the notes on the northern peninsula stumpage. Orde felt perfectly easy in his mind. He was in the position of many of our rich men's sons who, quite sincerely and earnestly, go penniless to the city to make their way. They live on their nine dollars a week, and go hungry when they lose their jobs. They stand on their own feet, and yet—in case of severe illness or actual starvation —the old man is there! It gives them a courage to be contented on nothing. So Orde would have gone to almost any lengths to keep free " Bobby's tract," but it stood always between himself and disaster. And a loan on western timber could be paid off just as easily as a loan on eastern timber, when you came right down to that. Even could he have known his partner's intentions, they would, on this account, have caused him no uneasiness, however angry they would have made him, or however determined to break the partnership. Even though Newmark destroyed utterly the firm's profits for the remaining year and a half the notes had to run, he could not thereby ruin Orde's chances. A loan on the California timber would solve all problems now. In this reasoning Orde would have committed the mistake of all large and generous temperaments when called upon to measure natures more subtle than their own. He would have underestimated both Newmark's resources and his own grasp of situations.*

---

* The author has considered it useless to burden the course of the narrative with a detailed account of Newmark's financial manœuvres. Realising, however, that a large class of his readers might be interested in the exact particulars, he herewith gives a sketch of the transactions.

It will be remembered that at the time—1878—Orde first came in need of money for the purpose of buying the California timber, the firm, Newmark & Orde, owned in the northern peninsula 300,000,000 feet of pine. On this they had paid $150,000, and owed still a like amount. They borrowed $75,000 on it, giving a note secured by mortgage due in 1883. Orde took

Affairs stood thus in the autumn before the year the notes would come due. The weather had been beautiful. A perpetual summer seemed to have embalmed the world in its forgetfulness of times and seasons. Navigation remained open through October and into November. No severe storms had as yet swept the lakes. The barge and her two tows had made one more trip than had been thought possible. It had been the intention to lay them up for the

this, giving in return his note secured by the Boom Company's stock. In 1879 and 1880 they made the two final payments on the timber; so that by the latter date they owned the land free of encumbrance save for the mortgage of $75,000. Since Newmark's plan had always contemplated the eventual foreclosure of this mortgage, it now became necessary further to encumber the property. Otherwise, since a property worth considerably above $300,000 carried only a $75,000 mortgage, it would be possible, when the latter came due, to borrow a further sum on a second mortgage with which to meet the obligations of the first. Therefore Newmark, in 1881, approached Orde with the request that the firm raise $70,000 by means of a second mortgage on the timber. This $70,000 he proposed to borrow personally, giving his note due in 1885 and putting up the same collateral as Orde had—that is to say, his stock in the Boom Company. To this Orde could hardly in reason oppose an objection, as it nearly duplicated his own transaction of 1878. Newmark therefore, through Heinzman, lent this sum to himself.

It may now be permitted to forecast events in the line of Newmark's reasoning.

If his plans should work out, this is what would happen: in 1883 the firm's note for $75,000 would come due. Orde would be unable to pay it. Therefore at once his stock in the Boom Company would become the property of Newmark & Orde. Newmark would profess himself unable to raise enough from the firm to pay the mortgage. The second mortgage from which he had drawn his personal loan would render it impossible for the firm to raise more money on the land. A foreclosure would follow. Through Heinzman, Newmark would buy in. As he had himself loaned the money to himself—again through Heinzman—on the second mortgage, the latter would occasion him no loss.

The net results of the whole transaction would be: first, that Newmark would have acquired personally the 300,000,000 feet of northern peninsula timber; and, second, that Orde's personal share in the stock company would now be held in partnership by the two. Thus, in order to gain so large a stake, it would pay Newmark to suffer considerable loss jointly with Orde in the induced misfortunes of the firm.

Incidentally it might be remarked that Newmark, of course, purposed paying his own note to the firm when it should fall due in 1885, thus saving for himself the Boom Company stock which he had put up as collateral.

winter, but the weather continued so mild that Orde suggested they be laden with a consignment for Jones &
Mabley, of Chicago.

"Did intend to ship by rail," said he. "They're all 'uppers,' so it would pay all right. But we can save all kinds
of money by water, and they ought to skip over there in
twelve to fifteen hours."

Accordingly, the three vessels were laid alongside the
wharves at the mill, and as fast as possible the selected
lumber was passed into their holds. Orde departed for the
woods to start the cutting as soon as the first belated snow
should fall.

This condition seemed, however, to delay. During each
night it grew cold. The leaves, after their blaze and riot
of colour, turned crisp and crackly and brown. Some of the
little, still puddles were filmed with what was almost, but
not quite ice. A sheen of frost whitened the house roofs
and silvered each separate blade of grass on the lawns.
But by noon the sun, rising red in the veil of smoke that
hung low in the snappy air, had mellowed the atmosphere
until it lay on the cheek like a caress. No breath of wind
stirred. Sounds came clearly from a distance. Long V-
shaped flights of geese swept athwart the sky, very high
up, but their honking came faintly to the ear. And yet,
when the sun, swollen to the great dimensions of the rising
moon, dipped blood-red through the haze, the first premonitory tingle of cold warned one that the grateful
warmth of the day had been but an illusion of a season
that had gone. This was not summer, but, in the quaint
old phrase, Indian summer, and its end would be as though
the necromancer had waved his wand.

To Newmark, sitting at his desk, reported Captain Floyd
of the steam barge *North Star*.

"All loaded by noon, sir," he said.

Newmark looked up in surprise.

" Well, why do you tell me? " he inquired.

" I want your orders."

" My orders? Why? "

" This is a bad time of year," explained Captain Floyd, " and the storm signal's up. All the signs are right for a blow."

Newmark whirled in his chair.

" A blow! " he cried. " What of it? You don't come in every time it blows, do you? "

" You don't know the lakes, sir, at this time of year," insisted Captain Floyd.

" Are you afraid? " sneered Newmark.

Captain Floyd's countenance burned a dark red.

" I only want your orders," was all he said. " I thought we might wait to see."

" Then go," snapped Newmark. " That lumber must get to the market. You heard Mr. Orde's orders to sail as soon as you were loaded."

Captain Floyd nodded curtly and went out without further comment.

Newmark arose and looked out of the window. The sun shone as balmily soft as ever. English sparrows twittered and fought outside. The warm smell of pine shingles rose from the street. Only close down to the horizon lurked cold, flat, greasy-looking clouds; and in the direction of the Government flag-pole he caught the flash of red from the lazily floating signal. He was little weatherwise, and he shook his head sceptically. Nevertheless it was a chance, and he took it, as he had taken a great many others.

XXXIV

TO Carroll's delight, Orde returned unexpectedly from the woods late that night. He was so busy these days that she welcomed any chance to see him. Much to his disappointment, Bobby had been taken duck-hunting by his old friend, Mr. Kincaid. Next morning, however, Orde told Carroll his stay would be short and that his day would be occupied.

"I'd take old Prince and get some air," he advised. "You're too much indoors. Get some friend and drive around. It's fine and blowy out, and you'll get some colour in your cheeks."

After breakfast Carroll accompanied her husband to the front door. When they opened it a blast of air rushed in, whirling some dead leaves with it.

"I guess the fine weather's over," said Orde, looking up at the sky.

A dull lead colour had succeeded the soft gray of the preceding balmy days. The heavens seemed to have settled down closer to the earth. A rising wind whistled through the branches of the big maple trees, snatching the remaining leaves in handfuls and tossing them into the air. The tops swayed like whips. Whirlwinds scurried among the piles of dead leaves on the lawns, scattering them, chasing them madly around and around in circles.

"B-r-r-r!" shivered Carroll. "Winter's coming."

She kept herself busy about the house all the morning; ate her lunch in solitude. Outside, the fierce wind, rising in a crescendo shriek, howled around the eaves. The day darkened, but no rain fell. At last Carroll resolved to take her husband's advice. She stopped for Mina Heinzman, and the two walked around to the stable, where the men harnessed old Prince into the phaeton.

They drove, the wind at their backs, across the drawbridge, past the ship-yards, and out beyond the mills to the Marsh Road. There, on either side the causeway, miles and miles of cat-tails and reeds bent and recovered under the snatches of the wind. Here and there showed glimpses of ponds or little inlets, the surface of the water ruffled and dark blue. Occasionally one of these bayous swung in across the road. Then the two girls could see plainly the fan-like cat's-paws skittering here and there as though panic-stricken by the swooping, invisible monster that pursued them.

Carroll and Mina Heinzman had a good time. They liked each other very much, and always saw a great deal to laugh at in the things about them and in the subjects about which they talked. When, however, they turned toward home, they were forced silent by the mighty power of the wind against them. The tears ran from their eyes as though they were crying; they had to lower their heads. Hardly could Carroll command vision clear enough to see the road along which she was driving. This was really unnecessary, for Prince was buffeted to a walk. Thus they crawled along until they reached the turn-bridge, where the right-angled change in direction gave them relief. The river was full of choppy waves, considerable in size. As they crossed, the *Sprite* darted beneath them, lowering her smokestack as she went under the bridge.

They entered Main Street, where was a great banging and clanging of swinging signs and a few loose shutters. All the sidewalk displays of vegetables and other goods had been taken in, and the doors, customarily wide open, were now shut fast. This alone lent to the street quite a deserted air, which was emphasised by the fact that actually not a rig of any sort stood at the curbs. Up the empty roadway whirled one after the other clouds of dust hurried by the wind.

"I wonder where all the farmers' wagons are?" marvelled the practical Mina. "Surely they would not stay home Saturday afternoon just for this wind!"

Opposite Randall's hardware store her curiosity quite mastered her.

"Do stop!" she urged Carroll. "I want to run in and see what's the matter."

She was gone but a moment, and returned, her eyes shining with excitement.

"Oh, Carroll!" she cried, "there are three vessels gone ashore off the piers. Everybody's gone to see."

"Jump in!" said Carroll. "We'll drive out. Perhaps they'll get out the life-saving crew."

They drove up the plank road over the sand-hill, through the beech woods, to the bluff above the shore. In the woods they were somewhat sheltered from the wind, although even there the crash of falling branches and the whirl of twigs and dead leaves advertised that the powers of the air were abroad; but when they topped the last rise, the unobstructed blast from the open Lake hit them square between the eyes.

Probably a hundred vehicles of all descriptions were hitched to trees just within the fringe of woods. Carroll, however, drove straight ahead until Prince stood at the top of the plank road that led down to the bath houses. Here she pulled up.

Carroll saw the lake, slate blue and angry, with white-capped billows to the limit of vision. Along the shore were rows and rows of breakers, leaping, breaking, and gathering again, until they were lost in a tumble of white foam that rushed and receded on the sands. These did not look to be very large until she noticed the twin piers reaching out from the river's mouth. Each billow, as it came in, rose sullenly above them, broke tempestuously to overwhelm the entire structure of their ends, and ripped inshore along their lengths, the crest submerging as it ran every foot of the massive structures. The piers and the light-houses at their ends looked like little toys, and the compact black crowd of people on the shore below were as small as Bobby's tin soldiers.

"Look there—out farther!" pointed Mina.

Carroll looked, and rose to her feet in excitement.

Three little toy ships—or so they seemed compared to the mountains of water—lay broadside-to, just inside the farthest line of breakers. Two were sailing schooners. These had been thrown on their beam ends, their masts pointing at an angle toward the beach. Each wave, as it reached, stirred them a trifle, then broke in a deluge of water that for a moment covered their hulls completely from sight. With a mighty suction the billow drained away, carrying with it wreckage. The third vessel was a steam barge. She, too, was broadside to the seas, but had caught in some hole in the bar so that she lay far down by the head. The shoreward side of her upper works had, for some freakish reason, given away first, so now the interior of her staterooms and saloons was exposed to view as in the cross-section of a model ship. Over her, too, the great waves hurled themselves, each carrying away its spoil. To Carroll it seemed fantastically as though the barge were made of sugar, and that each sea melted her precisely as Bobby loved to melt the lump in his chocolate by raising and lowering it in a spoon.

And the queer part of it all was that these waves, so mighty in their effects, appeared to the woman no different from those she had often watched in the light summer blows that for a few hours raise the "white caps" on the

lake. They came in from the open in the same swift yet
deliberate ranks; they gathered with the same leisurely
pauses; they broke with the same rush and roar. They
seemed no larger, but everything else had been struck
small—the tiny ships, the toy piers, the ant-like swarm of
people on the shore. She looked on it as a spectacle. It had
as yet no human significance.

" Poor fellows! " cried Mina.

" What? " asked Carroll.

" Don't you see them? " queried the other.

Carroll looked, and in the rigging of the schooner she
made out a number of black objects.

" Are those men?—up the masts? " she cried.

She set Prince in motion toward the beach.

At the foot of the bluff the plank road ran out into the
deep sand. Through this the phaeton made its way heavily.
The fine particles were blown in the air like a spray, ming-
ling with the spume from the lake, stinging Carroll's face
like so many needles. Already the beach was strewn with
pieces of wreckage, some of it cast high above the wash,
others still thrown up and sucked back by each wave,
others again rising and falling in the billows. This wreckage constituted a miscellaneous jumble, although most of it
was lumber from the deck-loads of the vessels. Inter-
mingled with the split and broken yellow boards were bits
of carving and of painted wood. Carroll saw one piece half
buried in the sand which bore in gilt two huge letters, A R.
A little farther, bent and twisted, projected the ornamental
spear which had pointed the way before the steamer's bow.
Portions of the usual miscellaneous freight cargo carried
on every voyage were scattered along the shore—boxes,
barrels, and crates. Five or six men had rolled a whisky
barrel beyond the reach of the water, had broached it, and
now were drinking in turn from a broken and dingy frag-
ment of a beer-schooner. They were very dirty; their hair

had fallen over their eyes, which were bloodshot; the expression of their faces was imbecile. As the phaeton passed, they hailed its occupants in thick voices, shouting against the wind maudlin invitations to drink.

The crowd gathered at the pier comprised fully half the population of Monrovia. It centred about the life saving crew, whose mortar was being loaded. A stove-in lifeboat mutely attested the failure of other efforts. The men worked busily, ramming home the powder sack, placing the projectile with the light line attached, attending that the reel ran freely. Their chief watched the seas and winds through his glasses. When the preparations were finished, he adjusted the mortar, and pulled the string. Carroll had seen this done in practice. Now, with the recollection of that experience in mind, she was astonished at the feeble report of the piece, and its freedom from the dense white clouds of smoke that should have enveloped it. The wind snatched both noise and vapour away almost as soon as they were born. The dart with its trailer of line rose on a long graceful curve. The reel sang. Every member of the crowd unconsciously leaned forward in attention. But the resistance of the wind and the line early made itself felt. Slower and slower hummed the reel. There came a time when the missile seemed to hesitate, then fairly to stand in equilibrium. Finally, in an increasingly abrupt curve, it descended into the sea. By a good three hundred yards the shot had failed to carry the line over the vessels.

"There's Mr. Bradford," said Carroll, waving her hand. "I wish he'd come and tell us something about it."

The banjo-playing village Brummell saw the signal and came, his face grave.

"Couldn't they get the lifeboats out to them?" asked Carroll as he approached.

"You see that one," said Bradford, pointing. "Well, the other's in kindling wood farther up the beach."

" Anybody drowned? " asked Mina quickly.

" No, we got 'em out. Mr. Carn's shoulder is broken."
He glanced down at himself comically, and the girls for
the first time noticed that beneath the heavy overcoat his
garments were dripping.

" But surely they'll never get a line over with the mortar! " said Carroll. " That last shot fell so far short! "

" They know it. They've shot a dozen times. Might as
well do something."

" I should think," said Mina, " that they'd shoot from
the end of the pier. They'd be ever so much nearer."

" Tried it," replied Bradford succintly. " Nearly lost the
whole business."

Nobody said anything for some time, but all looked
helplessly to where the vessels—from this elevation insig-
nificant among the tumbling waters—were pounding to
pieces.

At this moment from the river a trail of black smoke
became visible over the point of sand-hill that ran down to
the pier. A smokestack darted into view, slowed down, and
came to rest well inside the river-channel. There it rose and
fell regularly under the influence of the swell that swung
in from the lake. The crowd uttered a cheer, and streamed
in the direction of the smokestack.

" Come and see what's up," suggested Bradford.

He hitched Prince to a log sticking up at an angle from
the sand, and led the way to the pier.

There they had difficulty in getting close enough to
see ; but Bradford, preceding the two women, succeeded
by patience and diplomacy in forcing a way. The *Sprite* was
lying close under the pier, the top of her pilot-house just
about level with the feet of the people watching her. She
rose and fell with the restless waters. Fat rope-yarn
bumpers interposed between her sides and the piling. The
pilot-house was empty, but Harvey, the negro engineer,

leaned, elbows crossed against the sill of his little square door, smoking his pipe.

"I wouldn't go out there for a million dollars!" cried a man excitedly to Carroll and Bradford. "Nothing on earth could live in that sea! Nothing! I've run a tug myself in my time, and I know what I'm talking about!"

"What are they going to do?" asked Carroll.

"Haven't you heard!" cried the other, turning to her. "Where you been? This is one of Orde's tugs, and she's going to try to get a line to them vessels. But I wouldn't——"

Bradford did not wait for him to finish. He turned abruptly, and with an air of authority brushed toward the tug, followed closely by Carroll and Mina. At the edge of the pier was the tug's captain, Marsh, listening to earnest expostulation by a half-dozen of the leading men of the town, among whom were both Newmark and Orde.

As the three came within earshot Captain Marsh spit forth the stump of cigar he had been chewing.

"Gentlemen," said he crisply, "that isn't the question. I think I can do it; and I'm entirely willing to take all personal risks. The thing is hazardous and it's Mr. Orde's tug. It's for him to say whether he wants to risk her."

"Good Lord, man, what's the tug in a case like this!" cried Orde, who was standing near. Carroll looked at him proudly, but she did not attempt to make her presence known.

"I thought so," replied Captain Marsh. "So it's settled. I'll take her out, if I can get a crew. Harvey, step up here!"

The engineer slowly hoisted his long figure through the breast-high doorway, dragged his legs under him, and then with extraordinary agility swung to the pier, his teeth shining like ivory in his black face.

"Yas, suh!" said he.

" Harvey," said Captain Marsh briskly, " we're going to try to get a line aboard those vessels out there. It's dangerous. You don't have to go if you don't want to. Will you go? "

Harvey removed his cap and scratched his wool. The grin faded from his good-natured countenance.

" You-all goin', suh? " he asked.

" Of course."

" I reckon I'll done haif to go, too," said Harvey simply. Without further word he swung lightly back to the uneasy craft below him, and began to toss the slabs from the deck into the hold.

" I want a man with me at the wheel, two to handle the lines, and one to fire for Harvey," said Captain Marsh to the crowd in general.

" That's our job," announced the life-saving captain.

" Well, come on then. No use in delay," said Captain Marsh.

The four men from the life-saving service dropped aboard. The five then went over the tug from stem to stern, tossing aside all movables, and lashing tight all essentials. From the pilot-house Captain Marsh distributed life preservers. Harvey declined his.

" Whaf-for I want dat? " he inquired. " Lots of good he gwine do me down here! "

Then all hatches were battened down. Captain Marsh reached up to shake the hand which Orde, stooping, offered him.

" I'll try to bring her back all right, sir," said he.

" To hell with the tug! " cried Orde, impatient at this insistence on the mere property aspect. " Bring yourself back."

Captain Marsh deliberately lit another cigar and entered the pilot-house with the other men.

" Cast off! " he cried; and the silent crowd heard clearly

the single sharp bell ringing for attention, and then the "jangler" that called for full speed ahead. Awed, they watched the tiny sturdy craft move out into the stream and point to the fury of the open lake.

"Brave chaps! Brave chaps!" said Dr. McMullen to Carroll as they turned away. The physician drew his tall slender figure to its height. "Brave chaps, every one of them. But, do you know, to my mind, the bravest of them all are that nigger—and his fireman—nailed down in the hold where they can't see nor know what's going on, and if—if— " the good doctor blew his nose vigorously five or six times—"well, it's just like a rat in a hole." He shook his head vigorously and looked out to sea. "I read last evening, sir," said he to Bradford, "in a blasted fool medical journal I take, that the race is degenerating. Good God!"

The tug had rounded the end of the pier. The first of her thousand enemies, sweeping in from the open, had struck her fair. A great sheet of white water, slanting back and up, shot with terrific impact against the house and beyond. For an instant the little craft seemed buried; but almost immediately the gleam of her black hull showed her plunging forward dauntlessly.

"That's nothin'!" said the tug captain who had first spoken. "Wait 'til she gets outside!" The watchers streamed down from the pier for a better view. Carroll and Miss Heinzman followed. They saw the staunch little craft drive into three big seas, each of which appeared to bury her completely, save for her upper works. She managed, however, to keep her headway.

"She can stand that, all right," said one of the life-saving crew who had been watching her critically. "The trouble will come when she drops down to the vessels."

In spite of the heavy smashing of head-on seas the *Sprite* held her course straight out.

"Where's she going, anyway?" marvelled little Mr. Smith, the stationer. "She's away beyond the wrecks already."

"Probably Marsh has found the seas heavier than he thought and is afraid to turn her broadside," guessed his companion.

"Afraid, hell!" snorted a riverman who overheard.

Nevertheless the *Sprite* was now so distant that the loom of the great seas on the horizon swallowed her from view, save when she rose on the crest of some mighty billow.

"Well, what is he doing 'way out there then?" challenged Mr. Smith's friend with some asperity.

"Do'no," replied the riverman, "but whatever it is, it's all right as long as Buck Marsh is at the wheel."

"There, she's turned now," Mr. Smith interposed.

Beneath the trail of black smoke she had shifted direction. And then with startling swiftness the *Sprite* darted out of the horizon into full view. For the first time the spectators realised the size and weight of the seas. Not even the sullen pounding to pieces of the vessels on the bar had so impressed them as the sight of the tug coasting with railroad speed down the rush of a comber like a child's toy-boat in the surf. One moment the whole of her deck was visible as she was borne with the wave; the next her bow alone showed high as the back suction caught her and dragged her from the crest into the hollow. A sea rose behind. Nothing of the tug was to be seen. It seemed that no power or skill could prevent her feeling overwhelmed. Yet somehow always she staggered out of the gulf until she caught the force of the billow and was again cast forward like a chip.

"Maybe they ain't catchin' p'ticular hell at that wheel to hold her from yawing!" muttered the tug captain to his neighbour, who happened to be Mr. Duncan, the minister.

Almost before Carroll had time to see that the little craft

was coming in, she had arrived at the outer line of breakers. Here the combers, dragged by the bar underneath, crested, curled over, and fell with a roar, just as in milder weather the surf breaks on the beach. When the *Sprite* rushed at this outer line of white-water, a woman in the crowd screamed.

But at the edge of destruction the *Sprite* came to a shuddering stop. Her powerful propellers had been set to the reverse. They could not hold her against the forward fling of the water, but what she lost thus she regained on the seaward slopes of the waves and in their hollows. Thus she hovered on the edge of the breakers, awaiting her chance.

As long as the seas rolled in steadily, and nothing broke, she was safe. But if one of the waves should happen to crest and break, as many of them did, the weight of water catching the tug on her flat, broad stern deck would indubitably bury her. The situation was awful in its extreme simplicity. Would Captain Marsh see his opportunity before the law of chances would bring along the wave that would overwhelm him?

A realisation of the crisis came to the crowd on the beach. At once the terrible strain of suspense tugged at their souls. Each conducted himself according to his nature. The hardy men of the river and the woods set their teeth until the cheek muscles turned white, and blasphemed softly and steadily. Two or three of the townsmen walked up and down the space of a dozen feet. One, the woman who had screamed, prayed aloud in short hysterical sentences:

" O God! Save them, O Lord! O Lord! "

Orde stood on top of a half-buried log, his hat in his hand, his entire being concentrated on the manœuvre being executed. Only Newmark apparently remained as calm as ever, leaning against an upright timber, his arms folded, and an unlighted cigar as usual between his lips.

Methodically every few moments he removed his eye-glasses and wiped the lenses free of spray.

Suddenly, without warning, occurred one of those inexplicable lulls that interpose often amid the wildest uproars. For the briefest instant other sounds than the roar of the wind and surf were permitted the multitude on the beach. They heard the grinding of timbers from the stricken ships, and the draining away of waters. And distinctly they heard the faint, far tinkle of the jangler calling again for " full speed ahead."

Between two waves the *Sprite* darted forward directly for the nearest of the wrecks. Straight as an arrow's flight she held until from the crowd went up a groan.

" She'll collide ! " some one put it into words.

But at the latest moment the tug swerved, raced past, and turned on a long diagonal across the end of the bar toward the piers.

Captain Marsh had chosen his moment with exactitude. To the utmost he had taken advantage of the brief lull of jumbled seas after the " three largest waves " had swept by. Yet in shallow water and with the strong inshore set, even that lull was all too short. The *Sprite* was staggered by the buffets of the smaller breakers ; her speed was checked, her stern was dragged around. For an instant it seemed that the back suction would hold her in its grip. She tore herself from the grasp of the current. Enveloped in a blinding hail of spray she struggled desperately to extricate herself from the maelstrom in which she was involved before the resumption of the larger seas should roll her over and over to destruction.

Already these larger seas were racing in from the open. To Carroll, watching breathless and wide-eyed in that strange passive and receptive state peculiar to imaginative natures, they seemed alive. And the *Sprite,* too, appeared to be, not a fabric and a mechanism controlled by men, but a sentient creature struggling gallantly on her own volition.

Far out in the lake against the tumbling horizon she saw heave up for a second the shoulder of a mighty wave. And instinctively she perceived this wave as a deadly enemy of the little tug, and saw it bending all its great energies to hurrying in on time to catch the victim before it could escape. To this wave she gave all her attention, watching for it after it had sunk momentarily below its fellows, recognising it instantly as it rose again. The spasms of dismay and relief among the crowd about her she did not share at all. The crises they indicated did not exist for her. Until the wave came in, Carroll knew, the *Sprite,* no matter how battered and tossed, would be safe. Her whole being was concentrated in a continually shifting calculation of the respective distances between the tug and the piers, the tug and the relentlessly advancing wave.

" Oh, go! " she exhorted the *Sprite* under her breath.

Then the crowd, too, caught with its slower perceptions the import of the wave. Carroll felt the electric thrill of apprehension shiver through it. Huge and towering, green and flecked with foam the wave came on now calmly and deliberately as though sure. The *Sprite* was off the end of the pier when the wave lifted her, just in the position her enemy would have selected to crush her life out against the cribs. Slowly the tug rose against its shoulder, was lifted onward, poised; and then with a swift forward thrust the wave broke, smothering the pier and lighthouse beneath tons of water.

A low, agonised wail broke from the crowd. And then— and then—over beyond the pier down which the wave, broken and spent but formidable still, was ripping its way, they saw gliding a battered black stack from which still poured defiantly clouds of gray smoke.

For ten seconds the spectators could not believe their

eyes. They had distinctly seen the *Sprite* caught between a resistless wall of water and the pier; where she should have been crushed like the proverbial egg-shell. Yet there she was—or her ghost.

Then a great cheer rose up against the wind. The crowd went crazy. Mere acquaintances hugged each other and danced around and around through the heavy sands. Several women had hysterics. The riverman next to Mr. Duncan opened his mouth and swore so picturesquely that, as he afterward told his chum, " I must 've been plumb inspired for the occasion." Yet it never entered Mr. Duncan's ministerial head to reprove the blasphemy. Orde jumped down from his half-buried log and clapped his hat on his head. Newmark did not alter his attitude nor his expression.

The *Sprite* was safe. For the few moments before she glided the length of the long pier to stiller water this fact sufficed.

" I wonder if she got the line aboard," speculated the tug-boat captain at last.

The crowd surged over to the piers again. Below them rose and fell the *Sprite*. All the fancy scroll-work of her upper works, the cornice of her deck house, the light rigging of her cabin had disappeared, leaving raw and splintered wood to mark their attachments. The tall smokestack was bent awry, but its supports had held, which was fortunate since otherwise the fires would have been drowned out. At the moment, Captain Marsh was bending over examining a bad break in the overhang—the only material damage the tug had sustained.

At sight of him the crowd set up a yell. He paid no attention. One of the life-saving men tossed a mooring line ashore. It was seized by a dozen men. Then for the first time somebody noticed that although the tug had come to a standstill, her screw was still turning slowly over and over, holding her against the erratic strong jerking of a slender rope that ran through her stern chocks and into the water.

"He got it aboard!" yelled the man, pointing.

Another cheer broke out. The life-saving crew leaped to the deck. They were immediately followed by a crowd of enthusiasts eager to congratulate and question. But Captain Marsh would have none of them.

"Get off my tug!" he shouted. "Do you want to swamp her? What do you suppose we put that line aboard for? Fun? Get busy and use it! Rescue that crew now!"

Abashed, the enthusiasts scrambled back. The life-saving crew took charge. It was necessary to pass the line around the end of the pier and back to the beach. This was a dangerous job, and one requiring considerable power and ingenuity, for the strain on the line imposed by the waters was terrific; and the breaking seas rendered work on the piers extremely hazardous. However, the life-saving captain took charge confidently enough. His crew began to struggle out the pier, while volunteers, under his personal direction, manipulated the reel.

A number of the curious lingered about the *Sprite*. Marsh and Orde were in consultation over the smashed stern, and did not look as though they cared to be disturbed. Harvey leaned out his little square door.

"Don' know nuffin 'bout it," said he, "'ceptin' she done rolled 'way over 'bout foh times. Yass she did, suh! I know. I felt her doin' it.

"No," he answered a query. "I wasn't what you-all would call scairt, that is, not really *scairt*—jess a little ne'vous. All I had to do was to feed her slabs and listen foh my bell. You see, Cap'n Ma'sh, he was in cha'ge."

"No, sir," Captain Marsh was saying emphatically to his employer. "I can't figure it out except on one thing. You see it's stove from *underneath*. A sea would have smashed it from above."

" Perhaps you grounded in between seas out there," suggested Orde.

Marsh smiled grimly.

" I reckon I'd have known it," said he. " No, sir! It sounds wild, but it's the only possible guess. That last sea must 've lifted us bodily right over the corner of the pier."

" Well—maybe," assented Orde doubtfully.

" Sure thing," repeated Marsh with conviction.

" Well, you'd better not tell 'em so unless you want to rank in with Old Man Ananias," ended Orde. " It was a good job. Pretty dusty out there, wasn't it? "

" Pretty dusty," grinned Marsh.

They turned away together and were at once pounced on by Leopold Lincoln Bunn, the local reporter, a callow youth aflame with the chance for a big story of more than local interest.

" Oh, Captain Marsh! " he cried. " How did you get around the pier? It looked as though the wave had you caught."

Orde glanced at his companion in curiosity.

" On roller skates," replied Marsh.

Leopold tittered nervously.

" Could you tell me how you felt when you were out there in the worst of it? " he inquired.

" Oh, hell! " said Marsh grumpily, stalking away.

" Don't interview for a cent, does he? " grinned Orde.

" Oh, Mr. Orde! Perhaps you—— "

" Don't you think we'd better lend a hand below? " suggested Orde, pointing to the beach.

The wild and picturesque work of rescue was under way. The line had been successfully brought to the left of the lighthouse. To it had been attached the rope, and to that the heavy cable. These the crew of the schooner had dragged out and made fast to a mast. The shore end passed over a tall scissors. When the cable was tightened the breeches

buoy was put into commission, and before long the first
member of the crew was hauled ashore, plunging in and out
of the waves as the rope tightened or slackened. He was a
flaxen-haired Norwegian, who stamped his feet, shook his
body and grinned comically at those about him. He accepted
with equanimity a dozen drinks of whisky thrust at him
from all sides, swigged a mug of the coffee a few practical
women were making over an open fire, and opposed to
Leopold Lincoln Bunn's frantic efforts a stolid and baffling
density. Of none of these attentions did he seem to stand
in especial need.

The crew and its volunteers worked quickly. When the
last man had come ashore, the captain of the life-saving
service entered the breeches buoy and caused himself to be
hauled through the smother to the wreck. After an interval,
a signal jerked back. The buoy was pulled in empty and
the surf car substituted. In it were piled various utensils of
equipment. One man went with it, and several more on its
next trip, until nearly the whole crew were aboard the
wreck.

Carroll and Mina stayed until dusk and after, watching
the long heavy labour of rescue. Lines had to be rocketed
from the schooner to the other vessels. Then by their means
cable communication had to be established with the shore.
After this it was really a matter of routine to run the crew
to the beach, though cruel, hard work, and dangerous. The
wrecks were continually swept by the great seas; and at any
moment the tortured fabrics might give way, might dis-
solve completely in the elements that so battered them. The
women making the hot coffee found their services becoming
valuable. Big fires of driftwood were ignited. They were
useful for light as well as warmth.

By their illumination finally Orde discovered the two
girls standing, and paused long enough in his own heavy
labour of assistance to draw Carroll one side.

"You'd better go home now, sweetheart," said he. "Bobby'll be waiting for you, and the girls may be here in the crowd somewhere. There'll be nobody to take care of him."

"I suppose so," she assented. "But hasn't it been exciting? Whose vessels were they; do you know?"

Orde glanced at her strangely.

"They were ours," said he.

She looked up at him, catching quickly the wrinkles of his brow and the harassed anxiety in his eyes. Impulsively she pulled him down to her and kissed him.

"Never mind, dear," said she. "I care only if you do."

She patted his great shoulders lightly and smiled up at him.

"Run, help!" she cried. "And come home as soon as you can. I'll have something nice and hot all ready for you."

She turned away, the smile still on her lips; but as soon as she was out of sight, her face fell grave.

"Come, Mina!" she said to the younger girl. "Time to go."

They toiled through the heavy sand to where, hours ago, they had left Prince. That faithful animal dozed in his tracks and awoke reluctantly.

Carroll looked back. The fires leaped red and yellow. Against them were the silhouettes of people, and in the farther circle of their illumination were more people cast in bronze that flickered red. In contrast to their glow the night was very dark. Only from the lake there disengaged a faint gray light where the waters broke. The strength of the failing wind still lifted the finer particles of sand. The organ of the pounding surf filled the night with the grandeur of its music.

XXXV

ORDE mounted the office stairs next day with a very heavy step. The loss of the *North Star* and of the two schooners meant a great deal to him at that time.

"It kicks us into somewhat of a hole," he grumbled to Newmark.

"A loss is never pleasant," replied the latter, "and it puts us out of the carrying business for awhile. But we're insured."

"I can't understand why Floyd started," said Orde. "He ought to know better than to face sure prospects of a fall blow. I'll tan his soul for that, all right!"

"I'm afraid I'm partly responsible for his going," put in Newmark.

"You!" cried Orde.

"Yes. You see that Smith & Mabley shipment was important enough to strain a point for—and it's only twenty-four hours or so—and it certainly didn't look to see me as if it were going to blow very soon. Poor Floyd feels bad enough. He's about sick."

Orde for the first time began to appreciate the pressure of his circumstances. The loss on the cargo of "uppers" reached about 8,000,000 feet; which represented $20,000 in money. As for the *North Star* and her consorts, save for the insurance, they were simply eliminated. They had represented property. Now they were gone. The loss of $60,000 or so on them, however, did not mean a diminution of the company's present cash resources to that amount; and so did not immediately affect Orde's calculations as to the payment of the notes which were now soon to come due.

At this time the woods work increasingly demanded his attention. He disappeared for a week, his organising abilities claimed for the distribution of the road crews. When he returned to the office, Newmark, with an air of small triumph, showed him contracts for the construction of three new vessels.

"I get them for $55,000," said he, "with $30,000 of it on long time."

"Without consulting me!" cried Orde.

Newmark explained carefully that the action, seemingly so abrupt, had really been taking advantage of a lucky opportunity.

"Otherwise," he finished, "we shouldn't have been able to get the job done for another year, at least. If that big Cronin contract goes through—well, you know what that would mean in the shipyards—nobody would get even a look-in. And McLeod is willing, in the meantime, to give us a price to keep his men busy. So you see I had to close at once. You can see what a short chance it was."

"It's a good chance, all right," admitted Orde; "but—why—that is, I thought perhaps we'd job our own freighting for awhile—it never occurred to me we'd build any more vessels until we'd recovered a little."

"Recovered," Newmark repeated coldly. "I don't see what 'recovered' has to do with it. If the mill burned down, we'd rebuild, wouldn't we? Even if we were embarrassed—which we're not—we'd hardly care to acknowledge publicly that we couldn't keep up our equipment. And as we're making twelve or fifteen thousand a year out of our freighting, it seems to me too good a business to let slip into other hands."

"I suppose so," agreed Orde, a trifle helplessly.

"Therefore I had to act without you," Newmark finished. " I knew you'd agree. That's right: isn't it? " he insisted.

" Yes, that's right," agreed Orde drearily.

" You'll find copies of the contract on your desk," Newmark closed the matter. " And there's the tax lists. I wish you'd run them over."

" Joe," replied Orde, " I—I don't think I'll stay down town this morning. I——"

Newmark glanced up keenly.

" You don't look a bit well," said he ; " kind of pale around the gills. Bilious. Don't believe that camp grub quite agrees with you for a steady diet."

" Yes, that must be it," assented Orde.

He closed his desk and went out. Newmark turned back to his papers. His face was expressionless. From an inner pocket he produced a cigar which he thrust between his teeth. The corners of his mouth slowly curved in a grim smile.

Orde did not go home. Instead, he walked down Main Street to the docks where he jumped into a rowboat lying in a slip, and with a few rapid strokes shot out on the stream. In his younger days he had belonged to a boat club, and had rowed in the " four." He still loved the oar, and though his racing days were past, he maintained a clean-lined, rather unstable little craft which it was his delight to propel rapidly with long spoon-oars whenever he needed exercise. To-day, however, he was content to drift.

The morning was still and golden. The crispness of late fall had infused a wine into the air. The sky was a soft, blue-gray ; the sand-hills were a dazzling yellow. Orde did not try to think ; he merely faced the situation, staring it in the face until it should shrink to its true significance.

One thing he felt distinctly ; yet could not without a struggle bring himself to see. The California lands must be mortgaged. If he could raise a reasonable sum of money on them, he would still be perfectly able to meet his notes. He hated fiercely to raise that money.

It was entirely a matter of sentiment. Orde realised the fact clearly, and browbeat his other self with a savage contempt. Nevertheless his dream had been to keep the western timber free and unencumbered—for Bobby. Dreams are harder to give up than realities.

He fell into the deepest reflections which were broken only when the pounding of surf warned him he had drifted almost to the open lake. After all, there was no essential difference between owing money to a man in Michigan and to a man in California. That was the net result of his struggle.

"When the time comes, we'll just borrow that money on a long-time mortgage, like sensible people," he said aloud, "and quit this everlasting scrabbling."

Back to town he pulled with long vigorous strokes, skittering his feathered spoon-oars lightly over the tops of the wavelets. At the slip he made fast the boat, and a few minutes later reëntered the office, his step springy, his face glowing. Newmark glanced up.

"Hullo!" said he. "Back again? You look better."

"Exercise," said Orde, in his hearty manner. "Exercise, old boy! You ought to try it. Greatest thing in the world. Just took a row to the end of the piers and back, and I'm as fit as a fiddle!"

XXXVI

ORDE immediately set into motion the machinery of banking to borrow on the California timber. Taylor took charge of this, as the only man in Monrovia who had Orde's confidence. At the end of a necessary delay Orde received notice that the West had been heard from. He stepped across the hall to the lawyer's office.

"Well, Frank," said he, "glad we managed to push it through with so little trouble."

Taylor arose, shut carefully the door into his outer office, walked to the window, looked contemplatively out upon the hotel backyard, and returned to his desk.

"But there is trouble," said he curtly.

"What's the matter?" asked Orde.

"The banks refuse the loan."

Orde stared at him in blank astonishment.

"Refuse!" he echoed.

"Absolutely."

"What grounds can they possibly have for that?"

"I can't make out exactly from these advices. It's something about the title."

"But I thought you went over the title."

"I did," stated Taylor emphatically; "and I'll stake my reputation as a lawyer that everything is straight and clear from the Land Office itself. I've wired for an explanation; and we ought surely to know something definite by tomorrow."

With this uncertainty Orde was forced to be content. For the first time in his business career a real anxiety gnawed at his vitals. He had been in many tight places; but somehow heretofore success or failure had seemed to him about immaterial, like points gained or conceded in the game; a fresh start was always so easy, and what had been already won as yet unreal. Now the game itself was at issue. Property, reputation, and the family's future were at stake. When the three had lived in the tiny house by the church, it had seemed that no adversity could touch them. But now that long use had accustomed them to larger quarters, servants, luxuries, Orde could not conceive the possibility of Carroll's ever returning to that simplest existence. Carroll could have told him otherwise; but of course he did not as yet bring the possibility before her. She had economised closely, these last few years. Orde was proud of her. He was also fiercely resentful that his own foolishness, or untoward circumstances, or a combination of both should jeopardise her future. Therefore he awaited further news with the greatest impatience.

The message came the following day, as Taylor had predicted. Taylor handed it to him without comment.

"Land Office under investigation," Orde read. "Fraudulent entries suspected. All titles clouded until decision is reached."

"What do you suppose that means?" asked Orde, although he knew well enough.

Taylor glanced up at his dull eyes with commiseration.

"They simply won't lend good money on an uncertainty," said he.

"Frank," said Orde, rousing himself with an effort, "I've got to be here. I couldn't get away this winter if my life depended on it. And I won't even have time to pay much attention to it from here. I want you to go to California and look after those interests for me. Never mind your practice, man," as Taylor tried to interrupt him. "Make what arrangements you please; but go. It'll be like a sort of vacation to you. You need one. And I'll make it worth your while. Take Clara with you. She'll like California. Now don't say no. It's important. Straighten it out as quick as you can: and the minute it *is* straight borrow that money on it, and send it on p. d. q."

Taylor thoughtfully tapped his palm with the edge of his eye-glasses.

"All right," he said at last.

"Good!" cried Orde, rising and holding out his hand.

He descended the dark stairs to the street, where he turned down toward the river. There he sat on a pile for nearly an hour, quite oblivious to the keen wind of latter November which swept up over the scum ice from the Lake. At length he hopped down and made his way to the office of the Welton Lumber Co.

"Look here, Welton," he demanded abruptly when he had reached that operator's private office, "how much of a cut are you going to make this year?"

"About twenty million," replied Welton. "Why?"

"Just figuring on the drive," said Orde, nodding a farewell.

He had the team harnessed, and, assuming his buffalo-fur coat, drove to the offices of all the men owning timber up and down the river. When he had collected his statistics, he returned to his desk, where he filled the backs of several envelopes with his characteristically minute figures. At the close of his calculations he nodded his head vigorously several times.

"Joe," he called across to his partner, "I'm going to cut that whole forty million we have left."

Newmark did not turn. After a moment his dry expressionless voice came back.

"I thought that we figured that as a two-years' job."

Quite Oblivious to the Keen Wind

" We did, but I'm going to clean up the whole thing this year."

" Do you think you can do it?"

" Sure thing," replied Orde. Then under his breath, and quite to himself, he added: " I've got to!"

XXXVII

THE duel had now come to grapples. Orde was fighting for his very life. The notes given by Newmark & Orde would come due by the beginning of the following summer. Before that time Orde must be able to meet them personally, or, as by the agreement with Newmark, his stock in the Boom Company would be turned in to the firm. This would, of course, spell nearly a total loss of it, as far as Orde was concerned.

The chief anxiety under which the riverman laboured, however, was the imminent prospect of losing under the mortgage all the Northern Peninsula timber. He had thought that the firm would be able to step in for its redemption, even if he personally found himself unable to meet the obligation. Three hundred million feet would seem to be too important a matter to let go under so small a mortgage. Now as the time approached, he realised that if he could not pay the notes, the firm would certainly be unable to do so. What with the second mortgage, due two years later, and to be met by Newmark; with the outstanding obligations; with the new enterprise of the vessels ordered from Duncan McLeod, Newmark & Orde would be unable to raise anything like the necessary amount. To his personal anxieties Orde added a deep and bitter self-reproach at having involved his partner in what amounted to a total loss.

Spurred doubly by these considerations, then, he fell upon the woods work with unparalleled ferocity. A cut and sale of the forty million feet remaining of the firm's up-river holdings, together with the tolls to be collected for driving the river that spring would, if everything went right and no change in the situation took place, bring Orde through the venture almost literally by "the skin of his teeth." To cut forty million feet, even in these latter days of improvements then unknown, would be a task to strain to the utmost every resource of energy, pluck, equipment and organisation. In 1880-81 the operators on the river laughed good-humouredly over an evident madness.

Nevertheless Orde accomplished the task. To be sure he was largely helped by a favourable winter. The cold weather came early and continued late. Freezing preceded the snow, which was deep enough for good travoying and to assure abundant freshet water in the spring, but not too deep to interfere with the work. Orde increased his woods force; and, contrary to his custom, he drove them mercilessly. He was that winter his own walking-boss, and lived constantly in the woods. The Rough Red had charge of the banking, where his aggressive, brutal personality kept the rollways free from congestion. For congestion there means delay in unloading the sleighs; and that in turn means a drag in the woods work near the skidways at the other end of the line. Tom North and Tim Nolan and Johnny Sims and Jim Denning were foremen back in the forest. Every one had an idea, more or less vague, that the Old Fellow had his back to the wall. Late into the night the rude torches, made quite simply from brown stone jugs full of oil and with wicks in their necks, cast their flickering glare over the ice of the haul-roads. And though generally in that part of Michigan the thaws begin by the first or second week in March, this year zero weather continued even to the eighth of April. When the drive started, far up toward headwaters, the cut was banked for miles along the stream, forty million feet of it to the last timber.

The strain over, Orde slept the clock around and awoke to the further but familiar task of driving the river. He was very tired; but his spirit was at peace. As always after the event, he looked back on his anxieties with a faint amusement over their futility.

From Taylor he had several communications. The lawyer confessed himself baffled as to the purpose and basis of the Land Office investigation. The whole affair appeared to be tangled in a maze of technicalities and a snarl of red-tape which it would take some time to unravel. In the meantime Taylor was enjoying himself; and was almost extravagant in his delight over the climate and attractions of Southern California.

Orde did not much care for this delay. He saw his way clear to meeting his obligations without the necessity of hypothecating the California timber; and was the better pleased for it. With the break-up of spring he started confidently with the largest drive in the history of the river, a matter of over two hundred million feet.

This tremendous mass of timber moved practically in three sections. The first, and smallest, comprised probably thirty millions. It started from the lowermost rollways on the river, drove rapidly through the more unobstructed reaches, and was early pocketed above Monrovia in the Company's distributing booms. The second and largest section of a hundred million came from the main river and its largest tributaries. It too made a safe drive; and was brought to rest in the main booms and in a series of temporary or emergency booms built along the right bank and upstream from the main works. The third section containing a remainder of about seventy million had by the twenty-sixth of June reached the slack water above the city of Redding.

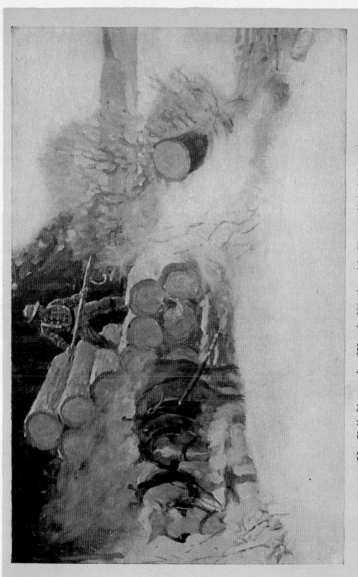

He Fell Upon the Woods Work with Unparalleled Ferocity

XXXVIII

THE morning of June twenty-sixth dawned clear.
Orde was early on the road before the heat of the
day. He drove his buckboard rapidly over the
twelve miles that separated his home from the distributing
booms, for he wanted at once to avoid the heat of the first
sun and to arrive at the commencement of the day's work.
After a glance at the river, he entered the tiny office and set
about the examination of the tally sheets left by the foreman.
While he was engaged in this checking, the foreman, Tom
North, entered.

"The river's rising a little," he remarked conversationally
as he reached for the second set of tally boards.

"You're crazy," muttered Orde, without looking up. "It's
clear as a bell; and there have been no rains reported from
anywhere."

"It's rising a little, just the same," insisted North, going
out.

An hour later Orde, having finished his clerical work,
walked out over the booms. The water certainly had risen;
and considerably at that. A decided current sucked through
the interstices in the piling. The penned logs moved uneasily.

"I should think it was rising!" said Orde to himself, as
he watched the slowly moving water. "I wonder what's up.
It can't be merely those rains three days ago."

He called one of the younger boys to him, Jimmy Powers
by name.

"Here, Jimmy," said he, "mark one of these piles and
keep track of how fast the water rises."

For some time the river remained stationary, then resumed its slow increase. Orde shook his head.

" I don't like June floods," he told Tom North. " A fellow can understand an ordinary spring freshet, and knows about how far it will go; but these summer floods are so confounded mysterious. I can't figure out what's struck the old stream, unless they're having almighty heavy rains up near headwaters."

By three o'clock in the afternoon Jimmy Powers reported a rise since morning of six inches. The current had proportionately increased in power.

" Tom," said Orde to the old riverman, " I'm going to send Marsh down for the pile-drivers and some cable. The barge company has some fifteen inch manilla."

North laughed.

" What in blazes do you expect to do with that? " he inquired.

" We may need them," Orde stated with conviction. " Everything's safe enough now; and probably will continue so; but I can't afford to take chances. If those logs ever break through they'll go on out to Lake Michigan and there they wouldn't be worth the salvage."

Tom North stared at his principal in surprise.

" That's a mighty long chance," he commented. " Never knew you to come so near croaking before, Jack."

" If this drive goes out, it surely busts me," replied Orde, " and I'm not taking even long chances."

Captain Marsh, returning with the *Sprite,* brought an evening paper and news from the telegraph offices. A cloudburst in the China Creek district followed by continued heavy rains was responsible for the increased water. The papers mentioned this only incidentally, and in explanation. Their columns were filled with an account of the big log jam that had formed above the iron railroad bridge. The planing mill's booms had given way under pressure and the contents had piled down stream against the buttresses. Before steps could be taken to clear the way, the head of the drive, hurried by the excess water, had piled in on top. Immediately a jam formed, increasing in weight each moment, until practically the entire third section had piled up back of the bridge.

The papers occupied themselves with the picturesque side of the affair. None expressed any anxiety as to the bridge. It was a new structure, each of whose bents weighed over a hundred tons. A fall of a few inches only would suffice to lock the jam solidly, thus relieving whatever pressure the mass exerted against the iron bridge. That the water would shortly go down was of course inevitable at this time of year. It would be a big jam for the rivermen to break, however.

"Do you think you'll go up there?" asked North.

Orde shook his head.

"They're in a nice pickle," he acknowledged; "but Nolan's in charge and will do his best. I think we may have troubles of our own right here at home."

He slept that night at the booms. The water, contrary to all expectation, rose steadily. By morning it had crept so far up the piles that there began to be danger that it would overflow their tops. In that case, of course, the logs in the booms would also run out.

"Guess it's time we did a little work," remarked Orde.

He set a crew of men to raising the height of the piling by tying logs firmly to the bolted timbers atop. This would take care of an extra two feet of water; a two feet beyond all previous records. Another crew stretched the fifteen inch manilla cables across the field of logs in order to segregate them into several units of mass, and so prevent them from piling up at the down-stream end of the enclosure. The pile-driver began to drop its hammer at spots of weakness. In spite of the accelerated current and the increased volume of the river, everything was soon shipshape and safe.

"We're all right now," said Orde. "The only thing I'm a little uneasy about is those confounded temporary booms upstream. Still they're all right unless they get to piling up. Then we'll have to see what we can do to hold them. I think as soon as the driver is through down at the sorting end, she'd better drive a few clumps of piles to strengthen the swing when it is shut. Then if the logs pile down on us from above, we can hold them there."

About two hours later the pile-driver moved up. The swing was opened; and the men began to drive clumps of piles in such a position as to strengthen the swing when the latter should be shut. It was a slow job. Each pile had to be taken from the raft at the stern of the scow, erected in the "carrier," and pounded into place by the heavy hammer raised and let drop in the derrick at the bow.

Long before the task was finished, the logs in the temporary booms had begun to slide atop one another, to cross and tangle, until at last the river bed inside the booms was filled with a jam of formidable dimensions. From beneath it the water boiled in eddies. Orde, looking at it, roused himself to sudden activity.

"Get a move on," he advised Captain Aspinwall of the driver. "If that jam breaks on us, we want to be ready; and if it don't break before you get this swing strengthened, maybe we can hold her where she is. There's no earthly doubt that those boom piles will never stand up when they get the full pressure of the freshet."

He departed up river on a tour of inspection from which he returned almost immediately.

"Hurry up! Hurry up!" he cried. "She can't last much longer!"

Indeed even to the men on the pile-driver, evidences of the pressure sustained by the slender boom piles were not wanting. Above the steady gurgle of the water and the intermittent puffing and other noises of the work, they could hear a creaking and groaning of timbers full of portent to those who could read the signs.

The driver's crew laboured desperately, hoisting the piles into the carriage, tripping the heavy hammer, sending it aloft again, binding feverishly the clumps of piles together by means of cables. Each man worked with an eye over his shoulder, fearful of the power that menaced him.

Two of the clumps had been placed and bound; a third was nearly finished, when suddenly, with a crack and a roar the upper booms gave way, projecting their logs upon the opening and the driver.

The half dozen members of the crew, caught utterly unaware in spite of the half warning they had been receiving for an hour past, were scattered by the winds of a panic. Two or three flung themselves on their faces; several ran from one end of the scow to the other; one leaped into the river! Imminent destruction seemed upon them.

Tom North, at the winch that operated the arm of the swing, however, retained his presence of mind. At the first sag outward of the boom piles he set in operation the machinery that closed the gate. Clumsy and slow as was his mechanism, he nevertheless succeeded in getting the long arm started. The logs, rushing in back of it, hurried it shut. Immediately they jammed again, and heaped up in a formidable tangle behind the barrier. Tom North, his little black pipe between his teeth, stood calm, the lever of his winch in his hand. A short three feet from the spot on which he stood, the first saw log of the many that might have overwhelmed him thrust forward its ugly head. The wash of the water lifted the huge pile-driver bodily and deposited it with a crash half on the bank and half in the water.

Instantly after the first break Orde had commenced running out over the booms from the shore.

"Good boy, Tom!" he shot at North as he passed.

Across the breast of the jam he hurried, and to the other bank where the pile-driver lay. The crew had recovered from their panic, and were ashore gazing curiously underneath the scow. Captain Aspinwall examined the supports of the derrick on deck.

"That was lucky," said Orde briefly to Aspinwall. "How's the damage? Stove you in?"

"I—I don't think so," replied the captain, turning a rather perturbed face to Orde.

"That's good. I'll send over the tug to help get her afloat. We've got our work cut out for us now. As soon as you're afloat, blow your whistle and I'll come over to tell you what to do."

"You don't expect me to work my driver under the face of that jam!" cried the captain.

"Certainly," snapped Orde, wheeling.

"Not me!" said Aspinwall positively. "I know when I've got enough!"

"What's the matter?" asked Orde.

"It isn't safe," replied the captain; "and I don't intend to risk my men or my driver."

Orde stood for a moment stock-still; then with a snort of anger he leaped to the deck, seized the man by the neck and thrust him bodily over the side to the bank.

"Safe, you white-livered skunk!" he roared. "Safe! Go over in the middle of that ten-acre lot and lie down on your face and see if you feel safe there! Get out; the whole pack of you! I'm in charge here now."

Captain Aspinwall picked himself up, his face red with anger.

"Get off my driver," he snarled. "Put that man off."

Orde seized a short heavy bar.

"This driver is requisitioned," said he. "Get out! I haven't time to fool with you. I've got to save my logs."

They hesitated; and while they did so Tom North and some others of the crew came running across the jam.

" Get a cable to the winch," Orde shouted at these as soon as they were within hearing. " And get Marsh up here with the *Sprite*. We've got to get afloat."

He paid no more attention to the ejected crew. The latter, overawed by the rivermen, who now gathered in full force, took the part of spectators.

A few minutes' hard work put the driver afloat. Fortunately its raft of piles had not become detached in the upheaval.

" Tom," said Orde briskly to North, " you know the pile-driver business. Pick out your crew, and take charge."

In ten seconds of time the situation had changed from one of comparative safety to one of extreme gravity. The logs, broken loose from the upper temporary booms, now jammed against the swing and against the other logs already filling the main booms. Already the pressure was beginning to tell, as the water banked up behind the mass. The fifteen-inch cables tightened slowly but mightily; some of the piles began to groan and rub one against the other; here and there a log deliberately up-ended above the level.

Orde took charge of the situation in its entirety, as a general might. He set North immediately to driving clumps each of sixteen piles, bound to solidity by chains, and so arranged in angles and slants as to direct the enormous pressure toward either bank, thus splitting the enemy's power. The small driver owned by the Boom Company drove similar clumps here, there and everywhere that need arose or weakness developed. Seventy-five men opposed, to the weight of twenty million tons of logs and a river of water, the expedients invented by determination and desperation.

As in a virulent disease, the symptoms developed rapidly when once the course of the malady was assured. After the first rush, when the upper booms broke, nothing spectacular occurred. Steadily and relentlessly the logs, packed close together down to the very bed of the stream, pressed outward against the frail defences. Orde soon found himself forced from the consideration of definite plans of campaign. He gave over formal defences, and threw his energies to saving the weak places which rapidly developed. By the most tremendous exertions he seemed but just able to keep even. So closely balanced was the equilibrium between the improvisation of defence and the increase of pressure behind the jam that it seemed as if even a moment's breathing spell would bring the deluge. Piles quivered, bent slowly outward—immediately, before the logs behind them could stir, the pile-driver must do its work. Back and forth darted the *Sprite* and her sister-tug the *Spray* towing the pile-drivers or the strings of piles. Under the frowning destruction that a breath might loosen, the crews had to do their work. And if ever that breath should come, there would be no chance for escape. Crushed and buried, the men and their craft alike would be borne with the breaking jam to an unknown grave in the Lake. Every man knew it.

Darkness came. No one stopped for food. By the light of lanterns the struggle went on, doubly terrifying in the mystery of night. By day the men, practised in such matters, could at least judge of the probabilities of a break. At night they had to work blindly, uncertain at what moment the forces they could not see would cut loose to overwhelm them.

Morning found no change in the situation. The water rose steadily; the logs grew more and more restive; the defences weaker and more inadequate. Orde brought out steaming pails of coffee which the men gulped down between moments. No one thought of quitting. They were afire with the flame of combat, and were set obstinately on winning even in the face of odds. About ten o'clock they were reinforced by men from the mills downstream. The owners of those mills had no mind to lose their logs. Another pile-driver was also sent up from the Government work. Without this assistance the jam must surely have gone out. Spectators marvelled how it held as it did. The mass seemed constantly to quiver on the edge of motion. Here and there over the surface of the jam single logs could be seen popping suddenly into the air, propelled as an apple seed is projected from between a boy's thumb and forefinger. Some of the fifteen-inch cables stretched to the shore parted. One, which passed once around an oak tree before reaching its shore anchorage, actually buried itself out of sight in the hard wood. Bunches of piles bent, twisted, or were cut off as though they had been but shocks of Indian corn. The current had become so swift that the tugs could not hold the drivers against it; and as a consequence, before commencing operations, special mooring piles had to be driven. Each minute threatened to bring an end to the jam, yet it held; and without rest the dogged little insects under its face toiled to gain an inch on the waters.

XXXIX

ALL that day and the next night the fight was hand to hand, without the opportunity of a breathing space. Then Orde, bareheaded and dishevelled, strung to a high excitement, but cool as a veteran under fire, began to be harassed by annoyances. The piles provided for the drivers gave out. Newmark left, ostensibly to purchase more. He did not return. Tom North and Jim Denning, their eyes burning deep in their heads for lack of sleep, came to Orde holding to him symbolically their empty hands.

" No more piles," they said briefly.

" Get 'em," said Orde with equal brevity. " Newmark will have enough here shortly. In the meantime, get them."

North and his friend disappeared, taking with them the crews of the drivers and the two tugs. After an interval they returned towing small rafts of the long timbers. Orde did not make any inquiries; nor until days later did he see a copy of the newspaper telling how a lawless gang of rivermen had driven away the railroad men and stolen the railroad's property. These piles lasted five or six hours. Tom North placed and drove them accurately and deliberately, quite unmindful of the constant danger. A cold fire seemed to consume the man, inflaming his courage and his dogged obstinacy. Once a wing of the jam broke suddenly just as his crew had placed a pile in the carrier. The scow was picked up, whirled around, carried bodily a hundred feet, and deposited finally with a crash. The instant the craft steadied and even before any one could tell whether or no the danger was past, Tom cut loose the hammer and drove that pile!

"I put you in that carrier to be *drove!*" he shouted viciously, "and drove you'll be, if we *are* goin' to hell!"

When the *Spray* shouldered the scow back to position that one pile was left standing upright in the channel, a monument to the blind determination of the man.

Fortunately the wing break carried with it but a few logs; but it sufficed to show, if demonstration were needed, what would happen if any more serious break should occur.

Orde was everywhere. Long since he had lost his hat; and over his forehead and into his eyes the strands of his hair whipped tousled and unkempt. Miles and miles he travelled; running along the tops of the booms, over the surface of the jam, spying the weakening places, and hurrying to them a rescue. He seemed tireless, omnipresent, alive to every need. It was as though his personality alone held in correlation these struggling forces; as though were he to relax for an instant his effort they would burst forth with the explosion of long-pent energies.

Toward noon the piles gave out again.

"Where in *hell* is Newmark!" exploded Orde, and immediately was himself again, controlled and resourceful. He sent North and a crew of men to cut piles from standing timber in farm wood lots near the river.

"Haul them out with your winch," said he. "If the owners object, stand them off with your peavies. Get them anyway."

About three of the afternoon the *Lucy Belle* splattered up stream from the village, carrying an excursion to see the jam. Captain Simpson brought her as close in as possible. The waves raised by her awkward paddle-wheel and her clumsy lines surged among the logs and piles. Orde looked on this with distrust.

"Go tell him to pull out of that," he instructed Jimmy Powers. "The confounded old fool ought to know better than that. Tell him it's dangerous. If the jam goes out, it'll carry him to Kingdom Come."

Jimmy Powers returned red-faced from his interview.

" He told me to go to hell," he said shortly.

" Oh, he did," snapped Orde. " I should think we had enough without that old idiot! "

With the short nervous leaps of a suppressed anger he ran down to where the *Sprite* had just towed the Number One driver into a new position.

"Lay me alongside the *Lucy Belle*," he told Marsh.

But Simpson, in a position of importance at last, was disinclined to listen. He had worn his blue clothes and brass buttons for a good many years in charge only of boxes and barrels. Now at a stroke he found himself commander over tenscore people. Likewise, at fifty cents a head, he foresaw a good thing as long as high water should last. He had risen nobly to the occasion; for he had even hoisted his bunting and brought with him the local brass band. Orde, brusque in his desire to hurry through an affair of minor importance, rubbed the man the wrong way.

" I reckon I've some rights on this river," Captain Simpson concluded the argument, " and I ain't agoin' to be bull-dozed out of them."

The excursionists, typical " trippers " from Redding, Holland, Monrovia and Muskegon, cheered this sentiment and jeered at Orde.

Orde nodded briefly.

" Marsh," said he to his captain in a low voice, " get a crew and take them in charge. Run 'em off."

As soon as the tug touched the piling, he was off and away, paying no further attention to a matter already settled. Captain Marsh called a dozen rivermen to him; laid the *Sprite* alongside the *Lucy Belle,* and in spite of Simpson's scandalised protests and an incipient panic among the passengers, thrust aside the regular crew of the steamship and took charge. Quite calmly he surveyed the scene. From the height of the steamer's bridge he could see abroad over the country. A warm June sun flooded the landscape which was filled with the peace of early summer. The river seemed to flow smoothly and quietly enough, in spite of the swiftness of its current and the swollen volume of its waters. Only up stream where the big jam shrugged and groaned did any element jar on the peace of the scene; and even that, in contrast to the rest of the landscape, afforded small hint to the inexperienced eye of the imminence of a mighty destruction.

Captain Marsh paid little attention to all this. His eye swept rapidly up and down where the banks used to be until he saw a cross current deeper than the rest sweeping in athwart the inundated fields. He swung over the wheel and rang to the engine-room for half speed ahead. Slowly the *Lucy Belle* answered. Quite calmly Captain Marsh rammed her through the opening and out over the cornfields. The *Lucy Belle* was a typical river steamboat, built light in the draught in order to slide over the numerous shifting bars to be encountered in her customary business. When Captain Marsh saw that he had hit the opening, he rang for full speed, and rammed the poor old *Lucy Belle* hard aground in about a foot of water through which a few mournful dried cornstalks were showing their heads. Then, his hands in his pockets, he sauntered out of the pilot-house to the deck.

"Now if you want to picnic," he told the astonished and frightened excursionists, "go to it!"

With entire indifference to the water, he vaulted over the low rail and splashed away. The rivermen and the engineer who had accompanied him lingered only long enough to start up the band.

"Now you're safe as a cow tied to a brick wall," said the Rough Red, whose appearance alone had gone far toward overawing the passengers. " Be joyful. Start up the music. Start her up, I tell you! "

The band hastily began to squawk, very much out of time, and somewhat out of tune.

" That's right," grinned the Rough Red savagely, " keep her up. If you quit before I get back to work, I'll come back and take you apart."

They waded through the shallow water in the cornfield. After them wafted the rather disorganised strains of *Whoa, Emma.* Captain Simpson was indulging in what resembled heat apoplexy. After a time the *Lucy Belle's* crew recovered their scattered wits sufficiently to transport the passengers in small boats to a point near the county road, whence all trudged to town. The *Lucy Belle* grew in the cornfield until several weeks later, when time was found to pull her off on rollers.

Arrived at the booms Captain Marsh shook the loose water from his legs.

" All right, sir," he reported to Orde. " I ran 'em ashore yonder."

Orde looked up, brushing the hair from his eyes. He glanced in the direction of the cornfield, and a quick grin flickered across the absorbed expression of his face.

" I should think you did," said he briefly. " I guess that'll end the excursion business. Now take Number Two up below the swing; and then run down and see if you can discover Tom. He went somewhere after piles about an hour ago."

Down river the various mill owners were busy with what men they had left in stringing defences across the river in case Orde's works should go out. When Orde heard this he swore vigourously.

" Crazy fools," he spat out. " They'd be a lot better off helping here. If this goes out, their little booms won't amount to a whiff of wind."

He sent word to that effect; but, lacking the enforcement of his personal presence his messages did not carry conviction, and the panic-stricken owners continued to labour, each according to his ideas, on what Orde's clearer vision saw to be a series of almost comical futilities. However, Welton answered the summons. Orde hailed his coming with a shout.

"I want a dredge," he yelled, as soon as the lumberman was within distance. "I believe we can relieve the pressure somewhat by a channel into Stearn's bayou. Get that Government dredge up and through the bayou as soon as you can."

"All right," said Welton briefly. "Can you hold her?"

"I've got to hold her," replied Orde between his clenched teeth. "Have you seen Newmark? Where in *hell* is Newmark? I need him for fifty things, and he's disappeared off the face of the earth! Purdy! that second cable! She's snapped a strand! Get a reinforcing line on her!" He ran in the direction of the new danger without another thought of Welton.

By the late afternoon casual spectators from the countryside had gathered in some number. The bolder or more curious of these added a further touch of anxiety to the situation by clambering out over the jam for a better view. Orde issued instructions that these should keep off the logs; but in spite of that, with the impertinent perseverance of the sight-seer, many persisted from time to time, when the rivermen were too busily engaged to attend to them, in venturing out where they were not only in danger but also in the way. Tom North would have none of this on his pile-driver. If a man was not actually working, he had no business on Number One.

"But," protested a spectator mildly, "I *own* this driver. I haven't any objections to your grabbing her in this emergency, even if you did manhandle my captain; but surely you are not going to keep me off my own property?"

"I don't give a tinker's damn who you are," replied North sturdily. "If you're not working, you get off."

And get off he did.

The broad deck of the pile-driver scow was a tempting point from which to survey the work, and the ugly jam, and the water boiling angrily, and the hollow-eyed, dishevelled maniacs who worked doggedly with set teeth as though they had not already gone without two nights' sleep. North had often to order ashore intruders, until his temper shortened to the vanishing point. One big hulking countryman attempted to argue the point. North promptly knocked him overboard into the shallow water between the driver and the bank. He did not rise; so North fished for him in the most matter-of-fact way with a boat hook, threw him on the bank unconscious, and went on driving piles! The incident raised a laugh among the men.

But flesh and blood has its limit of endurance; and that limit was almost reached. Orde heard the first premonitions of reaction in the mild grumblings that arose. He knew these men well from his long experience with them. Although the need for struggle against the tireless dynamics of the river was as insistent as ever; although it seemed certain that a moment's cessation of effort would permit the enemy an irretrievable gain, he called a halt on the whole work.

"Boys," said he, irrelevantly, "let's have a smoke."

He set the example by throwing himself full length against a slanting pile and most leisurely filling his pipe. The men stared a moment; then followed his example. A great peace of evening filled the sky. The horizon lay low and black against the afterglow. Beneath it the river shone like silver. Only the groaning, the heave and shrugging of the jam, and the low threatening gurgle of hurrying waters reminded the toil-weary men of the enemy's continued activity. Over beyond the rise of land that lay between the river and Stearn's Bayou could be seen the cloud of mingled smoke and steam that marked the activities of the dredge. For ten minutes they rested in the solace of tobacco. Orde was apparently more at ease than any of the rest, but each instant he expected to hear the premonitory *crack* that would sound the end of everything. Finally he yawned, knocked the ashes from his pipe, and got to his feet.

"Now," said he, a new ring in his voice, "come on and let's get something *done!*"

They responded to a man.

XL

BY midnight the water seemed to have gone down slightly. Half the crew snatched a little sleep. For several hours more the issue hung aggravatingly in equilibrium. Then, with the opening of the channel into Stearn's Bayou the heaviest pressure was relieved. For the moment the acute danger point was passed.

Orde spent the next two days in strengthening the defences. The men were able to take their quota of meals and of sleep. Merely the working hours were longer than usual. Orde himself slept little, and was still possessed by a feverish activity. The flood continued at about the same volume. Until the water should subside, the danger could not be considered completely over with.

In these few days of comparative leisure Orde had time to look about him and to receive news. The jam had been successfully held at the iron railroad bridge above Redding; but only by the most strenuous efforts. Braces of oak beams had been slanted where they would do the most good; chains strengthened the weaker spots; and on top of all ton after ton of railroad iron held the whole immovably. Nolan had enjoyed the advantage of a "floating" jam; of convenient facilities incident to a large city; and of an aroused public sentiment that proffered him all the help he could use. Monrovia, little village that it was, had not grasped the situation. Redding saw it clearly. The loss of the timber alone —representing some millions of dollars' worth of the sawed product—would mean failure of mill companies, of banks holding their paper, and so of firms in other lines of business; and besides would throw thousands of men out of employment. Furthermore, what was quite as serious, should the iron bridge give way, the wooden bridges below could hardly fail to go out. Railroad communication between eastern and western Michigan would be entirely cut off. For a season industry of every description would be practically paralysed. Therefore Nolan had all the help he required. Every device known was employed to strengthen the jam. For only a few hours was the result in doubt. Then as the *Clarion* jubilantly expressed it, " It's a hundred dollars to an old hat she holds! "

Orde received all this with satisfaction, but with a slight scepticism.

" It's a floating jam; and it gets a push from underneath," he pointed out. " It's probably safe; but another flood might send it out."

" The floods are going down," said North.

" Good Lord; I hope so! " said Orde.

Newmark sent word that a sudden fit of sickness had confined him to the house.

" Didn't think of a little thing like piles," said Orde to himself. " Well, that's hardly fair. Joe couldn't have realised when he left here just how bad things were."

For two days, as has been said, nothing happened. Then Orde decided to break out a channel through the jam itself. This was a necessary preliminary to getting the logs in shape for distribution. An opening was made in the piles, and the rivermen, with pike-pole and peavy, began cautiously to dig their way through the tangled timbers. The Government pile-driver, which had finally been sent up from below, began placing five extra booms at intervals down stream to capture the drift as fast as it was turned loose. From the mills and private booms crews came to assist in the labour. The troubles appeared to be quite over, when word came from Redding that the waters were again rising. Ten minutes later Leopold Lincoln Bunn, the local reporter, came flapping in on Randall's old white horse, like a second Paul Revere, crying that the iron bridge had gone, and the logs were racing down river toward the booms.

"It just went out!" he answered the eager exclamations of the men who crowded around him. "That's all I know. It went out! And the other bridges! Sure! All but the Lake Shore! Don't know why that didn't go out. No; the logs didn't jam there; just slid right under!"

"That settles it," said Welton, turning away.

"You aren't going to quit!" cried Orde.

"Certainly. You're crazy!" said Welton with some asperity. "If they can't stop a little jam with iron, what are your wooden defences going to amount to against the whole accumulation? When those logs hit the tail of this jam, she'll go out before you can wink."

He refused to listen to argument.

"It's sure death," said he, "and I'm not going to sacrifice my men for nothing, even if they'd stay."

Other owners among the bystanders said the same thing. An air of profound discouragement had fallen on them all. The strain of the fight was now telling. The utmost that human flesh and blood was capable of had been accomplished; a hard-won victory had been gained by the narrowest of narrow margins. In this new struggle the old odds were still against them, and in addition the strength that had pushed aside Redding's best effort, augmented by the momentum of a powerful current. It was small wonder they gave up.

Already the news was spreading among the workers on the jams. As man shouted to man, each shouldered his peavy and came running ashore, eager question on his lips. Orde saw the Government driver below casting loose from her moorings. A moment later her tug towed her away to some side bayou of safety out of the expected rush to the Lake.

"But we can hold her!" cried Orde in desperation. "Have a little nerve with you. You aren't going to quit like that!"

He swept them with his eye; then turned away from them with a gesture of despair. They watched him gravely and silently.

"It's no use, boy," said old Carlin; "it's sure death."

"Sure death!" Orde laughed bitterly. "All right; sure death, then. Isn't there a man in this crowd that will tackle this sort of sure death with me?"

"I'm with you." "And me," said North and the Rough Red in a breath.

"Good!" cried Orde. "You, too, Johnny Sims? and Purdy? and Jimmy Powers? Bully boys!"

"I reckon you'll need the tug," said Marsh.

A dozen more of Orde's personal following volunteered. At once his good humour returned; and his easy leisurely confidence in himself.

"We've got to close that opening, first thing," said he. "Marsh, tow the pile-driver up there."

He caused a heavy line to be run from a tree, situated around the bend down stream, to the stern of the driver.

"Now if you have to," he told North, who had charge, "let go all holds, and the line will probably swing you around out of danger. We on the tug will get out as best we can."

The opening was to be closed by piles driven in groups of sixteen bound together by chains. The clumps were connected one to the other by a system of boom logs and ropes to interpose a continuous barrier. The pile-driver placed the clumps; while the tug attended to the connecting defences.

"Now, boys," said Orde as his last word, "if she starts to go, save yourselves the best way you can. Never mind the driver. *Stay on top!*"

Slowly the tug and her consort nosed up through the boiling water.

"She's rising already," said Orde to Marsh, watching the water around the piles.

"Yes, and that jam's going out before many minutes," supplemented the tugboat captain grimly.

Both these statements were only too true. Although not fifteen minutes before, the jam had lain locked in perfect safety, now the slight rise of the waters had lifted and loosened the mass until it rose fairly on the quiver.

"Work fast!" Orde called to the men on the pile-driver. "If we can close the opening before those Redding logs hit us, we may be able to turn them into our new channel."

He did not add that if the opening were not closed before the jam broke, as break it would in a very few moments, the probabilities were that both pile-driver and tug would be destroyed. Every man knew that already.

Tom North ordered a pile placed in the carriage; the hammer descended. At once, like battering rams logs began to shoot up from the depths of the river end foremost all about them. These timbers were projected with tremendous force, leaping sometimes half their length above the surface of the water. If any of them had hit either the tug or the pile-driver squarely, it would have stove and sunk the craft. Fortunately this did not happen; but Marsh hastily towed the scow back to a better position. The pile had evidently been driven into the foot of the jam itself, thus loosening timbers lying at the bottom of the river.

The work went forward as rapidly as possible. Four times the jam shrugged and settled; but four times it paused on the brink of discharge. Three of the clumps had been placed and bound; and fifteen piles of the last clump had been driven.

"One more pile!" breathed Orde, his breath quickening a trifle as he glanced up stream.

The hammer in the high derrick ran smoothly to the top, paused, and fell. A half dozen times more it ripped. Then without delay the heavy chains were thrown around the winch, and the steam power began to draw the clumps together.

" Done ! " cried Tom North, straightening his back.

" And a job in time, too," said Johnny Sims, indicating the creaking and tottering jam.

North unmoored, and the driver dropped back with the current and around the bend where she was snubbed by the safety line already mentioned.

Immediately the tug churned forward to accomplish the last duty, that of binding the defences together by means of chains and cables. Two men leaped to the floating booms and moved her fore and aft. Orde and the Rough Red set about the task. Methodically they worked from either end toward the middle. When they met finally, Orde directed his assistant to get aboard the tug.

" I'll tie this one, Jimmy," said he.

Aboard the tug all was tense preparation. Marsh grasped alertly the spokes of the wheel. In the engine-room Harvey, his hand on the throttle, stood ready to throw her wide open at the signal. Armed with sharp axes two men prepared to cut the mooring lines on a sign from the Rough Red. They watched his upraised hand. When it should descend, their axes must fall.

" Look out," the Rough Red warned Orde, who was methodically tying the last cumbersome knot, " she's getting ready ! "

Orde folded the knot over without reply. Up stream the jam creaked, groaned, settled deliberately forward, cutting a clump of piles like straw.

" She's coming ! " cried the Rough Red.

" Give me every second you can," said Orde, without looking up. He was just making the last turns.

The mass toppled slowly, fell into the swift current, and leaped with a roar. The Rough Red watched with cat-like attention.

" Jump ! " he cried at last, and his right arm descended.

With the shout and the motion several things happened simultaneously. Orde leaped blindly for the rail, where he was seized and dragged aboard by the Rough Red; the axes fell, Marsh whirled over the wheel, Harvey threw open his throttle. The tug sprang from its leash like a hound. And behind the barrier the logs, tossing and tumbling, the white spray flying before their onslaught, beat in vain against the barrier, like raging wild beasts whose prey has escaped.

" Close call," said Orde briefly.

" Bet you," replied Marsh.

Neither referred to the tug's escape; but to the fortunate closing of the opening.

XLI

ORDE now took steps to deflect into the channel recently dredged to Stearn's Bayou the mass of the logs racing down stream from Redding. He estimated that he had still two hours or so in which to do the work. In this time he succeeded by the severest efforts in establishing a rough shunt into the new channel. The logs would come down running free. Only the shock of their impact against the tail of the jam already formed was to be feared. Orde hoped to be able to turn the bulk of them aside.

This at first he succeeded in doing; and very successfully as affecting the pressure on the jam below. The first logs came scattering. Then in a little while the surface of the river was covered with them; they shouldered each other aside in their eagerness to outstrip the rushing water; finally they crowded down more slowly, hardly able to make their way against the choking of the river banks, but putting forth in the very effort to proceed a tremendous power. To the crew working in the channel dredged through to Stearn's Bayou the affair was that of driving a rather narrow and swift stream, only exaggerated. By quick and skilful work they succeeded in keeping the logs in motion. A large proportion of the timbers found their way into the bayou. Those that continued on down the river could hardly have much effect on the jam.

The work was breathless in its speed. From one to another sweat-bathed, panting man the logs were handed on. As yet only the advance of the big jam had arrived at the dredged channel.

Orde looked about him and realised this.

"We can't keep this up when the main body hits us," he panted to his neighbour, Jim Denning. "We'll have to do some more pile-driver work."

He made a rapid excursion to the boom camp, whence he returned with thirty or forty of the men who had given up work on the jam below.

"Here, boys," said he, "you can at least keep these logs moving in this channel for a couple of hours. This isn't dangerous."

He spoke quite without sarcastic intent; but the rivermen, already over their first panic, looked at each other a trifle shamefacedly.

"I'll tie into her wherever you say," said one big fellow. "If you fellows are going back to the jam, I'm with you."

Two or three more volunteered. The remainder said nothing, but in silence took charge of the dredged channel.

Orde and his men now returned to the jam where, on the pile-driver, the tugs, and the booms, they set methodically to strengthening the defences as well as they were able.

"She's holding strong and dandy," said Orde to Tom North, examining critically the clumps of piles. "That channel helps a lot in more ways than one. It takes an awful lot of water out of the river. As long as those fellows keep the logs moving, I really believe we're all right."

But shortly the water began to rise again, this time fairly by leaps. In immediate response the jam increased its pressure. For the hundredth time the frail wooden defences opposed to millions of pounds were tested to the very extreme of their endurance. The clumps of piles sagged outward; the network of chains and cables tightened and tightened again, drawing ever nearer the snapping point. Suddenly, almost without warning, the situation had become desperate.

And for the first time Orde completely lost his poise and became fluently profane. He shook his fist against the mena-

cing logs; he apostrophised the river, the high water, the
jam, the deserters, Newmark and his illness, ending finally
in a general anathema against any and all streams, logs, and
floods. Then he stormed away to see if anything had gone
wrong at the dredged channel.

"Well," said Tom North, "they've got the old man real
good and mad this time."

The crew went on driving piles, stringing cables, binding
chains, although, now that the inspiration of Orde's combative spirit was withdrawn the labours seemed useless,
futile, a mere filling in of the time before the supreme moment when they would be called upon to pay the sacrifice
their persistence and loyalty had proffered for the altar of
self-respect and the invincibility of the human soul.

At the dredged channel Orde saw the rivermen standing
idle, and, half-blind with anger; he burst upon them de-
manding by this, that and the other what they meant. Then
he stopped short and stared.

Square across the dredged channel and completely block-
ing it lay a single span of an iron bridge. Although twisted
and misshapen, it was still intact, the framework of its
overhead truss-work retaining its cage-like shape. Behind
it the logs had of course piled up in a jam, which, sinking
rapidly to the bed of the channel, had dammed back the
water.

"Where in hell did that drop from?" cried Orde.

"Come down on top the jam," explained a riverman.
"Must have come way from Redding. We just couldn't
scare her out of here."

Orde, suddenly fallen into a cold rage, stared at the obstruction, both fists clenched at his side.

"Too bad, boy," said Welton at his elbow. "But don't
take it too hard. You've done more than any of the rest
of us could. And we're all losers together."

Orde looked at him strangely.

" That about settles it," repeated Welton.

" Settle!" cried Orde. " I should think not."

Welton smiled quaintly.

" Don't you know when you're licked?"

" Licked, hell!" said Orde. " We've just begun to fight."

" What can you do?"

" Get that bridge span out of there, of course."

" How?"

" Can't we blow her up with powder?"

" Ever try to blow up iron?"

" There must be some way."

" Oh, there is," replied Welton. " Of course—take her apart bolt by bolt and nut by nut."

" Send for the wrenches, then," snapped Orde.

" But it would take two or three days, even working night and day."

" What of it?"

" But it would be too late—it would do no good——"

" Perhaps not," interrupted Orde; " but it will be doing something, anyway. Look here, Welton, are you game? If you'll get that bridge out in two days I'll hold the jam."

" You can't hold that jam two hours, let alone two days," said Welton decidedly.

" That's my business. You're wasting time. Will you send for lanterns and wrenches and keep this crew working?"

" I will," said Welton.

" Then do it."

During the next two days the old scenes were all relived, with back of them the weight of the struggle that had gone before. The little crew worked as though mad. Excepting them, no one ventured on the river, for to be caught in the imminent break meant to die. Old spars, refuse timbers of all sorts—anything and everything was requisitioned that might help form an obstruction above or below water. Piles were taken where they could be found. Farmer's trees were cut down. Pines belonging to divers and protesting owners were felled and sharpened. Some were brought in by rail. Even the inviolate Government supply was commandeered. The Railroad Company had a fine lot which, with remarkable shortsightedness and lack of public spirit, they refused to sell at any price. The crew took them by force. Once Captain Marsh was found up to his waist in water, himself felling the trees of a wood, and dragging them to the river by a cable attached to the winch of his tug. Night followed day; and day night again. None of the crews realised the fact. The men were caught in the toils of a labour ceaseless and eternal. Never would it end, just as never had it begun. Always were they to handle piles, steam hammers and the implements of their trade, menaced by a jam on the point of breaking, wet by a swollen and angry flood, overarched by a clear calm sky or by the twinkling peaceful stars. Long since had they ceased to reckon with the results of what they did, the consequences either to themselves or to the jam. Mechanically they performed their labour. Perhaps the logs would kill them. Perhaps these long, black, dripping piles they drove were having some effect on the situation. Neither possibility mattered.

Then all at once, as though a faucet had been turned off, the floods slackened.

" They've opened the channel," said Orde dully. His voice sounded to himself very far away. Suddenly the external world, too, seemed removed to a distance, far from his centre of consciousness. He felt himself moving in strange and distorted surroundings; he heard himself repeating to each of a number of wavering, gigantic figures the talismanic words that had accomplished the dissolution of the earth for himself: " They've opened the channel." At last he felt hard planks beneath his feet, and, shaking his head with an effort, he made out the pilot-house of the *Sprite* and a hollow-eyed man leaning against it. " They've opened

the channel, Marsh," he repeated. " I guess that'll be all."
Then quite slowly he sank to the deck, sound asleep.

Welton, returning from his labours with the iron bridge
and the jam, found them thus. Men slept on the deck of
the tug, aboard the pile-driver. Two or three had even
curled up in the crevices of the jam, resting in the arms of
the monster they had subdued.

XLII

WHEN Newmark left, in the early stages of the jam, he gave scant thought to the errand on which he had ostensibly departed. Whether or not Orde got a supply of piles was to him a matter of indifference. His hope, or rather preference was that the jam should go out; but he saw clearly what Orde, blinded by the swift action of the struggle, was as yet unable to perceive. Even should the riverman succeed in stopping the jam, the extraordinary expenses incidental to the defence and to the subsequent salvaging, untangling and sorting would more than eat up the profits of the drive. Orde would then be forced to ask for an extension of time on his notes.

On arriving in Monrovia, he drove to his own house. To Mallock he issued orders.

"Go to the office and tell them I am ill," said he, "and then hunt up Mr. Heinzman, wherever he is, and tell him I want to see him immediately."

He did not trouble to send word directly to Orde, up river; but left him to be informed by the slow process of filtration through the bookkeepers. The interim of several hours before Heinzman appeared he spent very comfortably in his easy chair, dipping into a small volume of Montaigne.

At length the German was announced. He entered rather red and breathless, obviously surprised to find Newmark at home.

"Dot was a terrible jam," said he, mopping his brow and sinking into a chair. "I got lots of logs in it."

Newmark dismissed the subject with an abrupt flip of his unlighted cigar.

"Heinzman," said he, "in three weeks at the latest Orde will come to you asking for a renewal of the notes you hold against our firm. You must refuse to make such a renewal."

"All righdt," agreed Heinzman.

"He'll probably offer you higher interest. You must refuse that. Then when the notes are overdue you must begin suit in foreclosure."

"All righdt," repeated Heinzman a little restlessly. "Do you think he vill hold that jam?"

Newmark shrugged his shoulders swiftly.

"I got lots of logs in that jam. If that jam goes out I vill lose a heap of money."

"Well, you'll make quite a heap on this deal," said Newmark carelessly.

"Suppose he holds it," said Heinzman, pausing. "I hate like the mischief to joomp on him."

"Rot!" said Newmark decisively. "That's what he's there for." He looked at the German sharply. "I suppose you know just how deep you're in this?"

"Oh, I ain't backing oudt," negatived Heinzman. "Not a bit."

"Well, then, you know what to do," said Newmark, terminating the interview.

XLIII

LITTLE by little the water went down. The pressure, already considerably relieved by the channel into Stearn's Bayou, slackened every hour. Orde, still half dazed with his long-delayed sleep, drove back along the marsh road to town.

His faculties were still in the torpor that follows rest after exhaustion. The warm July sun, the breeze from the Lake, the flash of light from the roadside water, these were all he had room for among his perceptions. He was content to enjoy them, and to anticipate drowsily the keen pleasure of seeing Carroll again. In the rush of the jam he had heard nothing from her. For all he knew she and Bobby might have been among the spectators on the bank; he had hardly once left the river. It did not seem to him strange that Carroll should not have been there to welcome him after the struggle was over. Rarely did she get to the booms in ordinary circumstances. This episode of the big jam was, after all, nothing but part of the day's work to Orde; a crisis, exaggerated it is true, but like many other crises a man must meet and cope with on the river. There was no reason why Carroll should drive the twelve miles between Monrovia and the booms, unless curiosity should take her.

As the team left the marsh road for the county turnpike past the mills and lumberyards, Orde shook himself fully awake. He began to review the situation. As Newmark had accurately foreseen, he came almost immediately to a realisation that the firm would not be able to meet the notes given to Heinzman. Orde had depended on the profits

got home, but I missed you. Come in and sit down, and I'll tell you about it."

"You're quite sure Mrs. Orde is well?" insisted Orde.

"Absolutely. Never better. As well as you are."

"Where was she exposed?"

"Down at Heinzman's. You know—or perhaps you don't —that old Heinzman is the worst sort of anti-vaccination crank. Well, he's reaped the reward."

"Has he smallpox?" asked Orde. "Why, I thought I remembered seeing him up river only the other day."

"No; his daughter."

"Mina?"

"Yes. Lord knows where she got it. But get it she did. Mrs. Orde happened to be with her when she was taken with the fever and distressing symptoms that begin the disease. As a neighbourly deed she remained with the girl. Of course no one could tell it was smallpox at that time. Next day, however, the characteristic rash appeared on the thighs and armpits, and I diagnosed the case." Dr. Mc-Mullen laughed a little bitterly. "Lord, you ought to have seen them run! Servants, neighbours, friends—they all ske-daddled, and you coudn't have driven them back with a steam-roller! I telegraphed to Redding for a nurse. Until she came Mrs. Orde stayed by, like a brick. Don't know what I should have done without her. There was nobody to do anything at all. As soon as the nurse came Mrs. Orde gave up her post. I tell you," cried Doctor McMullen with as near an approach to enthusiasm as he ever permitted himself, "there's a sensible woman! None of your story-book twaddle about nursing through the illness, and all that. When her usefulness was ended, she knew enough to step aside gracefully. There was not much danger as far as she was concerned. I had vaccinated her myself, you know, last year. But she *might* take the contagion and she wanted to spare the youngster. Quite right. So I offered her quarters with us for a couple of weeks."

" How long ago was this?" asked Orde, who had listened with a warm glow of pride to the doctor's succinct statement.

" Seven days."

" How is Mina getting on?"

" She'll get well. It was a mild case. Fever never serious after the eruption appeared. I suppose I'll have old Heinzman on my hands, though."

" Why; has he taken it?"

" No; but he will. Emotional old German fool. Rushed right in when he heard his daughter was sick. Couldn't keep him out. And he's been with her or near her ever since."

" Then you think he's in for it?"

" Sure to be," replied Dr. McMullen. " Unless a man has been vaccinated, continuous exposure means infection in the great majority of cases."

" Hard luck," said Orde thoughtfully. " I'm going to step up to your house and see Mrs. Orde."

" You can telephone her," said the doctor. " And you can see her if you want to. Only in that case I should advise your remaining away from Bobby until we see how things turn out."

" I see," said Orde. " Well," he concluded with a sigh, after a moment's thought, " I suppose I'd better stay by the ship."

He called up Dr. McMullen's house on the telephone.

" Oh, it's good to hear your voice again," cried Carroll, " even if I can't see you! You must promise me right after lunch to walk up past the house so I can see you. I'll wave at you from the window."

" You're a dear, brave girl, and I'm proud of you," said Orde.

" Nonsense! There was no danger at all. I'd been vaccinated recently. And somebody had to take care of poor Mina until we could get help. How's Bobby?"

XLIV

AFTER lunch Orde went downtown to his office where for some time he sat idly looking over the mail. About three o'clock Newmark came in.

"Hullo, Joe," said Orde with a slight constraint, "sorry to hear you've been under the weather. You don't look very sick now."

"I'm better," replied Newmark, briefly; "this is my first appearance."

"Too bad you got sick just at that time," said Orde; "we needed you."

"So I hear. You may rest assured I'd have been there if possible."

"Sure thing," said Orde, heartily, his slight resentment dissipating, as always, in the presence of another's personality. "Well, we had a lively time, you bet, all right; and got through about by the skin of our teeth." He arose and walked over to Newmark's desk, on the edge of which he perched. "It's cost us considerable; and it's going to cost us a lot more, I'll have to get an extension on those notes."

"What's that?" asked Newmark, quickly.

Orde picked up a paper knife and turned it slowly between his fingers.

"I don't believe I'll be able to meet those notes. So many things have happened——"

"But," broke in Newmark, "the firm certainly cannot do so. I've been relying on your assurance that you would take them up personally. Our resources are all tied up."

"Can't we raise anything more on the Northern Peninsula timber?" asked Orde.

"You ought to know we can't," cried Newmark, with an appearance of growing excitement. "The last seventy-five thousand we borrowed for me finishes that."

"Can't you take up part of your note?"

"My note comes due in 1885," rejoined Newmark with cold disgust. "I expect to take it up then. But I can't until then. I hadn't expected anything like this."

"Well, don't get hot," said Orde vaguely. "I only thought that Northern Peninsula stuff might be worth saving any way we could figure it."

"Worth saving!" snorted Newmark, whirling in his chair.

"Well, keep your hair on," said Orde, on whom Newmark's manner was beginning to have its effect, as Newmark intended it should. "You have my Boom Company stock as security."

"Pretty security for the loss of a tract like the Upper Peninsula timber!"

"Well, it's the security you asked for, and suggested," said Orde.

"I thought you'd surely be able to pay it," retorted Newmark, now secure in the position he desired to take, that of putting Orde entirely in the wrong.

"Well, I expected to pay it; and I'll pay it yet," rejoined Orde. "I don't think Heinzman will stand in his own light rather than renew the notes."

He seized his hat and departed. Once in the street, however, his irritation passed. As was the habit of the man, he began more clearly to see Newmark's side, and so more emphatically to blame himself. After all, when he got right down to the essentials, he could not but acknowledge that Newmark's anger was justified. For his own private ends he had jeopardised the firm's property. More of a business man might have reflected that Newmark, as financial head, should have protected the firm against all contingencies;

should have seen to it that it met Heinzman's notes, instead of tying up its resources in unnecessary ways. Orde's own delinquency bulked too large in his eyes to admit his perception of this. By the time he had reached Heinzman's office, the last of his irritation had vanished. Only he realised clearly now that it would hardly do to ask Newmark for a renewal of the personal note on which depended his retention of his Boom Company stock unless he could renew the Heinzman note also. This is probably what Newmark intended.

" Mr. Heinzman? " he asked briefly of the first clerk.

" Mr. Heinzman is at home ill," replied the bookkeeper.

" Already! " said Orde. He drummed on the black walnut rail thoughtfully. The notes came due in ten days. " How bad is he? "

The clerk looked up curiously. " Can't say. Probably won't be back for a long time. It's smallpox, you know."

" True," said Orde. " Well, who's in charge? "

" Mr. Lambert. You'll find him in the private office."

Orde passed through the grill into the inner room.

" Hullo, Lambert," he addressed the individual seated at Heinzman's desk. " So you're the boss, eh? "

Lambert turned, showing a perfectly round face, ornamented by a dot of a nose, two dots of eyes set rather close together, and a pursed up mouth. His skin was very brown and shiny, and was so filled by the flesh beneath as to take the appearance of having been inflated.

" Yes, I'm the boss," said he non-committally.

Orde dropped into a chair.

" Heinzman holds some notes due against our people in ten days," said he. " I came in to see about their renewal. Can you attend to it? "

" Yes, I can attend to it," replied Lambert. He struck a bell; and to the bookkeeper who answered he said: " John, bring me those Newmark & Orde papers."

Orde heard the clang of the safe door. In a moment the clerk returned and handed to Lambert a long manilla envelope. Lambert opened this quite deliberately, spread its contents on his knee, and assumed a pair of round spectacles.

" Note for seventy-five thousand dollars with interest at ten per cent. Interest paid to January tenth. Mortgage deed on certain lands described herein."

" That's it," said Orde.

Lambert looked up over his spectacles.

" I want to renew the note for another year," Orde explained.

" Can't do it," replied Lambert, removing and folding the glasses.

" Why not? "

" Mr. Heinzman gave me especial instructions in regard to this matter just before his daughter was taken sick. He told me if you came when he was not here—he intended to go to Chicago yesterday—to tell you he would not renew."

" Why not? " asked Orde blankly.

" I don't know that."

" But I'll give him twelve per cent. for another year."

" He said not to renew, even if you offered higher interest."

" Do you happen to know whether he intends anything in regard to this mortgage? "

" He instructed me to begin suit in foreclosure immediately."

" I don't understand this," said Orde.

Lambert shook his head blandly. Orde thought for a moment.

" Where's your telephone? " he demanded abruptly.

He tried in vain to get Heinzman at his house. Finally the telephone girl informed him that although messages had come from the stricken household, she had been unable to get an answer to any of her numerous calls, and suspected the bell had been removed. Finally Orde left the office at a loss how to proceed next. Lambert, secretly overjoyed at this opportunity of exercising an unaccustomed and autocratic power, refused to see beyond his instructions. Heinzman's attitude puzzled Orde. A foreclosure could gain Heinzman no advantage of immediate cash. Orde was forced to the conclusion that the German saw here a good opportunity to acquire cheap a valuable property. In that case a personal appeal would avail little.

Orde tramped out to the end of the pier and back, mulling over the tangled problem. He was pressed on all sides—by the fatigue after his tremendous exertions of the past two weeks; by his natural uneasiness in regard to Carroll; and finally by this new complication which threatened the very basis of his prosperity. Nevertheless the natural optimism of the man finally won its ascendency.

"There's the year of redemption on that mortgage," he reminded himself. "We may be able to do something in that time. I don't know just what," he added whimsically, with a laugh at himself. He became grave. "Poor Joe," he said, "this is pretty tough on him. I'll have to make it up to him somehow. I can let him in on that California deal, when the titles are straightened out."

XLV

ORDE did not return to the office; he felt unwilling to face Newmark until he had a little more thoroughly digested the situation. He spent the rest of the afternoon about the place, picking up the tool house, playing with Bobby, training Duke, the black and white setter dog. Three or four times he called up Carroll by telephone; and three or four times he passed Dr. McMullen's house to shout his half of a long-distance and fragmentary conversation with her. He ate solemnly with Bobby at six o'clock, the two quite subdued over the vacant chair at the other end of the table. After dinner they sat on the porch until Bobby's bed-time. Orde put his small son to bed, and sat talking with the youngster as long as his conscience would permit. Then he retired to the library, where, for a long time, he sat in twilight and loneliness. Finally, when he could no longer distinguish objects across the room, he arose with a sigh, lit the lamp, and settled himself to read.

The last of the twilight drained from the world, and the window panes turned a burnished black. Through the half-open sashes sucked a warm little breeze, swaying the long lace curtains back and forth. The hum of lawn-sprinklers and the chirping of crickets and tree-frogs came with it.

One by one the lawn-sprinklers fell silent. Gradually there descended upon the world the deep slumbrous stillness of late night; a stillness compounded of a thousand and one mysterious little noises repeated monotonously over and over until their identity was lost in accustomedness. Occasionally the creak of timbers or the sharp scurrying of a

mouse in the wall served more to accentuate than to break
this night silence.

Orde sat lost in reverie, his book in his lap. At stated
intervals the student lamp at his elbow flared slightly, then
burned clear again after a swallow of satisfaction in its
reservoir. These regular replenishments of the oil supply
alone marked the flight of time.

Suddenly Orde leaned forward, his senses at the keenest
attention. After a moment he arose and quietly walked toward the open window. Just as he reached the casement and
looked out, a man looked in. The two stared at each other
not two feet apart.

"Good Lord! Heinzman!" cried Orde in a guarded voice.
He stepped decisively through the window, seized the
German by the arm, and drew him one side.

"What are you doing here?" he demanded.

Heinzman was trembling violently as though from a chill.

"Dake me somewheres," he whispered hoarsely. "Somewheres quick. I haf broke quarantine, and dey vill be after
me."

"The place for you is at your own house," said Orde, his
anger rising. "What do you mean by coming here and ex-
posing my house to infection?"

Heinzman began to blubber; choked, shivered all over,
and cried aloud with an expression of the greatest agony:

"You must dake me somewheres. I must talk with you
and your goot wife. I haf somedings to say to you." He in
his turn grasped Orde by the arm. "I haf broke quarantine
to gome and tell you. Dey are dere mit shotguns to kill me
if I broke quarantine. And I haf left my daughter, my
daughter Mina, all alone mit dose people to come and tell
you. And now you don't listen."

He wrung his hands dramatically, his soft pudgy body
shaking.

"Come with me," said Orde briefly.

He led the way around the house to the tool shed. Here he lit a lantern, thrust forward one nail keg, and sat down on another.

Heinzman sat down on the nail keg, almost immediately arose, walked up and down two or three times, and resumed his seat.

Orde looked at him curiously. He was half dressed, without a collar, his thin hair unkempt. The usual bright colour of his cheeks had become livid, and the flesh, ordinarily firm and elastic, had fallen in folds and wrinkles. His eyes burned bright as though from some internal fire. A great restlessness possessed him. Impulsively Orde leaned forward to touch his hand. It was dry and hot.

" What is it, Heinzman? " he asked quietly, fully prepared for the vagaries of a half delirium.

" Ach, Orde! " cried the German, " I am tortured mit *höllenqualle*—what you call?—hell's fire. You, whose wife comes in and saves my Mina when the others runs away. You, my best friends! It is *schrecklich*! She vas the noblest, the best, the most kindest——"

" If you mean Mrs. Orde's staying with Mina," broke in Orde, " it was only what any one should have done, in humanity; and I, for one, am only too glad she had the chance. You mustn't exaggerate. And now you'd better get home where you can be taken care of. You're sick."

" No, no, my friend," said Heinzman, vigourously shaking his head. " She might take the disease. She might die. It vas noble." He shuddered. " My Mina left to die all alone! "

Orde rose to his feet with decision.

" That is all right," said he. " Carroll was glad of the chance. Now let me get you home."

But Heinzman's excitement had suddenly died.

" No," said he, extending his trembling hand; " sit down. I want to talk business."

" You are in no condition to talk business," said Orde.

"No!" cried Heinzman with unexpected vigour. "Sit down! Listen to me! Dot's better. I haf your note for sefenty-five t'ousand dollars. No?"

Orde nodded.

"Dot money I never lent you. *No!* I'm not crazy. Sit still! I know my name is on dot note. But the money came from somewheres else. It came from your partner, Joseph Newmark."

Orde half rose from his keg.

"Why? What?" he asked in bewilderment.

"Den ven you could not pay the note, I vas to foreclose and hand over dot Northern Peninsula land to Joseph Newmark, your partner."

"Impossible!" cried Orde.

"I vas to get a share. It vas a trick."

"Go on," said Orde grimly.

"Dere is no go on. Dot is all."

"Why do you come to tell me now?"

"Because for more than one year now I say to mineself, 'Carl Heinzman, you vas one dirty scoundrel. You vas dishonest; a sneak; a thief'; I don't like to call myself names like dose. It iss all righdt to be smart; but to be a thief!"

"Why didn't you pull out?" asked Orde.

"I couldn't!" cried Heinzman piteously. "How could I? He haf me cold. I paid Stanford five hundred dollars for his vote on the charter; and Joseph Newmark, he know dot; he can *prove* it. He tell me if I don't do what he say, he put me in jail. Think of dot! All my friends go back on me; all my money gone; maybe my daughter Mina go back on me, too. How could I?"

"Well, he can still put you in prison," said Orde.

"Vot I care?" cried Heinzman, throwing up both his arms. "You and your wife are my friends. She save my Mina. *Du lieber Gott!* If my daughter had died, vot good iss friends and money? Vot good iss anything? I don't vant

His Eyes Burned Bright as Though from Some Internal Fire

tó live! And ven I sit dere by her always something ask me: 'Vy you do dot to the peoples dot safe your Mina?' And ven she look at me, her eyes say it; and in the night everything cry out at me; and I get sick, and I can't stand it no longer, and I don't care if he send me to prison or to hell, no more."

His excitement died. He sat listless, his eyes vacant, his hands between his knees.

" Vell, I go," he said at last.

" Have you that note?" asked Orde.

" Joseph Newmark, he keeps it most times," replied Heinzman, " but now it is at my office for the foreclosure. I vill not foreclose; he can send me to the penitentiary."

" Telephone Lambert in the morning to give it to me. No; here. Write an order in this notebook."

Heinzman wrote the required order.

" I go," said he, suddenly weary.

Orde accompanied him down the street. The German was again light-headed with the fever, mumbling about his daughter, the notes, Carroll, the voices that had driven him to righteousness. By some manœuvring Orde succeeded in slipping him through the improvised quarantine without discovery. Then the riverman with slow and thoughtful steps returned to where the lamp in the study still marked off with the spaced replenishments from its oil reservoir the early morning hours.

XLVI

MORNING found Orde still seated in the library chair. His head was sunk forward on his chest; his hands were extended listless, palms up, along the arms of the chair; his eyes were vacant and troubled. Hardly once in the long hours had he shifted by a hair's breadth his position. His body was suspended in an absolute inaction while his spirit battered at the walls of an impasse. For, strangely enough, Orde did not once, even for a single instant, give a thought to the business aspects of the situation—what it meant to him and his prospects or what he could do about it. Hurt to the soul he stared at the wreck of a friendship. Nothing will more deeply sicken the heart of a naturally loyal man than to discover baseless his faith in some one he has thoroughly trusted.

Orde had liked Newmark. He had admired heartily his clearness of vision, his financial skill, his knowledge of business intricacies, his imperturbable coolness, all the abilities that had brought him to success. With a man of Orde's temperament, to admire is to like; and to like is to invest with all good qualities. He had constructed his ideal of a friend, with Newmark as a basis; and now that this, which had seemed to him as solid a reality as a brick block, had dissolved into nothing, he found himself in the necessity of refashioning his whole world. He was not angry at Newmark. But he was grieved down to the depths of his being.

When the full sun shone into the library, he aroused himself to change his clothes. Then, carrying those he had just discarded, he slipped out of the house and down the street.

Duke, the black and white setter dog, begged to follow him. Orde welcomed the animal's company. He paused only long enough to telephone from the office telling Carroll he would be out of town all day. Then he set out at a long swinging gait over the hills. By the time the sun grew hot, he was some miles from the village and in the high beech woods. There he sat down, his back to a monster tree. A l day long he gazed steadily on the shifting shadows and splotches of sunlight; on the patches of blue sky, the dazzling white clouds that sailed across them; on the waving, whispering frond that over-arched him, and the deep cool shadows beneath. The woods creatures soon became accustomed to his presence. Squirrels of the several varieties that abounded in the Michigan forests scampered madly after each other in spirals around the tree trunks, or bounded across the ground in long undulating leaps. Birds flashed and called and disappeared mysteriously. A chewink, brave in his black and white and tan uniform, scratched mightily with great two-footed swoops that threw the vegetable mould over Orde's very feet. Blazoned butterflies—the yellow and black turnus, the dark troilus, the shade-loving nymphalis—flickered in and out of the patches of sunlight. Orde paid them no attention. The noon heat poured down through the forest isles like an incense. Overhead swung the sun, and down the slope until the long shafts of its light lifted wand-like across the tree trunks.

At this hint of evening Orde shook himself and arose. He was little nearer the readjustment he sought than he had been the previous night.

He reached home a little before six o'clock. To his surprise he found Taylor awaiting him. The lawyer had written nothing as to his return.

"I had things pretty well in shape," he said, after the first greetings had been exchanged, "and it would do no good to stay away any longer."

"Then the trouble is over?" asked Orde.

"I wouldn't say that," replied Taylor; "but you can rest easy as to the title to your lands. The investigation had no real basis to it. There may have been some small individual cases of false entry; but nothing on which to ground a real attack."

"When can I borrow on it?"

"Not for a year or two, I should say. There's an awful lot of red-tape to unwind, as there always is in such cases."

"Oh," said Orde in some disappointment.

Taylor hesitated, removed his eye-glasses, wiped them carefully, and replaced them. He glanced at Orde sidelong through his keen, shrewd eyes.

"I have something more to tell you; something that will be painful," said he.

Orde looked up quickly.

"Well; what is it?" he asked.

"The general cussedness of all this investigation business had me puzzled, until at last I made up my mind to do a little investigating on my own account. It all looked foolish to me. Somebody or something must be back of all this performance. I was at it all the time I was West, between times on regular business, of course. I didn't make much out of my direct efforts—they cover things up well in those matters—but at last I got on a clue by sheer accident. There was one man behind all this. He was——"

"Joe Newmark," said Orde quietly.

"How did you know that?" cried Taylor in astonishment.

"I didn't know, Frank; I just guessed."

"Well, you made a good guess. It was Newmark. He'd tied up the land in this trumped-up investigation so you could not borrow on it."

"How did he find out I owned any land?" asked Orde.

"That I couldn't tell you. Must have been a leak somewhere."

"Quite likely," said Orde calmly.

Taylor looked at his principal in some wonder.

"Well, I must say you take it coolly enough," said he at last.

Orde smiled.

"Do I?" said he.

"Of course," went on Taylor after a moment, "we have a strong presumption of conspiracy to get hold of your Boom Company stock, which I believe you put up as security. But I don't see how we have any incontestable proof of it."

"Proof? What more do we want?"

"We'd have no witness to any of these transactions; nor have we documentary proofs. It's merely moral certainty; and moral certainty isn't much in a court of law. I'll see him, if you say so, though, and scare him into some sort of an arrangement."

Orde shook his head.

"No," said he decidedly. "Rather not. I'll run this. Please say nothing."

"Of course not!" interjected Taylor, a trifle indignantly.

"And I'll figure out what I want to do."

Orde pressed Taylor to stay to supper; but the latter declined. After a few moments' conversation on general topics the lawyer took his departure, secretly marvelling over the phlegmatic way in which Orde had taken what had been to Taylor, when he first stumbled against it, a shocking piece of news.

XLVII

ORDE did not wish to return to the office until he had worked his problem out; so, to lend his absence the colour of naturalness, he drove back next morning to the booms. There he found enough to keep him occupied all that day and the next. As in those times the long distance telephone had not yet been attempted, he was cut off from casual communication with the village. Late in the afternoon he returned home.

A telephone to Carroll apprised him that all was well with her. A few moments later the call sounded, and Orde took a message that caused him to look grave and to whistle gently with surprise. He ate supper with Bobby. About star-time he took his hat and walked slowly down the street beneath the velvet darkness of the maples. At Newmark's he turned in between the oleanders.

Mallock answered his ring.

"No, sir, Mr. Newmark is out, sir," said Mallock. "I'll tell him you called, sir," and started respectfully but firmly to close the door.

But Orde thrust his foot and knee in the opening.

"I'll come in and wait," said he quietly.

"Yes, sir, this way, sir," said Mallock, trying to indicate the dining-room, where he wished Orde to sit until he could come at his master's wishes in the matter.

Orde caught the aroma of tobacco and the glimmer of light to the left. Without reply he turned the knob of the door and entered the library.

There he found Newmark in evening dress, seated in a

low easy chair beneath a lamp, smoking, and reading a magazine. At Orde's appearance in the doorway, he looked up calmly, his paper knife poised, keeping the place.

"Oh, it's you, Orde," said he.

"Your man told me you were not in," said Orde.

"He was mistaken. Won't you sit down?"

Orde entered the room and mechanically obeyed Newmark's suggestion, his manner preoccupied. For some time he stared with wrinkled brow at a point above the illumination of the lamp. Newmark, over the end of his cigar, poised a foot from his lips, watched the riverman with a cool calculation.

"Newmark," Orde began abruptly at last, "I know all about this deal."

"What deal?" asked Newmark, after a barely perceptible pause.

"This arrangement you made with Heinzman."

"I borrowed some money from Heinzman for the firm."

"Yes; and you supplied that money yourself."

Newmark's eyes narrowed, but he said nothing. Orde glanced toward him, then away again, as though ashamed.

"Well," said Newmark at last, "what of it?"

"If you had the money to lend why didn't you lend it direct?"

"Because it looks better to mortgage to an outside holder."

An expression of profound disgust flitted across Orde's countenance. Newmark smiled covertly, and puffed once or twice strongly on his nearly extinct cigar.

"That was not the reason," went on Orde. "You agreed with Heinzman to divide when you succeeded in foreclosing me out of the timber lands given as security. Furthermore you instructed Floyd to go out on the eve of that blow in spite of his warnings; and you contracted with McLeod for the new vessels; and you've tied us up right and left for the sole purpose of pinching us down where we couldn't meet those notes. That's the only reason you borrowed the seventy-five thousand on your own account; so we couldn't borrow it to save ourselves."

" It strikes me you are interesting but inconclusive," said Newmark, as Orde paused again.

" That sort of thing is somewhat of a facer," went on Orde without the slightest attention to the interjection. " It took me some days to work it out in all its details; but I believe I understand it all now. I don't quite understand how you discovered about my California timber. That ' investigation ' was a very pretty move."

" How the devil did you get onto that? " cried Newmark, startled for a moment out of his cool attitude of cynical aloofness.

" Then you acknowledge it? " shot in Orde quick as a flash.

Newmark laughed in amusement.

" Why shouldn't I? Of course Heinzman blabbed. You couldn't have got it all anywhere else."

Orde arose to his feet, and half sat again on the arm of his chair.

" Now I'll tell you what we will do in this matter," said he crisply.

But Newmark unexpectedly took the aggressive.

" We'll follow," said he, "the original programme, as laid down by myself. I'm tired of dealing with blundering fools. Heinzman's mortgage will be foreclosed; and you will hand over as per the agreement your Boom Company stock."

Orde stared at him in amazement.

" I must say you have good nerve," he said; " you don't seem to realise that you are pretty well tangled up. I don't know what they call it: criminal conspiracy, or something of that sort, I suppose. So far from handing over to you the bulk of my property, I can send you to the penitentiary."

" Nonsense," rejoined Newmark, leaning forward in his turn. " I know you too well, Jack Orde. You're a fool of more kinds than I care to count, and this is one of the kinds. Do you seriously mean to say that you dare try to prosecute me? Just as sure as you do, I'll put Heinzman in the pen too. I've got it on him, *cold*. He's a bribe giver—and somewhat of a criminal conspirator himself."

" Well," said Orde.

Newmark leaned back with an amused little chuckle. " If the man hadn't come to you and given the whole show away, you'd have lost every cent you owned. He did you the biggest favour in his power. And for your benefit I'll tell you what you can easily substantiate; I forced him into this deal with me. I had this bribery case on him; and in addition his own affairs were all tied up."

" I knew that," replied Orde.

" What had the man to gain by telling you? " pursued Newmark. " Nothing at all. What had he to lose? Everything: his property, his social position, his daughter's esteem, which the old fool holds higher than any of them. You could put me in the pen, perhaps—with Heinzman's testimony. But the minute Heinzman appears on the stand, I'll land him high and dry and gasping, without a chance to flop."

He paused a moment to puff at his cigar. Finding it had gone out, he laid the butt carefully on the ash tray at his elbow.

" I'm not much used to giving advice," he went on, " least of all when it is at all likely to be taken. But I'll offer you some. Throw Heinzman over. Let him go to the pen. He's been crooked, and a fool."

" That's what you'd do, I suppose," said Orde.

" Exactly that. You owe nothing to Heinzman; but something to what you would probably call repentance, but which is in reality a mawkish sentimentality of weakness. However, I know you, Jack Orde, from top to bottom; and I know you're fool enough not to do it. I'm so sure of it that I dare put it to you straight; you could never bring yourself to the point of destroying a man who had sacrificed himself for you."

"You seem to have this game all figured out," said Orde with contempt.

Newmark leaned back in his chair. Two bright red spots burned in his ordinarily sallow cheeks. He half closed his eyes.

"You're right," said he with an ill-concealed satisfaction. "If you play a game, play it through. Each man is different; for each a different treatment is required. The game is infinite, wonderful, fascinating to the skilful." He opened his eyes and looked over at Orde with a mild curiosity. "I suppose men are about all of one kind to you."

"Two," said Orde grimly; "the honest men and the scoundrels."

"Well," said the other, "let's settle this thing. The fact remains that the firm owes a note to Heinzman, which it cannot pay. You owe a note to the firm which you cannot pay. All this may be slightly irregular; but for private reasons you do not care to make public the irregularity. Am I right so far?"

Orde, who had been watching him with a slightly sardonic smile, nodded.

"Well, what I want out of this——"

"You might hear the other side," interrupted Orde. "In the first place," said he, producing a bundle of papers, "I have the note and the mortgage in my possession."

"Whence Heinzman will shortly rescue them, as soon as I get to see him," countered Newmark. "You acknowledge that I can force Heinzman; and you can hardly refuse him."

"If you force Heinzman, he'll land you," Orde pointed out.

" There is Canada for me, with no extradition. He travels with heavier baggage. I have the better trumps."

" You'd lose everything."

" Not quite," smiled Newmark. " And, as usual, you are forgetting the personal equation. Heinzman is—Heinzman. And I am I."

" Then I suppose this affidavit from Heinzman as to the details of all this is useless for the same reason? "

Newmark's thin lips parted in another smile.

" Correct," said he.

" But you're ready to compromise below the face of the note? "

" I am."

" Why? "

Newmark hesitated.

" I'll tell you," said he; " because I know you well enough to realise that there is a point where your loyalty to Heinzman would step aside in favour of your loyalty to your family."

" And you think you know where that point is? "

" It's the basis of my compromise."

Orde began softly to laugh. " Newmark, you're as clever as the devil," said he. " But aren't you afraid to lay out your cards this way? "

" Not with you," replied Newmark, boldly; " with anybody else on earth, yes. With you, no."

Orde continued to laugh, still in the low undertone.

" The worst of it is, I believe you're right," said he at last. " You have the thing sized up; and there isn't a flaw in your reasoning. I always said that you were the brains of this concern. If it were not for one thing, I'd compromise sure; and that one thing was beyond your power to foresee."

He paused. Newmark's eyes half-closed again, in a quick darting effort of his brain to run back over all the elements of the game he was playing. Orde waited in patience for him to speak.

"What is it?" asked Newmark at last.

"Heinzman died of smallpox at four o'clock this afternoon," said Orde.

XLVIII

NEWMARK did not alter his attitude nor his expression, but his face slowly went gray. For a full minute he sat absolutely motionless, his breath coming and going noisily through his contracted nostrils. Then he arose gropingly to his feet, and started toward one of the two doors leading from the room.

"Where are you going?" asked Orde quietly.

Newmark steadied himself with an effort.

"I'm going to get myself a drink in my bedroom," he snapped. "Any objections?"

"No," replied Orde. "None. After you get your drink, come back. I want to talk to you."

Newmark snarled at him: "You needn't be afraid I'll run away. How'd I get out of town?"

"I know it wouldn't pay you to run away," said Orde.

Newmark passed out through the door. Orde looked thoughtfully at Heinzman's affidavit, which, duly disinfected, had been handed him by Dr. McMullen as important; and thrust it and the other papers into his inside pocket. Then he arose to his feet and glided softly across the room to take a position close to the door through which Newmark had departed in quest of his drink. For a half minute he waited. Finally the door swung briskly inward. Like a panther, as quickly and as noiselessly, Orde sprang forward. A short but decisive struggle ensued. In less than ten seconds Orde had pinioned Newmark's arms to his side where he held them immovable with one of his own. The other hand he ran down Newmark's right arm to the pocket.

There followed an instant of silent resistance. Then with a sharp cry of mingled anger and pain Newmark snatched his hand out and gazed a trifle amazedly at the half crushed fingers. Orde drew forth the revolver Newmark had grasped concealed in the coat pocket.

Without hesitation he closed and locked the bedroom door; turned the key in the lock of the other; tried and fastened the window. The revolver he opened; spilled out the cartridges into his hand; and then tossed the empty weapon to Newmark, who had sunk into the chair by the lamp.

"There's your plaything," said he. "So you wanted that affidavit, did you? Now we have the place to ourselves; and we'll thresh this matter out."

He paused, collecting his thoughts.

"I don't need to tell you that I've got you about where you live," said he finally. "Nor what I think of you. The case is open and shut; and I can send you over the road for the best part of your natural days. Also I've got these notes and the mortgage."

"Quit it," growled Newmark, "you've got me. Send me up; and be damned."

"That's the question," went on Orde slowly. "I've been at it three days, without much time off for sleep. You hurt me pretty bad, Joe. I trusted you; and I thought of you as a friend."

Newmark stirred slightly with impatience.

"I had a hard time getting over that part of it; and about three-quarters of what was left in the world looked mighty like ashes for awhile. Then I began to see this thing a little clearer. We've been together a good many years now; and as near as I can make out you've been straight as a string with me for eight of them. Then I suppose the chance came and before you knew it you were in over your neck."

He looked, half-pleading toward Newmark. Newmark made no sign.

"I know that's the way it might be. A man thinks he's mighty brave; and so he is, as long as he can see what's coming, and get ready for it. But some day an emergency just comes up and touches him on the shoulder, and he turns around and sees it all of a sudden. Then he finds he's a coward. It's pretty hard for me to understand dishonesty, or how a man can be dishonest. I've tried, but I can't do it. Crookedness isn't my particular kind of fault. But I do know this: that we every one of us have something to be forgiven for by some one. I guess I've got a temper that makes me pretty sorry sometimes. Probably you don't see how it's possible for a man to get crazy mad about little things. That isn't your particular kind of fault."

"Oh, for God's sake, drop that preaching. It makes me sick!" broke out Newmark.

Orde smiled whimsically.

"I'm not preaching," he said; "and even if I were, I've paid a good many thousands of dollars, it seems, to buy the right to say what I damn please. And if you think I'm working up to a Christian forgiveness racket, you're very much mistaken. I'm not. I don't forgive you; and I surely despise your sort. But I'm explaining to you—no, to myself—just what I've been at for three days."

"Well, turn me over to your sheriff, and let's get through with this," said Newmark sullenly. "I suppose you've got that part of it all fixed."

Orde rose.

"Look here, Newmark, that's just what I've been coming to, just what I've had such a hard time to get hold of. I felt it, but I couldn't put my finger on it. Now I know. I'm not going to hand you over to any sheriff; I'm going to let you off. No," he continued, in response to Newmark's look of incredulous amazement, "it isn't from any fool notion of

forgiveness. I told you I didn't forgive you. But I'm not
going to burden my future life with you. That's just plain,
ordinary selfishness. I suppose I really ought to jug you;
but if I do, I'll always carry with me the thought that I've
taken it on myself to judge a man. And I don't believe any
man is competent to judge another. I told you why—or tried
to—a minute or so ago. I've lived clean, and I've enjoyed
the world as a clean open-air sort of proposition—like a
windy day—and I always hope to. I'd rather drop this
whole matter. In a short time I'd forget you; you'd pass
out of my life entirely. But if we carry this thing through
to a finish, I'd always have the thought with me that I'd
put you in the pen; that you are there now. I don't like
the notion. I'd rather finish this up right here and now and
get it over and done with and take a fresh start." He paused
and wiped his brow, wet with the unusual exertion of this
self-analysis. " I think a fellow ought to act always as if
he was making the world. He ought to try not to put things
in it that are going to make it an unpleasant or an evil
world. We don't always do it; but we ought to try. Now if
I were making a world, I wouldn't put a man in a penitentiary in it. Of course there's dangerous criminals." He
glanced at Newmark a little anxiously. " I don't believe
you're that. You're sharp and dishonest, and need punishment; but you don't need extinction. Anyway, I'm not going to bother my future with you."

Newmark, who had listened to this long and rambling
exposition with increasing curiosity and interest, broke into
a short laugh.

" You've convicted me," he said. " I'm a most awful failure. I thought I knew you; but this passes all belief."

Orde brushed this speech aside as irrelevant.

" Our association, of course, comes to an end. There remain the terms of settlement. I could fire you out of this
without a cent, and you'd have to git. But that wouldn't

"I'm Going to Give You About the Worst Licking You Ever Heard *Tell* Of"

be fair. I don't give a damn for you; but it wouldn't be fair to me. Now as for the Northern Peninsula timber, you have had seventy-five thousand out of that and have lent me the same amount. Call that quits. I will take up your note when it comes due; and destroy the one given to Heinzman. For all your holdings in our common business I will give you my note without interest and without time for one hundred thousand dollars. That is not its face value, nor anything like it, but you have caused me directly and indirectly considerable loss. I don't know how soon I can pay this note; but it will be paid."

" All right," agreed Newmark.

" Does that satisfy you? "

" I suppose it's got to."

" Very well. I have the papers here all made out. They need simply to be signed and witnessed. Timbull is the nearest notary."

He unlocked the outside door.

" Come," said he.

In silence the two walked the block and a half to the notary's house. Here they were forced to wait some time while Timbull dressed himself and called the necessary witnesses. Finally the papers were executed. In the street Newmark paused significantly. But Orde did not take the hint.

" Are you coming with me? " asked Newmark.

" I am," replied Orde. " There is one thing more."

In silence once more they returned to the shadowy low library filled with its evidences of good taste. Newmark threw himself into the armchair. He was quite recovered, once again the imperturbable, coldly calculating, cynical observer. Orde relocked the door, and turned to face him.

" You have five days to leave town," he said crisply. " Don't ever show up here again. Let me have your address for the payment of this note."

He took two steps forward.

" I've let you off from the pen because I didn't want my life bothered with the thought of you. But you've treated me like a hound. I've been loyal to the firm's interests from the start; and I've done my best by it. You knifed me in the back. You're a dirty, low-lived skunk. If you think you're going to get off scot-free, you're mightily mistaken."

He advanced two steps more. Newmark half arose.

" What do you mean? " he asked in some alarm.

" I mean that I'm going to give you about the worst licking you ever heard *tell* of," replied Orde, buttoning his coat.

XLIX

FIVE minutes later Orde emerged from Newmark's house, softly rubbing the palm of one hand over the knuckles of the other. At the front gate he paused to look up at the stars. Then he shut it decisively behind him.

Up through the maple shaded streets he walked at a brisk pace, breathing deep, unconsciously squaring back his shoulders. The incident was behind him. In his characteristic decisive manner he had wiped the whole disagreeable affair off the slate. The copartnership with its gains and losses, its struggles and easy sailing was a thing of the past. Only there remained, as after a flood the sediment, a final result of it all, the balance between successes and failures, a ground beneath the feet of new aspirations. Orde had the Northern Peninsula timber; the Boom Company; and the carrying trade. They were all burdened with debt, it is true, but the riverman felt surging within him the reawakened and powerful energy for which optimism is another name. He saw stretching before him a long life of endeavour, the sort of endeavour he enjoyed, exulted in; and in it he would be untrammelled and alone. The idea appealed to him. Suddenly he was impatient for the morrow that he might begin.

He turned out of the side street. His own house lay before him, dark save for the gas jet in the hallway and the single lamp in the library. A harmony of softly touched chords breathed out through the open window. He stopped; then stole forward softly until he stood looking in through the doorway.

Carroll sat leaning against the golden harp, her shining head with the soft shadows bent until it almost touched the strings. Her hands were straying idly over accustomed chords and rich modulations, the plaintive half-music of reverie. A soft light fell on her slender figure; half revealed the oval of her cheek and the sweep of her lashes.

Orde crept to her unheard. Gently he clasped her from behind. Unsurprised she relinquished the harp strings and sank back against his breast with a happy little sigh.

"Kind of fun being married, isn't it, sweetheart?" he repeated their quaint formula.

"Kind of," she replied; and raised her face to his.

THE END